A SCHOOL HISTORY OF THE UNITED STATES.

BY

W. H. VENABLE,
OF THE CHICKERING CLASSICAL AND SCIENTIFIC INSTITUTE.

WILSON, HINKLE & CO.,
CINCINNATI: 137 WALNUT ST.
NEW YORK: 28 BOND ST.

ELECTROTYPED AT
THE FRANKLIN TYPE FOUNDRY,
CINCINNATI.

PREFACE.

THE object aimed at in the preparation of this book was to produce a systematic, brief, clear, and authentic history of the United States for the use of schools.

The plan is simple. No arbitrary division into historical periods and eras is employed, but each chapter embraces associated events and forms a natural link in an unbroken chain. A strictly chronological order of arrangement is followed, whereby occurrences are shown in their true relation to one another, and to their causes. The most important dates are made prominent in the text by a peculiar type. A condensed record of general progress is placed at the end of almost every chapter, designed to interest the pupil in the civil and domestic character of the country, and in employments, institutions, and ideas not directly connected with wars, politics, or national legislation.

Brevity is secured not by shortening sentences to the last degree, but by rejecting comparatively unimportant matter. The tree has been pruned, but its outline remains unchanged.

The style of composition adopted is simple, plain, and direct, though anecdotes and rhetorical forms of expression are not entirely rejected. It has not been the author's experience that bald facts dryly stated are easily learned or long remembered by the young. A pleasing allusion, a well-chosen metaphor, or a pointed quotation often serves to fasten firmly in the memory information which, though useful, has in itself no attraction for the pupil. Even adult and disciplined minds derive great assistance from the embellishments of style. What reader could not more readily master one of the delightful works of Irving, Motley, or Prescott, than commit to memory a chronological table of its contents?

The sources from which this compilation is derived are the most trustworthy to be found, and neither time nor labor has been spared to verify the statements herein made.

The history of the nation as a whole is sketched, not the history of sections, states, special interests, or particular men.

Much information is scattered through the volume, relating to migration and the progress of settlement; to the history of parties and political questions; to religion, education, invention, art, and refinement.

The foot-notes are designed to stimulate a taste for reading and research, and to afford guidance in the selection of approved literary matter illustrative of American life and annals. They refer to accessible sources of standard history, biography, fiction, and poetry, and it is believed they will be of service in both the school-room and the home circle.

It will be conceded by all that the superior mechanical execution of this volume is in pleasing contrast with that of the great majority of similar works now in the market. The numerous maps are models of elegance and accuracy, and present in themselves a complete and correct idea of the progressive development of the United States. Their fidelity and beauty are due to the skill and taste of Mr. H. H. VAIL, whose service in this and other directions is here most gratefully acknowledged.

The author returns thanks to Mr. JOHN M. NEWTON for valuable assistance in collecting material for Chapter Fifteenth; and to Mr. ROBERT CLARKE, for the use of his excellent historical library.

Without further preliminary, this Manual is offered to the educational public in the hope that it may be found useful. The test of the recitation room must finally determine the merit of every school-book, and its consequent success or failure.

W. H. V.

MARCH 20, 1872.

CONTENTS.

LIST OF MAPS.

HISTORY

OF

THE UNITED STATES.

CHAPTER FIRST.

DISCOVERERS AND DISCOVERIES.

BOUT the close of the thirteenth century, Marco Polo, the Venetian traveler, and others who had journeyed beyond the Ganges, spread abroad dazzling accounts of the continental and island empires of remote eastern Asia, then vaguely known to Europeans under the general name India, or the *Indies*.* They represented Japan and China, then called Cipango and Cathay, as abounding in wealth and magnificence.

2. Navigators had begun to admit that the earth is a sphere, but they greatly underestimated its size, and supposed the eastern limits of Asia to reach near to the western

* See Marco Polo's Travels; also Irving's Columbus, Vol. III., Appendix.

QUESTIONS.—**1.** Who was Marco Polo? About how long ago did he live? What was the ancient name of Japan? Of China?

borders of Europe. It seemed possible "that ships might pass by the west into those rich eastern realms, where, according to the popular belief, the earth teemed with spices, and imperial palaces glittered with pearls and rubies, with diamonds and gold."

3. The first to attempt the actual experiment of crossing the Atlantic in search of a passage, by the west, to the Indies, was Christopher Columbus.* This illustrious man was born near Genoa (jĕn'-o-a), Italy, about the year 1435. Nearly forty years of his life were spent before he conceived, at first in dim outline, his grand scheme of discovery. After years of study and exalted meditation, he came to regard himself as an instrument divinely chosen to trace out for commerce a new route to the opulent East, and to convey the blessings of Christianity to benighted multitudes with whom he expected to establish intercourse.

Christopher Columbus.

4. To enable him to conduct a voyage of discovery,

* See Helps's Life of Columbus, and Prescott's Ferdinand and Isabella.

---

2. What was the belief in the thirteenth century respecting the shape and size of the earth? What attractions were supposed to belong to India?

3. When and where was Columbus born? At what age did he conceive the idea of a voyage of discovery? What objects had he in view?

Columbus applied for assistance, successively, but in vain, to the authorities of his native state, to John II. of Portugal, and to Henry VII. of England. Resolute in spite of repeated disappointment, he sought the court of Spain, and solicited aid of the sovereigns Ferdinand and Isabella. Tedious years elapsed. At length, by the gracious favor of the Spanish queen, means were provided for the prosecution of the long-deferred, but glorious enterprise, which enabled the greatest of maritime heroes to "give a new world to Castile and Leon," the kingdoms of which Ferdinand and Isabella were the sovereigns.

5. Columbus, exulting in spirit, at once made preparations for his first voyage of discovery. He himself furnished one small ship, besides which were procured "two light barks called caravels, not superior to river and coasting craft of more modern days." With difficulty, a sufficient number of mariners was obtained to man the vessels. The whole number of persons that embarked, comprising officers, mariners, and adventurers, was one hundred and twenty. The little squadron put to sea from the port of Palos (på'loce), on the morning of Friday, August 3, **1492.**

At about ten o'clock on the evening of October 11, Columbus, from the top of the cabin of his ship, gazing anxiously toward the west, beheld a light glimmering far away on the horizon, and at dawn on the following day he came in sight of land.* The land proved to be a productive island, called by the natives Guanahani (gwå-nä-hå'nee). It belongs to the group now known as the Bahamas (ba-hå'maṣ). Columbus took formal possession of it for Spain, piously naming it San Salvador (sån-sal-vå-dōr')—Holy Savior.

* See Irving's Columbus, Vol. I., Book III.; also Barlow's Columbiad, and poems on Columbus by Rogers and Lowell.

---

4. To whom did he apply for aid? By whose assistance was he finally fitted out?

5. Of what did his squadron consist? How many persons went on this first voyage? Whence and at what date did Columbus set sail? How many years ago is that? Give the particulars concerning the first discovery of land. What was the land discovered? What name did Columbus give it?

On the 28th of October, Cuba was discovered. Columbus believed this island to be the Cipango of which Marco Polo had told. Hayti was soon after discovered, and named Hispaniola (ēs-pån-yō′lå). Having made some further explorations among the West Indies, Columbus returned to Spain after an absence of nearly seven months.

6. In 1493, Columbus, with seventeen vessels and fifteen hundred men, put forth upon a second expedition, in which he discovered the Caribbean (kar-rib-bee′an) islands and Jamaica (ja-må′ka). He returned in 1496. Two years later he made a third voyage, from which, after discovering the main-land near the mouth of the Orinoco (o-re-nō′-ko), he was, through the treachery and malice of some of his jealous companions, sent home a prisoner in chains. He afterward made a fourth voyage, during which he cruised among the West Indies and explored a part of the coast of Darien.

7. Columbus died in comparative obscurity, at Valladolid (vål-yå-do-leed′), May 20, 1506, aged about seventy years. Ignorant of the real nature and importance of the service he had rendered mankind, he never doubted that he had reached the Indies by a western passage—never dreamed that he had discovered a new continent.

8. Giovanni Cabot (jo-vån′nee cab′-ot) and his son Sebastian, Venetians, sailing under a commission of Henry VII. of England, probably in 1497, discovered Cape Breton. This was nearly five years after Columbus had discovered Guanahani, and about one year before he beheld the main-land near the mouth of the Orinoco. Sebastian Cabot,

---

When was Cuba discovered? What name did Columbus give the island now called Hayti or San Domingo?

6. Give an account of the second expedition of Columbus. When did he make his third voyage? Where did he discover the main-land? What did he accomplish on his last voyage?

7. When, where, and at what age did Columbus die? What was his belief respecting his own discoveries?

8. What discovery did the Cabots make in 1497? Was this before or after the discoveries of Columbus? Under whose commission did the Cabots sail?

in 1498, probably discovered Labrador, though we have no distinct account of this.*

9. Amerigo Vespucci (ȧ-mȧ-ree'go vĕs-poot'chee), a Florentine merchant, it was claimed by an early German geographer, preceded every other European in the discovery of the Western Continent; but history establishes the fact that the earliest visit of Vespucci to the coast which he is said first to have seen was not until 1499. Vespucci's account of his voyages furnishes the earliest published description of the New World, which, on that account, was called by his name, Amerigo, or America.

10. Juan Ponce de Leon (hoo-ȧn pŏn'thȧ dȧ lȧ-ŏn')† a Spanish cavalier, set out in the year 1513, upon a romantic expedition in search of a fountain and a stream which existed, according to tradition, in some delightful island of the west, and which yielded waters possessing the remarkable property of conferring perpetual youth upon all who might drink of them. With strange credulity, De Leon, already old and war-worn, determined to seek this fabulous fountain and stream. Having fitted out a little squadron at his own cost, he put to sea from Porto Rico (pōr'to ree'ko), and directed his course to the unexplored west. Upon the 27th of March, Easter Sunday, called in Spanish Pasqua Florida, the *Feast of Flowers*, he came in sight of a region which he named Florida, a name afterward applied by the Spanish to an unlimited extent of territory which they claimed.

11. Spanish enterprise rapidly added discovery to discovery, and soon the entire coast of the Mexican Gulf was

* See Life of S. Cabot in Sparks's Am. Biog., Vol. IX, First Series.

† See Bancroft's Hist. U. S., Vol. I., pp. 31–4; Parkman's Pioneers of France in the New World, pp. 6–7.

---

9. When did Vespucci first visit the Western Continent? Why was America so named? By what name is it sometimes called in the language of poetry and oratory?

10. What induced Ponce de Leon to lead an expedition of discovery? What did he discover? When? What claim was founded on this discovery?

explored. Diego Velasquez (dē-ā'go vȧ-lȧs'kĕth), governor of Cuba, influenced by reports of rich realms and cities beyond the gulf, was induced to send Hernando Cortez upon the memorable expedition against Montezuma, which, in 1521, resulted in the subjugation of the Aztecs and the Spanish conquest of Mexico.*

12. It was not until 1524 that the French nation, at the public cost, sent out an expedition of discovery to the New World. In that year, Giovanni Verazzano (vĕr-rȧt-zȧ'no), a Florentine, after a stormy voyage of fifty days, reached the main-land of North America, in latitude 34°. He sailed under the patronage of Francis I., with a single caravel, in search of a north-west passage to Cathay. He traced the coast southward for fifty leagues, and then, returning, sailed northward as far as Nova Scotia. He entered and explored the harbors now known as New York and Newport, gathered knowledge concerning the products and inhabitants of the districts he visited, and claimed, for the French king, the whole country along the shores of which he had ranged, under the name of New France. On his return to Europe he prepared a written account of his voyages, which contains the earliest description extant of the eastern border of what is now the United States.

13. Ten years had elapsed since the voyage of Verazzano, when the French Admiral Chabot (shȧ-bō'), by consent of Francis I., dispatched Jacques Cartier (zhȧk kȧr'te-ȧ'), of St. Malo, with two ships, across the Atlantic, for the purpose of exploring and colonizing Newfoundland and the adjacent lands. Cartier set sail in April, 1534, and made the coast of Newfoundland in twenty days. Continuing

* See Prescott's Conquest of Mexico; and E. Maturin's Montezuma (fiction).

---

11. When was Mexico conquered? By whom?

12. In what year did Verazzano sail? Under whose commission? Where did he first discover land? What was the object of his voyage? What was the extent of his explorations? What claim was based on *his* discoveries?

13. When did Cartier make his first voyage? For what purpose?

his voyage, he discovered and named the bays of Chaleur (shå'loor') and Gaspé (gås-på'), and, supposing himself on the direct course to Cathay, sailed up the river St. Lawrence until he could see land on either side. In the next year, Cartier made a second voyage, and extended his discoveries to the island of Montreal (mŏn-tre-âwl'). He spent the winter at Orleans (or'lē-anz), which, as it abounded in grapes, he called the Isle of Bacchus. Cartier and others made persistent attempts at colonization; but sickness, scarcity, and severe weather long defeated all efforts to plant a permanent French colony in America.*

14. After Ponce de Leon's discovery was made known, many daring Spaniards cherished the desire to conquer Florida and explore its remote interior, lured by delusive hopes of finding "a second Mexico with its royal palace and sacred pyramids, or another Cuzco with its temple of the sun encircled with a frieze of gold." Hernando de Soto, a man at once ambitious, wealthy, and influential, obtained of Charles IV. a grant of Florida, on condition that he would colonize and explore it.

Having selected an army of over six hundred men from the much larger number who eagerly volunteered their services, and after making what he deemed ample provision for a grand expedition of conquest, De Soto set sail from Havana, in May, 1539, and, in due time, came to land at Tampa Bay. Abandoning his ships, he proceeded with his men, first northward and then westward, through the trackless and inhospitable wilderness. He had several fierce encounters with the Indians. Hardship, hunger, malaria, and the deadly arrow of lurking foes, daily

* See Parkman's Pioneers of France, p. 181, edition of 1868.

What discoveries did he make? What was accomplished by his second voyage? Where did he winter? What prevented Cartier and others from establishing colonies?

14. What motive induced the Spanish to attempt the exploration of Florida? Who was Hernando de Soto? What grant did he obtain from the King of Spain? Whence did he set sail, and where did he land? How long after De Leon's discovery? What course did De Soto take in his explorations? From what causes did the Spaniards suffer?

thinned the Spanish ranks, and the little army of proud invaders rapidly wasted away. At length, after a two years' march, De Soto came to the Mississippi somewhere near the point which now marks the southern boundary of Tennessee. This was in April, **1541.**

De Soto crossed the great river, and penetrated westward to the mountain region of Arkansas. He then descended to the junction of the Red River with the Mississippi. Here he was seized with a malignant fever, of which he died. His body was consigned to the bosom of the mighty stream he had discovered. His dejected companions, now reduced in number to three hundred, managed, by means of seven rude brigantines of their own construction, to make their way to a Spanish settlement near Tampico.*

15. In the years 1541–2 Francisco Vasquez (vås-kĕth') de Coronado, acting under the orders of Mendoza, Viceroy of Mexico, explored a considerable part of what are now New Mexico and Colorado, in search of the fabulous "seven cities of Cibola." Instead of these cities the river Gila (hē'lå) and the head-waters of the Rio del Norte (rē'o del nor'-tå) were discovered. Spanish adventurers explored the Pacific coast as far north as latitude 44°, hoping to find a passage across the continent to the Atlantic. They named the coast California.

16. The principal inducements that first led Europeans to come to America were: the hope of finding a western passage to India; eagerness to amass sudden fortunes by conquest or mining; curiosity and love of adventure; the prospect of profit from the Newfoundland fisheries, and from trade in train-oil, walrus-tusks, bear-skins, and beaver-

* See Bancroft's United States, Vol. I., Ch. 2; L. A. Wilmer's Life of De Soto; and W. G. Simms's Vasconselos (fiction).

When did De Soto discover the Mississippi? At what point? What were his subsequent movements? Where did he die? What became of his followers?

15. What were the discoveries of Vasquez? Of other Spanish explorers on the Pacific coast?

16. What inducements led Europeans to come to America?

skins; zeal to convert heathen peoples to Christianity; and the design of planting colonies.

GENERAL QUESTIONS AND DIRECTIONS.

How many years passed between the discovery of Guanahani and that of the Mississippi River? Under authority of what nations and sovereigns were discoveries made? Write in the order of time a list of the discoverers named in Chapter First. Tell the nationality of each discoverer, and the name of the power he served. What territorial claims were based upon the discoveries mentioned in Chapter First?

NOTE I.—Pupils should learn to spell and pronounce correctly all the unfamiliar proper names found in the text.

NOTE II.—The numerous references at the bottom of these pages are designed not to verify the author's statements, but to guide teacher and pupil in extending their knowledge beyond the necessarily narrow range of the text-book. Certain standard works should be placed within the students' reach — especially the histories of Hildreth, Bancroft, Lossing, Parkman, and Palfrey; Irving's Life of Washington, and Sparks's American Biographies. The collection of a library in every school district should be encouraged. In this age of books the chances are that, even where no libraries exist, the combined resources of teacher and pupils will furnish, each day, at least one good history, biography, essay, tale, or poem, illustrative of the history lesson. Should there be a little time to spare after the regular recitation, it may profitably be employed in reading selected passages aloud.

CHAPTER SECOND.

THE INDIANS.

THE natural aspect of North America three hundred years ago was wild and grand. From the Atlantic to the Alleghanies, and south of 40°, even to the Mississippi, extended one unbroken forest. Thousands of square miles of forest also lay north of the Great Lakes. From the Mexican Gulf to the Arctic Ocean stretched a region of plains, spreading westward in some places to the Rocky Mountains, part barren, and part covered with rank grass. East of the Mississippi these plains were interspersed with forests, the wooded and the grassy lands there being of about equal extent. West of the Rocky Mountains were both plains and forests, the latter prevailing on the Pacific slope.

18. The forests abounded with bears, deer, and many species of smaller quadrupeds. The prairies of the Missouri were covered with bison. The lakes and streams of the continent were full of fish. Innumerable wild fowl frequented woodland, water-side, and prairie.

19. The American Aborigines were fit denizens of the

QUESTIONS.—**17.** Locate the forest region of aboriginal North America. What portions of the continent were covered by plains? What was the character of these plains?

18. Mention the principal animal life of the primeval forests, plains, and streams.

primeval wilderness. Children of nature, the Red men were akin to all that is rude, savage, and unreclaimable. These strange people, of unknown origin, were scattered sparsely over the whole continent. Their number within the limits of what is now the United States was at no time, since the discovery of America, above 400,000 individuals. Those dwelling east of the Mississippi River numbered, perhaps, 180,000.

The North American Indians may be divided into eleven families, each distinguished by peculiarities of language: the Iroquois, the Algonquins, the Cherokees, the Catawbas, the Mobilians, the Dakotas, the Athapascans, the Shoshones, the Eskimos, the Aztecs, and the Mayas.* The location of these families is shown on the map facing page 23. Each family was divided into tribes or nations; each tribe, into numerous villages and bands. Independently of their local subdivisions, many of the tribes were divided into clans, each designated by a specific name, as the clan of the Hawk, or the clan of the Wolf.

Our knowledge of the geographical distribution of the Indians, and of their early migrations, is scanty and uncertain. "America, when it became known to Europeans, was, as it had long been, a scene of wide-spread revolution. North and south, tribe was giving place to tribe, language to language; for the Indian, hopelessly unchanging in respect to individual and social development, was, as regarded tribal relations and local haunts, mutable as the wind."

By far the best known of the Indian families are the Iroquois† and the Algonquins. It is from the study of these that history is enabled to delineate Indian life and character with fidelity. These exhibit the highest and most

* See D. G. Brinton's Myths of the New World, Chap. II.

† See L. H. Morgan's League of the Iroquois.

19. In what part of North America did Indians live? How great was their number? How many were east of the Mississippi? Upon what distinction are the Indian families based? Name the eleven families. How are these families divided and sub-divided? What are clans? What is known of the early geographical distribution of the Indians? Which of the Indian families do we know most about?

interesting types of the American savage. Of the Iroquois, Brinton says: "They are more like ancient Romans than Indians, and are leading figures in the colonial wars." To this formidable family belonged Red Jacket, Joseph Brant, and many other celebrated warriors. The fame of the Algonquins is perpetuated in the history of King Philip, Pontiac, Tecumseh, Black Hawk, and Pocahontas, the daughter of Powhatan.*

Red Jacket.

20. In person, the Indians were tall, straight, well-formed, and athletic. They were of a copper color, had high cheekbones, small, dark eyes, straight, black hair, and no beard. In summer they went almost naked; their winter dress was made of the skins of wild animals. They were fond of ornament, and decorated their bodies profusely with feathers, trinkets, and paint. Some of the tribes lived in villages covering a space of from one to ten acres. Their houses were rudely constructed of saplings, and covered with roofs of bark. Other tribes lived in huts, called

* See Stone's Life and Times of Red Jacket, and Life of Brant; Drake's Life of Tecumseh, and of Black Hawk; Parkman's Conspiracy of Pontiac; Philip of Pokanoket, in Irving's Sketch Book; Halleck's Red Jacket, and Sands's Yamoyden (poems).

What does Brinton say of the Iroquois? Mention some celebrated Iroquois. What famous Algonquins can you name?

20. What was the personal appearance of the Indians? How did they dress and adorn themselves?

wigwams, made of skins stretched over a framework o. poles.

The Indians subsisted mainly on the fruits of the chase, on fish, and the spontaneous products of the soil; though maize, beans, pumpkins, and tobacco were cultivated in many localities. To the women, or *squaws,* fell the task of tilling the soil and gathering the harvest. To them, indeed, fell all drudgery, such as collecting fire-wood, preparing food, and making fishing-nets. When not employed in their favorite pursuits of war or the hunt, the men sometimes engaged in the building of houses, or the manufacture of weapons, pipes, and canoes; but for the most part they were idle, or else whiling their time in dancing, gambling, and feasting.

Even among savages, necessity enforces commercial relations, and a kind of traffic in skins, corn, nets, fish, etc., was regularly carried on. The Indian currency, called *wampum,* consisted of a sort of long beads cut from the inside of certain shells. Wampum fastened upon strings or belts was used as an ornament, as a token of agreement in treaties, and for various other purposes.

21. The Red men held war to be the most desirable and glorious of employments. Tribe warred against tribe, village against village, personal enemy against enemy. Stratagem, surprise, and the basest treachery were approved and practiced even by the bravest. Language can not exaggerate the ferocity of Indian battle, or the revolting cruelty practiced upon the captive of war. The very words tomahawk, scalping-knife, and torture-scaffold fill the fancy with dire images; and to say "as savage as an Iroquois warrior" is to exhaust the power of simile.

22. Imbued by nature and habit with hatred of restraint, the Indian would tolerate no government that interfered with absolute personal freedom. Yet, of choice, he placed

---

Describe their habitations. What was their food? How were the squaws employed? How, the men? In what articles did they traffic? What is wampum?

21. How did the Indians regard war? How did they conduct warfare? What was their treatment of prisoners?

ımself under some political and social regulations, both for his individual and for the general good. His self-control was remarkable. Each tribe had its *sachem*, or *sagamore*, who held over it a general directing power. Sub-tribes, bands, and villages followed the leadership of inferior chiefs. These chiefs held their position by a species of hereditary descent, but they were deposed for incompetency or cowardice, and their authority was always proportional to their personal prowess and success in war.

Questions in which many were interested, such as related to the making of war or peace, or to the disposal of prisoners, were discussed in a council composed of chiefs and leading warriors. The deliberations of the council were carried on with the utmost decorum. There, professional orators engaged in long debates, and sometimes the grave circle of listening braves was thrilled and persuaded by true eloquence. The decision of the council became temporary law.

23. The Indians were gross sensualists, and usually followed the leading of their baser propensities. They were wasteful and improvident. They were generally destitute of fine sentiment, modesty, or delicate moral perceptions. Their religion was a sort of Pantheism, full of extravagant superstitions, and lacking in spirituality. They had good traits—were brave, independent, hospitable, and in some sense generous and grateful. On the other hand, they were lazy, mean, and treacherous. They were distinguished for jealousy and revenge.*

24. Hispaniola, at the time of its discovery, was popu-

* See Parkman's brilliant volumes; Catlin's Notes and Letters on the North American Indians; Drake's Indian Biography; also Cooper's Leather Stocking Tales, and Wyandotte; Longfellow's Song of Hiawatha; and Whittier's Mogg Megone.

22. How did the Indians regard freedom? Did they admit of any system of government? What was the office and power of chiefs? How did chiefs retain power? What was the object of Indian councils? How were they conducted?

23. What was the moral and intellectual character of the Indians? What was their religion?

lated by at least a million of inhabitants, whom Columbus described as peculiarly mild and friendly, though feeble. They were reduced to sixteen thousand in fifteen years. This fearful mortality was the effect of Spanish cruelty, which extorted intolerable labor from the natives, in the gold-mines and under the task-master's lash. In order to supply the deficiency of laborers, the Spanish decoyed into Hispaniola forty thousand of the inhabitants of the Lucayo, now Bahama, islands. Six-sevenths of these perished within nine years. The whole aboriginal population of the West Indies soon became extinct under the iron rule of the Spanish.

How different this result from that contemplated by the philanthropic mind of Columbus! Pizarro in Peru, and Cortez in Mexico, extended usurpation and havoc to unoffending nations on the continent. Ponce de Leon, De Soto, and indeed all the Spanish discoverers, outraged every sentiment of justice and humanity in their conduct toward the Indians. They enslaved them, they compelled them to perform the most degrading work, they used them as beasts of burden, they loaded them with chains, they tortured them for complaining, and killed them without compunction; they burned villages and pursued the flying inhabitants with blood-hounds. They kidnapped ship-loads of Indians and sold them into slavery.

Nor was the treatment which the Indians received at the hands of the English discoverers either conciliatory or humane. The French, however, except in a few cases, met the children of the forest with kindness and courtesy, and often succeeded in winning their confidence and aid. As might have been expected, a general mistrust of white men soon spread among the Indians. Those who had actually suffered at the hands of European invaders, cherished in

---

24. How many Indians were in Hispaniola at the time of its discovery? What became of them? How did the Spanish employ them? What was the conduct of the Spanish generally toward the Indians? Enumerate the cruelties practiced by the Spanish discoverers. How did the English treat the Indians? How did the French? What was the prevalent feeling of the Indians with respect to the white men?

unforgiving hearts a fierce desire for revenge. The violent and unjust course pursued by the Spaniards in their treatment of the natives was the origin of a series of struggles, which has continued to the present day.

The Indian nations were destined to a swift and melancholy destruction. They vanished before the advancing power of the white man. They are fast becoming extinct. The names they gave still cling, like vague epitaphs, to our mountains, lakes, and rivers, and even to many of our political divisions and towns;—

> "But they are gone,
> With their old forests wide and deep,
> And we have built our homes upon
> Fields where their generations sleep."

Map Questions and Geographical Review.

Bound North America. Why was it called the New World? Why America? What parts of North America were originally covered by forests? What by prairies? Give the different names of the island first discovered by Columbus. What is the modern name of Hispaniola? Of the Lucayo islands?

In what latitude is Cuba? What did Columbus suppose Cuba to be? Where is Jamaica? When did the Cabots first visit America? What discovery was made by Ponce de Leon? When? What part of the continent did Verazzano explore? When? Who explored the St. Lawrence? When and by whom was the Mississippi discovered?

When and by whom were the head-waters of the Rio Grande discovered? When and by whom was the Pacific coast first explored? When and by whom was Yucatan discovered? When and by whom was Florida discovered? What discovery was made in 1494? In 1541? In 1542? In 1534?

How many Indian families inhabited North America? Of which is most known? Give the location of the Mayas. The Aztecs. The Eskimos. The Shoshones. The Athapascans. The Dakotas. The Mobilians. The Catawbas. The Cherokees. The Algonquins. The Iroquois. What nation dwelt in Mexico? In Yucatan? Within the present limits of New York? Of New England? Of Florida?

With which families did the Spanish come in collision? What families dwelt west of 90°? What south of 40°? What family occupied the prairie region? Were the West Indies inhabited? How many Indians were there in all?

NOTE.—The pupil should compare the maps in this book with corresponding maps on which present political divisions, towns, and geographical names are correctly given.

CHAPTER THIRD.

EARLIEST SETTLEMENTS IN NORTH AMERICA.

HE French Admiral Gaspard de Coligny (ko-leen′-ye), desirous of affording French Protestants a place of refuge from religious persecution, obtained the consent of Charles IX. to plant a colony in the New World. Accordingly, a company of Huguenots* (hū′ge-nots), led by Jean Ribaut† (rė-bȯ′), crossed the Atlantic in 1562, and, landing at Port Royal, built a fort and garrisoned it with a party of thirty men. "From the North Pole to the Gulf of Mexico there was no Christian denizen but they." Owing to various causes, the colony became dissatisfied. Their provisions failing, they, in desperation, embarked for France in a frail boat. Hunger reduced them to the horrible necessity of sacrificing one of their own number for food.

26. Not discouraged by one failure, Coligny, in 1564, sent forth, under the command of Rene de Laudonnière (rẹh-nȧ′ dȧ lō-dŏn′ne-air), another and larger body of Hu-

* See the Huguenots, by Samuel Smiles; and W. G. Simms's Lily and Totem (fiction).

† See Sparks's Am. Biog., Second Series, Vol. VII.

QUESTIONS.—**25.** By whose influence were the Huguenots led to seek America? Who were the Huguenots? Give a full account of Ribaut's colony. When did Ribaut make his voyage?

26. Who commanded Coligny's second body of colonists?

guenot emigrants. These, having chosen the bank of the St. John, by them called the River of May, as a place of lodgment, erected another fort, named, as that at Port Royal had been, Fort Caroline, in honor of the French king.

But Spain had no thought of relinquishing her claim to Florida, and the bigoted Philip II.* readily entered into a compact with Pedro Menendez, by which the latter was bound to extirpate the French colony and establish in its stead a settlement of Spanish. Menendez equipped several vessels at his own expense, and, with a number of soldiers and emigrants, put to sea.

Pedro Menendez.
(From Parkman's Pioneers of France.)

Arriving at Florida in September, **1564,** he proclaimed Philip monarch of all North America, and immediately laid the foundation of St. Augustine (sån aw'-gŭs-teen), the oldest town in the United States. He next proceeded with 500 soldiers against the Huguenot colony, surprised Fort Caroline, and massacred 142 men, women, and children—not, as he declared, because they were French, but because they were Protestants. Several hundred more of the French, who had taken ship, expecting to encounter the Spanish by sea, were wrecked, and they gave themselves up to Menendez, relying on his promise that their lives

* See Prescott's Philip the Second.

Where did these establish themselves? What bargain did Philip make with Menendez? When did Menendez arrive at Florida? What was his first action? Describe his proceedings against the Huguenots.

should be spared. The Spaniard, basely treacherous, caused them to be slain in cold blood. Laudonnière and a few others escaped to France.

The friends of the murdered colonists applied in vain to the crown for means of retribution. It was reserved to the bold Gascon, Dominique de Gourgues, (do-me-nēk' dȧ goorg) to render blood for blood. By selling his own property, he procured three vessels, and with 150 resolute men put to sea in April, 1567, and reached Florida in May. He surprised and, by the help of Indians, captured the Spanish forts upon the River of May. The prisoners taken were hanged upon the trees under which Menendez had slaughtered the Huguenots. His purpose fulfilled, De Gourgues returned to France. The victims of Spanish violence and bigotry were avenged.*

27. Augustin Ruyz (rīth), in 1580, and Antonio Espejo (ĕs-pā'ho), in 1581, re-explored the region first visited by Vasquez. Espejo named it New Mexico. In 1582, the Spanish founded, on a branch of the Rio Grande, the town of Santa Fé (săn'tȧ fā), next to St. Augustine the oldest town in the United States.

28. In 1578, Sir Humphrey Gilbert† obtained a patent from Elizabeth, Queen of England, to plant a colony in North America; and during the same year he led an expedition to Newfoundland, and went through the ceremony of claiming that island for his sovereign. But he failed to establish a settlement. On his return voyage his ship foundered at midnight in a stormy sea, and he and his crew were lost.

* See Theodore Irving's Conquest of Florida, and Helps's Spanish Conquest of America.

† See Barrow's Naval Worthies, and Longfellow's Sir Humphrey Gilbert (poem).

Relate the deeds of Dominique de Gourgues.

27. By whom and in what years was New Mexico re-explored? When was Santa Fe founded? How long after St. Augustine?

28. In what year did Sir Humphrey Gilbert obtain a patent to colonize America? Of whom? What did Gilbert accomplish? What was the manner of his death?

29. Six years later, the famous Sir Walter Raleigh* (raw'le), a step-brother of Gilbert, having received of Elizabeth an ample patent, renewed the attempt to found an English colony in America. In 1584 he dispatched Philip Ami'das and Arthur Barlow, with two vessels, to seek, in a mild latitude, some suitable place to make a settlement.

Sir Walter Raleigh.

The expedition made land near Cape Fear, coasted northward along the Carolina shore, and visited the sounds of Pamlico and Albemarle, and the neighboring islands of Wococon and Roanoke. With these islands the voyagers were much delighted. They found the natives gentle and hospitable. Upon returning to England, Amidas and Barlow described their discoveries in glowing terms, and Elizabeth named the region they had visited Virginia. Raleigh was knighted for his discoveries, and, possessing both wealth and influence, he vigorously pushed forward the work of colonization. A squadron of seven ships, commanded by Sir Richard Grenville, conveyed his first company of emigrants to

* See Edwards's, W. Oldys's, and P. F. Tytler's Life of Raleigh; and Southey's Lives of British Admirals.

29. What Englishman next after Gilbert attempted to colonize America? Give an account of the voyage of Amidas and Barlow. What name was given to the region visited by them?

Virginia in 1585. A colony of 110 men, with Ralph Lane as governor, was left at Roanoke Island; but, the next year, discouraged and homesick, the whole colony returned to England.

A second band of fifteen men, left also by Grenville at Roanoke, in 1586, was totally destroyed by the Indians. A third company of eighty-nine men, women, and children, organized to found "the city of Raleigh," came to Virginia in 1587; but, when, in 1590, an expedition conveyed supplies to their place of settlement, not a single person could be found. Nothing was ever learned of the fate of this colony, the last that Raleigh undertook to establish.

30. In 1602, Bartholomew Gosnold, sailing in the employ of Raleigh's assignees, visited the American coast, named Cape Cod and the Elizabeth Islands, and then returned to England with a cargo of furs, skins, and sassafras. The next year Martin Pring, in the service of some merchants of Bristol, entered Penobscot Bay with two small vessels and coasted southward as far as Martha's Vineyard. He also carried home peltries, and sassafras, an article then highly valued in medicine.

We learn from the foregoing facts that the earliest attempts to colonize the New World were made by the French, the Spanish, and the English, and that the Spanish founded the first permanent settlements on this continent. The English undertook to plant themselves north of Florida. Their schemes were commercial and agricultural. They entertained ambitious designs of building cities and organizing states.

The English at first held amicable relations with their dusky neighbors. But the Indians were proud, punctilious, and quick to take offense, and it was not long before the

---

When did Raleigh send his first colony to Virginia? Under what governor? What was the history of this colony? Of the second colony at Roanoke? Of what did the third colony consist? What was the design of this colony? What was its fate?

30. Narrate the facts concerning Gosnold's voyage to America. With what did he load his ships? What points did Pring visit? What was the object of his voyage?

English excited their hostility. It is probable that Raleigh's colonists of 1587 perished by the tomahawk and the knife.

Many and great were the difficulties that beset the men who cast their lot as first residents of the wild forest that bordered the Atlantic. It is not surprising that failure after failure marks the history of colonization. When a hundred years had elapsed after the voyage of Columbus, America had no white population north of 30°, excepting a handful of Spaniards at Santa Fé.

GENERAL QUESTIONS AND DIRECTIONS.

How many years elapsed from the time of the discovery of America to that of Martin Pring's voyage? What permanent settlements had been made in the New World in the year 1600? By what nation? Under what king? Under what French sovereign were attempts at colonization made? Under what English sovereign? What part did the Indians take in relation to the early settlements in Florida? In Virginia? Prepare a list of the names of the leaders of the various expeditions mentioned in Chapter Third. Tell the nationality of each leader. Arrange in chronological order the dates given in Chapter Third, and opposite each date briefly write the principal event to which it refers.

CHAPTER FOURTH.

THE SETTLEMENT OF VIRGINIA.

1606—1643.

Ruins of Jamestown.

IN April, 1606, two rival companies, the London and the Plymouth, obtained of James I., the successor of Queen Elizabeth, a joint charter granting the privilege of establishing colonies in America. The proposed colonies were to be under the general control of a Council of Virginia resident in England, and each under the special management of a local council resident in America. All council members were to be appointed by the king.

32. The London Company sent out three ships and 105 colonists under the command of Christopher Newport. The adventurers made for Roanoke, but a storm drove them northward, and they entered the Chesapeake Bay. They ascended a stream called by the natives the Powhatan′, on the north bank of which, about fifty miles from the bay, they selected a spot for a settlement, loyally naming it Jamestown. This was on the 13th of May, **1607.**

These first colonists were quite unfit to found a community in the wilderness. Forty-eight of them were indolent

---

QUESTIONS.—**31.** When were the London and the Plymouth companies chartered? By whom? How were the proposed colonies to be governed? How were council members to be appointed?

32. Which company first sent out a colony? Of how many? Under whose command? Where did they finally settle? When?

"gentlemen;" only twelve were field laborers; only four, mechanics; the rest were soldiers and servants. Among the names of those whom the king had selected to form the local council was that of Captain John Smith.* On a false charge, Smith was excluded from the council, and his accuser, the jealous and mercenary Edward Wingfield, was chosen first president.

Captain John Smith.

In June, Newport returned to England. Want of food and of good water induced sickness, of which half the colonists died. Wingfield put the public stores to his private use, and, being accused of "living in luxury while the others were starving," he was deposed. His successor, one Ratcliffe, proved inefficient. Smith was honorably restored to his place in the council, and on him the management of the affairs of the colony devolved. This brave man, while on an expedition up the Chickahominy, hoping to find a passage to Cathay, was captured by the Indians. He was carried before an Algonquin chief, Powhatan, and by him condemned to die. It is related in a narrative, attributed to Smith's own pen, that "Pocahontas,

* See Hillard's Life of John Smith in Sparks's Am Biog., Vol. II.

What was the character of these first settlers? What unjust treatment did Captain John Smith suffer? What was Wingfield's relation to the colony? Who was his successor? What stream did Smith explore, and with what object? Relate the anecdote of Smith and Pocahontas.

the king's dearest daughter, got his head in her armes, and laid her owne upon his to save him from death." *

Pocahontas was subsequently married to a young Englishman, John Rolfe, who took her to England, where she died, leaving a son, from whom some of the leading families in Virginia trace their pedigree. Released from captivity, Smith returned to Jamestown, and found the colony reduced to less than fifty persons. To these were presently added 120 more, most of whom were vagabond gentlemen, goldsmiths, and others equally inefficient as pioneers. In the autumn of 1608, Smith made an exploration of Chesapeake Bay. Soon after this he was chosen president of the council.

Again the colony received an accession, this time of seventy persons, two of whom were women. Smith administered with sense and vigor, securing to the colony all the prosperity that circumstances would permit. He is to be regarded as the central figure about which all others concerned in the settlement of Virginia group in subordination. Says Bancroft: "He was the Father of Virginia, the true leader who first planted the Saxon race within the borders of the United States."

33. In May, 1609, a new charter was granted, in which the powers before exercised by the king were transferred to the London Company, and the local council was superseded by a governor. The company elected Lord de La Warr governor for life; but his affairs detaining him awhile in England, Newport, Sir Thomas Gates, and Sir George Somers were appointed to act temporarily in his stead. They put to sea with nine vessels, on which embarked

* The authenticity of this beautiful anecdote has been called in question by several recent authorities. See S. Hopkins's Youth of the Old Dominion; also M. W. Moseby's Pocahontas, Seba Smith's Powhatan, and Mrs. Sigourney's Pocahontas.

What was the after history of Pocahontas? What second exploration did Smith make? What does the historian Bancroft say of Smith?

33. What change was made in the government of Virginia in 1609? Who was elected governor? Who were appointed governors *pro tem.?* With how many vessels did they put to sea?

more than 500 emigrants, much of a sort with those that had preceded them—"ruined gentlemen, prodigal sons, disreputable retainers, debauched tradesmen." The ship which carried the deputy governors was wrecked on the shore of Bermuda; the others arrived safely in Virginia.

The new-comers at first disputed the authority of Smith, who, nevertheless, continued to rule, until, disabled by an accidental discharge of gunpowder, he was obliged to cross the sea for surgical aid. The colony, now presided over by Captain Percy, who was prostrated by sickness, fell into confusion. Laziness and vice prevailed, and were speedily followed by famine, disease, and recklessness. Some resorted to piracy. This period in the history of Jamestown is known as the *Starving Time.* The colony in six months dwindled away until it numbered only sixty souls. These were unexpectedly gladdened by the arrival of the party that had been wrecked at Bermuda. So general was the discontent that the deputy governors were persuaded to abandon Virginia, and the whole colony took ship and set out for Newfoundland; but, meeting Lord de La Warr near the mouth of James River with men and provisions, they were induced to return, and the deserted village was re-occupied.

The settlement grew more prosperous, but the governor was taken sick, and returned to England, leaving Percy again in authority. Shortly afterward Sir Thomas Dale came to Jamestown with supplies and 300 settlers. He assumed the government and proclaimed a severe code of laws, which continued in force for eight years. Dale was superseded by Sir Thomas Gates, who established the settlements of Henrico and New Bermuda, and who instituted the right of private property, greatly to the good of the colonists. In 1617 Samuel Argall became governor of Vir-

---

With how many emigrants, and of what description? What happened at Bermuda? What befell the colony when Smith left it? How many died during the "starving time?" What did the rest do? Was De La Warr's presence favorable to the prosperity of the colony? Why did he return to England? Who took his place? What kind of laws did Dale establish? Who superseded Dale, and what service did he render the colonists?

ginia, much against the will of the settlers, whom he oppressed and defrauded.

George Yeardley was soon appointed in his place. He it was who called the first Colonial Assembly of Virginia, composed of the governor, the council, and two burgesses from each of the eleven plantations into which the colony was divided. Edwin Sandys, treasurer of the London Company during the year 1621, sent 800 emigrants to Virginia. Among these were ninety young women, who were disposed of as wives to those of the planters who paid their passage. From 100 to 150 pounds of tobacco was "the cost of a wife." Sandys soon resigned his office, and the Earl of Southampton, a friend and patron of Shakespeare, was appointed treasurer in his place.

In August, **1620**, a Dutch ship brought to Jamestown twenty Africans, who were sold to the colonists; and thus negro slavery was introduced into the English colonies.* A year later an ordinance was enacted by the London Company granting a colonial constitution to Virginia, by which the people, except in local matters, were subject to laws essentially the same as those of England. Sir Thomas Wyatt was, at the same time, appointed to supersede Yeardley as governor.

34. Very friendly relations existed between the colonists and the Indians up to the time of Powhatan's death. But Opechancánough, the son of Powhatan, proved a bold, cunning, and inveterate foe to the white men. He planned the destruction of all the Virginia settlements. At noon on March 12, 1622, the scattered plantations were attacked by the savages, and 350 men, women, and children were massacred. The inhabitants of Jamestown, forewarned, de-

* The Spanish had already introduced black slaves into Florida. Negro hands helped to lay the foundation of St. Augustine.

Who followed Argall? What important act marks his administration? How many emigrants did Sandys send to Virginia? How were the women disposed of? By whom were negro slaves first brought to Virginia?

34. What was the character of Powhatan's son and successor? What plot did he devise? How was it executed?

fended themselves without much loss of life. The colonists now entered upon a war of extermination. Gradually the Indians were driven away or destroyed.

35. In 1624 the first colonial statutes of Virginia were enacted. About the same time the king, displeased at the growing power of the London Company, took such action as resulted in the forfeiture of the charter, and Virginia became a royal province. Wyatt was continued at the head of affairs, and no marked changes were made in the government. James I. died in March, 1625, and Charles I. ascended the English throne. An unsuccessful attempt was made by the new monarch to secure a royal monopoly of the tobacco trade, by far the most profitable part of American commerce at that time. In 1634 the colony was divided into eight counties.*

36. Painfully slow was the progress of Virginia for the first dozen years after the planting of Jamestown. But, like a hardy tree, having once taken root, she began steadily to grow. Her early laws, though severe in the letter, were in spirit mild, and her citizens enjoyed a large degree of political freedom. "Virginia was the first state in the world, composed of separate boroughs diffused over an extensive surface, where the government was organized on the principle of universal suffrage." All tax payers were allowed to vote. Conformity to the Church of England was required, and neither Catholics, Quakers, nor Puritans were tolerated, though persecutions did not arise as in New England.

* See Charles Campbell's History of the Colony and Ancient Dominion of Virginia; R. R. Howison's History of Virginia; Thomas Jefferson's Notes on Virginia.

---

35. When were the first colonial statutes enacted? What change took place in the government of the colony at nearly the same date? When did James I. die? Who then became King of England?

36. What was the character of the early laws of Virginia? The condition of the people politically? Who were voters? What was the established religion? What social distinction existed? How were the lands worked? What was the chief agricultural product of Virginia?

Class distinctions existed, society being divided into persons of "quality," or aristocrats, and the common people. A generous hospitality characterized all ranks. There were no towns of any size in Virginia, and no manufactories. There were few churches and no public schools. The plantations were worked by indented servants and slaves. Tobacco, the chief agricultural product, was largely exported. It was also used as the circulating medium at home. Indeed, tobacco sustained the colony, the material profit derived from it being the inducement to migration.

GENERAL QUESTIONS AND DIRECTIONS.

Under what British sovereign was the colonization of Virginia attempted? Chiefly by whom? Under what sovereign was it accomplished? Chiefly by whom? How long after the discovery of America was Jamestown founded? How long after the founding of St. Augustine? Write in chronological order a list of the names of the presidents and governors of Virginia as given in Chapter Fourth. Prepare a chronological table of the dated events given in Chapter Fourth.

NOTE.—The pupil should copy and preserve in a blank book the various lists, tables, etc., which he is directed to prepare. In recitation the blackboard may be used to exhibit his work.

CHAPTER FIFTH.

SETTLEMENT OF NEW ENGLAND.

1620—1643.

I. PLYMOUTH.

THE Plymouth Company made an unsuccessful attempt, in **1607**, to establish a settlement in North Virginia, as the country between latitude 38° and 45° was then called. Seven years later Captain John Smith surveyed the coast from Cape Cod to Penobscot Bay, and made a map of the country which he named *New England*. Through the influence of Sir Francis Gorges and others, a patent was obtained of James I., in November, **1620**, incorporating the Council for New England, to which was granted the territory from latitude 40° to 48°, and from the Atlantic to the Pacific.

38. Independently of this council, and but a few days after the issuing of its patent, 100 Puritans (the Pilgrims) anchored their ship in the harbor of Cape Cod, and soon

---

QUESTIONS.—**37.** Did the Plymouth Company establish any colony in America? To what region was the name North Virginia applied? What enterprise did Captain Smith accomplish in 1614? When was the Council for New England incorporated? What territory was granted to this organization?

afterward they planted the first permanent New England colony at Plymouth. Natives of England, many of them had been living for eleven years at Leyden (lī′dẹn), Holland, whither, on account of religious persecution, they had fled with their revered minister, John Robinson. Not contented to remain in Holland, they resolved to seek civil and religious liberty in the New World. After a stormy voyage of sixty-four days, in the Mayflower, "they came in sight of the white sand banks of Cape Cod." They disembarked to begin their settlement, December 21, **1620.***

Before they landed a solemn compact was drawn up and signed by all the men, forty in number, by which they were organized into a body politic. John Carver was unanimously chosen governor. The little colony was divided into nineteen families. They at once began to cut trees and build huts. The winter proved mild, but before warm weather returned John Carver and nearly half of his associates had died from exposure and bad food. William Bradford was elected governor. He continued in office until 1632, when Edward Winslow was elected in his place.

The pilgrims were not daunted by peril, hardship, or famine. For several years there was alarming scarcity of food and general prevalence of sickness. The colony was occasionally increased by immigration, but when four years had passed Plymouth "consisted of only thirty-two cabins, inhabited by one hundred and eighty persons." In 1623 the establishment of private property was inaugurated, and it proved, as in Virginia, very stimulating to industry. Friendly relations were early established with the Indians,

* See Holmes's Robinson of Leyden and Mrs. Hemans's Landing of the Pilgrim Fathers, poems.

38. Where was the first permanent New England settlement made? Give the history of the Pilgrims. What action was taken on board the Mayflower before landing? Who was first governor of Plymouth, and for how long? How did the colonists employ themselves? Who succeeded Carver as governor? What evils beset the young colony? What were the size and population of Plymouth in 1624? What relations existed between the colony and the Indians?

especially the Wampano'ags, whose chief, Mas'sas-soit, entered into a treaty of peace, which was kept inviolate for nearly half a century.

Such of the Indians as manifested hostility were intimidated by the firmness of Bradford, the address of Winslow, and the bravery of Miles Standish, the military head of the colony. The settlers had not passed their second winter at Plymouth before they were alarmed by rumors that the Narragansett Indians meditated war against them. We are told by Bradford that they "built a fort with good timber, both strong and comely, which was of good defense, made with a flat roof and battlements, on which their ordnance were mounted. It served them also for a meeting-house, and was fitted accordingly for that use." The government of Plymouth was, for more than eighteen years, a pure democracy both in church and state. It then took a representative form, the increase of population making the change desirable.*

II. MASSACHUSETTS BAY COLONY.

39. As early as 1623 some Devonshire fishermen had started a settlement at Cape Ann. This did not succeed, but it was the forerunner of a permanent plantation at Salem, undertaken by the Massachusetts Bay Company and begun by John Endicott and about fifty or sixty others, September, 1628. Endicott was one of six patentees who obtained of the council for New England a grant, afterward confirmed in a royal charter, of lands extending from three miles north of the Merrimac to three miles south of the

* See Palfrey's Hist. of N. E., Vol. I., Ch. V. and VI.; Banvard's Plymouth and the Pilgrims; Young's Chronicles of the Pilgrim Fathers; Cheever's Journal of the Pilgrims; also L. M. Child's Hobomok, Cheney's Peep at the Pilgrims, J. L. Motley's Merry Mount, E. H. Sears's Picture of the Olden Time, fictions; and Longfellow's Courtship of Miles Standish, poem.

What form of government did the Pilgrims adopt?

39. When and by whom was Salem settled? Under what grant? What was the council for New England?

Charles, and from ocean to ocean. The colony was organized, and Endicott was elected governor.

The next year the colony received an accession of "eighty women and maids, twenty-six children, and three hundred men," most of them devoted Puritans. A branch settlement was soon made at Charlestown. In August, 1629, an important change took place, by which the government and patent of the colonies were transferred from the company to the resident colonists in New England. John Winthrop was now chosen governor, with a deputy and eighteen assistants.*

John Winthrop, Senior.

40. Early in 1630 the new officers reached Salem, accompanied by about a thousand colonists, many of whom were persons of wealth, influence, and education. Scarcity of food prevailed for a time, and many sickened and died. Charlestown was presently selected as the capital of the colony, and there the court of Assistants convened from time to time and enacted laws; but the seat of government was

* See R. C. Winthrop's Life of John Winthrop.

Who was first governor of the Salem colony? What important transfer took place in 1629? Why important? Who was the second governor of the colony? How was his power supplemented?

40. What accession of numbers did the colony receive in 1630? What was the character of the immigrants?

transferred to Boston, October 19. Already eight settlements had sprung up about Boston Bay.

The colonial laws were stringent; the government was theocratic in form. The power of the governor and his assistants was at first almost supreme. They and their adherents were opposed to rotation in office; but the majority of the people, availing themselves of the right guaranteed them by their charter, elected Thomas Dudley governor in Winthrop's place, in the year 1634. Thus early began the conflict of free thought in America, and the formation of political parties. In 1635 the council for New England resigned its charter to the king, and its territory was granted to twelve individuals. The change scarcely affected the Massachusetts colonies at all.

41. It was at about this time that Roger Williams,* afterward so celebrated as the principal founder of the state of Rhode Island, came to America. A young and promising minister, he was for a time settled over the Salem church; but, on account of disagreement with the magistrates and dissent from some intolerant views of the ecclesiastics, he was exiled from the colony. Dudley was succeeded in office by John Haines, and he by the famous Sir Harry Vane.† In 1637 Winthrop was again elected. Soon after this, John Wheelwright and Mrs. Anne Hutchinson were banished for the dissemination of religious opinions of a liberal character, thought by the authorities to be dangerous.‡ Wheelwright, with thirty-five companions, settled on a branch of the Piscat'aqua, and founded Exeter.

Small settlements had previously been made at Portsmouth and Dover. John Mason obtained a patent for the

* See R. Elton's and J. D. Knowles's Life of Roger Williams.

† See Forster's Life of Vane.

‡ See Sparks's Am. Biog., Vol. VI., Second Series.

What political contest occurred in 1634? How did it result? What became of the council for New England?

41. Who was Roger Williams? Narrate the events of his ministry and exile. Give the facts in regard to Wheelwright and Mrs. Hutchinson. By whom was New Hampshire named?

land lying between Massachusetts and the Piscat'aqua, and named it New Hampshire. Mason died, and New Hampshire reverted to different proprietors. Three years after Wheelwright's settlement was started, the province was united with Massachusetts. In 1640 Dudley was again elected over Winthrop. Richard Bellingham was elected the next year, and at the end of his term Winthrop was once more elected. In **1643** the settlements or towns of Massachusetts, thirty in number, were distributed into four counties, and the government was divided into two legislative branches.*

III. THE CONNECTICUT COLONY.

42. Lord Saye and Sele and Lord Brooke, patentees of Connecticut, dispatched John Winthrop, son of the governor of Massachusetts, and almost as much distinguished as his father, to occupy their territory, and in October, 1635, Fort Saybrook was begun at the mouth of the Connecticut River. A small party from Plymouth had fortified a station further up the river a year before.

43. Connecticut was mainly colonized by emigrants from Massachusetts. Thomas Hooker and Samuel Stone,† ministers of Newtown, led the enterprise, and in June, 1636, removed with their congregations to the then "far West," and settled at Hartford. Wethersfield and Windsor were early founded, and within a year the population of the three towns reached about 800.

* See Palfrey's N. E.; Bancroft's and Hildreth's U. S.; Drake's History of Boston; Young's Chronicles of Massachusetts Bay; Barber's N. E.; D. Bacon's Tales of the Puritans, J. Banvard's Priscilla, J. G. Holland's Bay Path, fictions.

† See E. W. Hooker's Life of Thomas Hooker.

When was it annexed to Massachusetts? What geographical divisions were erected in Massachusetts in 1643?

42. Give the history of the founding of Fort Saybrook. Was Saybrook the first settlement in Connecticut?

43. How was Connecticut mainly colonized? Give an account of the settling of Hartford.

44. Not without provocation, the Pequot Indians, a tribe numbering 1000, who dwelt on the Thames, became involved in a war with the settlers. Their animosity once aroused, the Indians were implacable. At different times and in various ways the colonists were harassed, and as many as thirty had been killed before decided measures were taken for war. Plymouth and Massachusetts were at length solicited for aid. The former ordered a levy of forty, and the latter of a hundred and sixty men; but before these could be got into the field ninety Connecticut men, accompanied by a party of Mohegans and Narragansetts, set forth to destroy the Pequots.

The Mohegans were led by the celebrated chief Uncas. The rude fort of the Pequots, located about five miles from the present site of the village of Stonington, was surprised May, 1637, the inclosed wigwams were burned, and about five hundred Indians were slain. In a few days the troops from Massachusetts arrived. The remnant of the doomed nation were driven from their abodes and either captured, killed, or dispersed; and so the Pequot nation became extinct. Sassacus, their chief, was murdered by the Mohawks, to whom he fled for protection. "And from savage violence the land had rest forty years."*

45. Peace and security being restored, the colonists gave their attention to the founding of a permanent government. They framed a liberal constitution, which continued in force for 200 years—"the first example in history of a written constitution." No religious test restricted the ballot in Connecticut.† John Haines, who had been the third governor of Massachusetts, removed with his family to Hartford, and he was elected first governor of Connecticut, April 11, 1639.

* In Palfrey's History is a curious representation of the Pequot fort and village.

† See Trumbull's History of Connecticut.

---

44. Give an account of the war with the Pequot Indians.

45. What was the character of the Connecticut constitution? How long did it remain in force? Who were voters in Connecticut?

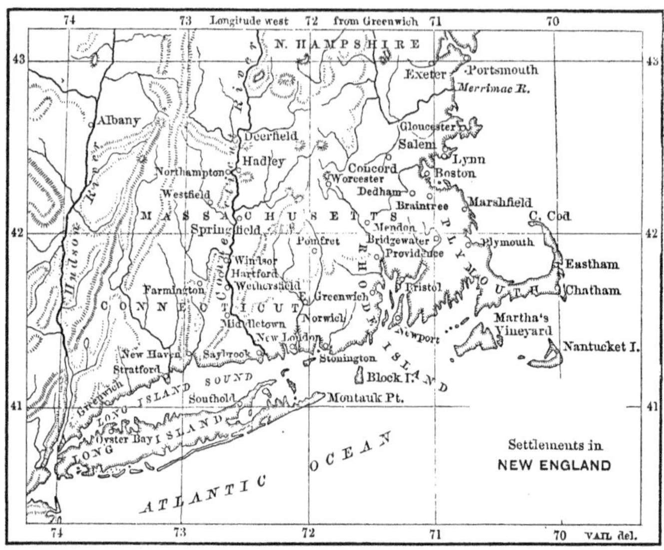

IV. NEW HAVEN.

46. A settlement was inaugurated at New Haven by John Davenport, a London Puritan minister, and a company of his friends, emigrants from England. Under an oak they held their first Sabbath service, April 15, 1638. The next year they organized a government allowing only church members to vote, and bound themselves to be subject only to the law of the Bible. Theophilus Eaton was chosen magistrate, and was annually re-elected for twenty years. He was assisted by four deputies. The early laws of New Haven were extremely rigid. By treaty with the Indians, the colonists obtained a title to the lands they occupied. They extended their possessions by successive purchases, and, in a few years, had settlements at Stamford, Southhold, and on Delaware Bay.

---

46. By whom was New Haven settled? In what year? What was the character of the New Haven government? Who was magistrate, and for how many years? What agreement did the colonists make with the Indians?

47. On the 10th of May, **1643,** the colonies of Plymouth, Massachusetts, Connecticut, and New Haven, the history of which we have thus far traced, were consolidated for mutual good, under the name of the United Colonies of New England.

V. PROVIDENCE AND RHODE ISLAND.

48. Roger Williams, banished from Massachusetts, as related, spent the winter with the Narragansett Indians, over whom he gained a remarkable influence. In June, 1638, with five companions, he laid the foundation of Providence. With the proceeds of his private property at Salem, which he sold, he purchased land of the aborigines, and freely gave it away to all who chose to join him in his settlement. The commonwealth which he established was a pure democracy.

49. A few of Anne Hutchinson's sympathizers went with Wheelwright to New Hampshire, but the larger number, led by John Clarke and William Coddington, settled on the island of Rhode Island, given to them, at the request of Williams, by Miantonomah, a Narrangsett chief. The settlements prospered, and the towns of Portsmouth and Newport were presently founded. A democratic constitution was adopted in March, 1641. Anne Hutchinson found refuge in the colony for awhile; but she subsequently removed to the dominion of the Dutch, and came to a violent death at the hands of the Indians.

50. The colonies of Providence and Rhode Island were not admitted into the union of New England in **1643,** but a royal charter was obtained for them through the aid of

---

47. What colonies formed the New England union? When?

48. Give an account of the founding of Providence. How did Roger Williams obtain the means of procuring land? How did he induce settlers to come to Providence? What kind of a government did he inaugurate?

49. Who settled the island of Rhode Island? Of whom did they obtain the island? Did their settlement succeed?

50. By whom was a royal charter obtained for Rhode Island and Providence? What is a royal charter?

Williams and the influence of Sir Henry Vane, then a member of the British Parliament. The two colonies were in time united in one, forming the present State of Rhode Island.*

VI. MAINE.

51. In 1622 the council for New England granted to John Mason and Ferdinando Gorges the province of Laconia, extending from the Merrimac to the Kennebec, and from the Atlantic to the St. Lawrence. In 1629 Laconia was divided, Gorges obtaining a separate patent for the northern part, which he named New Somerset. The coast had long been occupied at different points by small fishing hamlets. In 1639 Gorges obtained a royal charter for his province, and it was thenceforth called Maine. Thomas Gorges, deputy of the proprietor, was made governor of Maine in 1640. The province was divided into two counties, and an elaborate system of government was inaugurated, and sustained for years, while as yet the territory was almost without population. The first general court for Maine was held at Saco. In the course of events, Maine, like New Hampshire, was annexed to Massachusetts.†

PURITAN SOCIETY AND INSTITUTIONS.

52. The early progress of New England was rapid. The principles of self-government were practiced, and all the institutions essential to the common good, both civil and social, were organized. The laws were generally severe. The authority and dignity of magistrates were highly respected, and ministers of religion exercised great power in both private and public life. The relations of church and

* See S. G. Arnold's History of Rhode Island.

† See Sullivan's History of Maine.

---

51. Who obtained a royal charter for Maine? To what colony was Maine annexed?

52. What can you say of the progress of New England? Of Puritan laws? Of the magistrates? Of the clergy?

state were intimate. The franchise in several of the colonies was much restricted. The whole number of freemen or voters in Massachusetts was not over one-fifth of the population. In the same colony the citizens were under legal obligation to attend church.

The established religion was Puritanism, and forms of worship were conducted according to the Westminster Confession of Faith. There were, at first, two ministers to each church—a preacher and a pastor. No toleration was extended to other than the established church. Indeed, facts seem to justify the assertion of a recent able historian, that "New England Protestantism appealed to Liberty: then closed the door against her." The customs of the Puritans were austere, amusements were curtailed, and all holidays abolished. Even the eating of mince-pies on Christmas was considered wicked. Industry and frugality were prevalent virtues.

The land was divided into numerous small freeholds, by which means personal thrift and enterprise were promoted. There were many towns and villages. The manufacture of thread and yarn, and of linen, cotton, and woolen cloth, was early begun. Ship-building was also carried on. The chief exports were furs, lumber, and fish. The chief agricultural products were maize, oats, rye, barley, hay, peas, squashes, and pumpkins. Apples, pears, quinces, plums, and cherries were raised. The circulating medium was either corn, beaver-skins, or bullets, and these were employed even to pay taxes. In trade with the Indians, Yankee-made wampum was used.

"Among a people, a large portion of whom were well-informed, several of whom were learned, and a few rich, there could not have been a dearth of books." Public education early received attention in each of the colonies.

Of the ballot? Of attendance at religious service? Of intolerance? Of Puritan customs? How was the land divided? What articles were manufactured? What exported? What products were cultivated? What was the circulating medium? What was the literary condition of the colonists? The state of education? When was Harvard College founded? Where was the first printing-press set up?

Harvard College was founded in the year 1638. About the same time a printing-press was set up at Cambridge, the first in the United States.

" Within the first fifteen years (and there was never afterward any considerable increase from England) there came over 21,200 persons, or 4,000 families. Their descendants now are not far from 4,000,000. Each family has multiplied, on the average, to 1,000 souls. To New York and Ohio, where they constitute half the population, they have carried the Puritan system of free schools; and their example is spreading it through the civilized world."

GENERAL QUESTIONS AND DIRECTIONS.

Prepare a chronological table of the dated events given in Chapter Fifth. Name the colonies of New England organized between 1620 and 1643. Which of these were consolidated in 1643? Name the governors and principal men of Plymouth. Of the Massachusetts Bay settlements. Of the Connecticut colony. Of New Haven. Of Providence and Rhode Island. Of Maine. What was the principal inducement that led emigrants to New England? In what respect did the laws, customs, and institutions of New England differ from those of Virginia? What Indian chiefs are mentioned in Chapters Fourth and Fifth? What Indian wars?

NOTE.—Questions and directions like these, the ingenious teacher may multiply *ad libitum*.

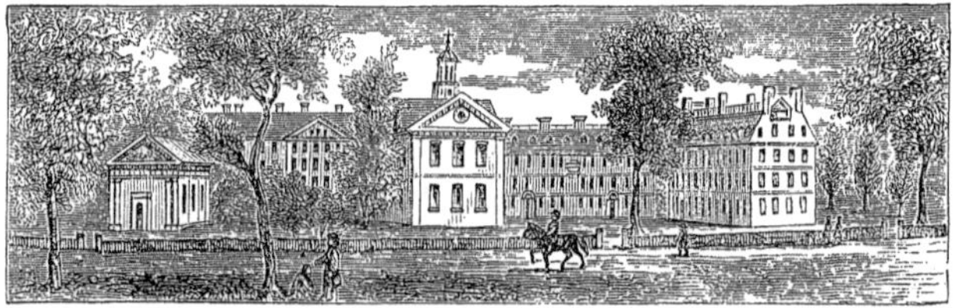

Harvard College in 1770.

Map Questions and Geographical Review.

What Indian tribes were located on the Atlantic coast? What tribes dwelt between 40° and 45°? What is the difference between a tribe and a family? Name the tribes belonging to the Iroquois family. With what tribe did the early Virginia settlers come in conflict? With what, the New England settlers? Locate the Andastes. The Abenakis. The Seminoles. The Powhatans. The Lenni-Lenape. The Mohegans. The Pequots. To what tribe did Pocahontas belong? Massassoit?

Where is Roanoke Island? What historical events are connected with it? What island lies near it? Where is Mount Desert Island? When and by whom was Newfoundland claimed for England? Where is Cape Fear? Where is Cape Cod? Who named Cape Cod? Who first settled at Cape Ann? Where is Chesapeake Bay? By whom was it first explored? Locate the River of May. North River. South River. What is the modern name of each of these rivers? What was the Indian name of the James River?

Why is the Chickahominy mentioned in the text? In what latitude is St. Augustine? Where was Fort Caroline? Port Royal? When, why, and by whom was Florida so named? Virginia? New England? Maine? New Hampshire? How much territory did the Spanish claim under the name of Florida? What region was once known as North Virginia? What part of the American coast was surveyed by Smith? What territory was granted to the council for New England?

Locate Jamestown. Plymouth. Boston. Salem. Portsmouth. New Haven. What is the origin of the name Saybrook? By whom was Providence founded? What other towns named in these chapters are marked on the map on p. 44? What Virginia settlements did Sir Thomas Gates establish? Who were the proprietors of Laconia? Where was New Somerset? Where are the Bermudas? Whence did the Pilgrims sail?

CHAPTER SIXTH.

NEW FRANCE, NEW NETHERLAND, AND NEW SWEDEN.

I. NEW FRANCE.

E LA ROCHE (lå rosh′), a French marquis, obtained, in 1598, a commission of his government to colonize Canada. He conveyed a party of forty desperadoes, most of them out of French prisons, to Sable Island. In five years all but twelve of these had perished, and the miserable remnant were carried to France. De La Roche died, and in 1600 a commission was granted to Chauvin (shō-vång′), a naval officer, who associated with him Pontgrave, a merchant, and the two carried on a profitable traffic in furs for a year or two, when Chauvin died. Aymar de Chastes (shå′tes) now obtained a patent of Henry IV. of France, and dispatched Pontgrave and Samuel de Champlain on a voyage of exploration up the St. Lawrence. During their absence De Chastes died, and the king issued to Pierre du Guast, Sieur de Monts (mōng), a patent granting him the governorship of all that part of North America lying between the 40th and 46th degrees of north latitude, under the name of Acadia.

54. In the spring of 1604 De Monts, accompanied by

QUESTIONS.—**53.** What enterprise did De La Roche attempt, and with what success? When did Chauvin obtain a commission? Who joined Chauvin? What did they do? What was done by De Chastes? Who was the next French patentee, and what was granted him?

Champlain, Pontgrave, Baron de Poutrincourt, and a number of colonists of good character, sailed for Acadia.* Seventy-nine men were left on a small island at the mouth of the St. Croix (sënt kroi) River, to begin a settlement. Thirty-five of these died before the next spring. In August, 1604, the site of the settlement was changed to Port Royal, now Annapolis, Nova Scotia. Here, first in the New World the attempt was made to establish a colony on an agricultural basis. Port Royal was destined to become a permanent settlement. It existed two years before the English had laid the foundation of Jamestown.

Samuel de Champlain.

55. In 1608 Champlain began the settlement of Quebec, and the next year he discovered the beautiful lake which bears his name. A few years later the Jesuit mission of St. Savior was established on Mt. Desert Island.

56. Samuel Argall, captain of an illicit trading vessel from Virginia, sailing in 1613 to obtain a supply of codfish, accidentally heard of this French settlement, and went out of his way to destroy it. On a second expedition he de-

* See Champlain and his Associates in Parkman's Pioneers of France in the New World, Chapters I. and II.

---

54. When did De Monts sail for Acadia? Who accompanied him? Narrate the history of the St. Croix settlement. Where was the first permanent French settlement made?

55. Who began the settlement of Quebec? In what year was Lake Champlain discovered? Where was the mission of St. Savior? What is a mission?

molished Port Royal, which, however, was soon rebuilt by the persevering French. Argall was for a time governor at Jamestown, as related in a preceding chapter.

57. Quebec became the most important French settlement in America. Thither the Jesuits repaired to carry on their missions with the Huron Indians. Champlain, the Father of New France, the Captain Smith of Canada, still cherishing the design of Columbus to discover a direct passage to the Indies, and to carry Christianity around the world, pushed his explorations to the north-west, discovering, in 1615, lakes Huron and Ontario. His rovings at an end, he was settled as governor of Quebec.

58. In 1627 Cardinal Richelieu (rĕsh′ẹ-loo) organized the company of the Hundred Associates, designed to monopolize the commerce and promote the colonization of Canada. Two years later, England became involved in a war with France, and sent out a force which easily succeeded in dispossessing the French of all their American possessions. Peace being declared, New France was restored, Quebec re-occupied, and the enterprise of the Hundred Associates resumed.

59. Emigration to Canada was permitted to French Catholics only, and Jesuit priests virtually ruled the colony. To those not engaged as agents of the Hundred Associates, the only motive to immigration was religious ardor—zeal to convert the Indians. "The scheme of English colonization made no account of the Indian tribes. In the scheme of French colonization they were all in all." Quebec was devoted to two objects—the fur trade and mission work. Its growth was slow, the entire population in 1640 not being

---

56. What do you know about Samuel Argall?

57. What sort of man was Champlain? What motive prompted his enterprises? What did he discover in 1615? Was New England settled at that date? Of what place was Champlain made governor?

58. Who organized the company of the Hundred Associates? For what purpose?

59. How was emigration to New France restricted? Who exercised the controlling influence in Canada? From what center? What was the population of Quebec in 1640?

much above 200. A college for French boys, with a mission school for Indian youth attached, was established in 1637, one year before Harvard College was founded.*

II. NEW NETHERLAND.

60. Almost cotemporaneously with the discovery of Lake Champlain, Henry Hudson discovered, and, in his little ship, the Half Moon, sailed far up the noble stream now known as the Hudson, but which he named the River of the Mountains, and the Dutch called sometimes the Mauritius, but generally the North River. Hudson,† though English born, was sailing in the employ of Holland merchants at the time of his American discoveries, on which account the Dutch claimed the territory between the Delaware River and Passamaquoddy Bay, under the name of New Netherland.

A small trading fort was built on Manhattan Island, and another, several years later, on the Hudson, at the head of navigation. Several Dutch navigators, among whom the principal were Adrian Block, Cornelius Mey, and Hendrick Christiansen, made explorations in the vicinity of Long Island, discovering the Housatonic (hoo'sa-ton'ik) the Connecticut, East River, and Narragansett Bay.

61. The English colonists, jealous of the encroachments of the Dutch, insisted that New Netherland was part of Virginia. Argall, on his return from Port Royal, compelled the occupants of Manhattan to haul down the Dutch

* See Parkman's Jesuits in North America; Shea's Charlevoix' History of New France.

† See Sparks's American Biography, Vol. IX.; J. M. Read's Historical Inquiries concerning Henry Hudson.

What means of education did the Jesuits provide?

60. When and by whom was the Hudson River discovered? What names have been given to this river? What claim was based on Hudson's discoveries? Where did the Dutch first build forts? What Dutch navigators made discoveries? What did they discover?

61. What incident connects the name of Argall with the history of New Netherland?

flag from their stockade; but they put it up again as soon as he had gone. Captain Dormer, in the service of Gorges, also touched at Manhattan in **1620,** and urged proprietary claims, which the Dutch denied. Complaints were made to the authorities in Holland, but without avail. Six months after the issuing of the charter for the Council for New England, a charter was granted by Holland to the Dutch West India Company. The management of Dutch interests in America fell into the hands of this corporation.

62. The first permanent Dutch colonies were begun in 1623. Fort Nassau (nas'saw) was erected on the Delaware; and Fort Orange, on the Hudson, where Albany now stands. The West India Company appointed Cornelius Mey director of New Netherland. He was succeeded by Wilhelm Verhulst, and he, in 1626, by Peter Minuet. Minuet bought Manhattan from the Indians for a sum equal to about twenty-four dollars. A block-house surrounded by palisades, called Fort Amsterdam, was built on the site of the present city of New York.

The title of *patroon* and extraordinary privileges were conferred on favored individuals, on condition that they should colonize lands granted them. But the patroons proved great monopolists, and rather hindered than helped immigration. Peter Minuet was recalled in 1632, and Wouter Van Twiller became director. He continued in office six years, when he gave place to Wilhelm Kieft.

63. The Dutch early established friendly relations with the Indians. Imprudently, they sold them fire-arms and intoxicating drinks. Kieft, violent and reckless, provoked the first serious conflict between the Dutch and the Indians. To his treachery is attributed the origin of a two years' war with the Algonquins, in which both parties suffered ex-

---

What event in the history of Manhattan occurred in 1620? When was the Dutch West India Company chartered?

62. Where was Fort Nassau erected? Where, Fort Orange? Who was director after Mey? What bargain did Minuet make with the Indians? What were patroons? Who was director after Minuet? Who after him?

63. What was Kieft's disposition? What calamity did he bring upon the colony?

tremely. Kieft, being very unpopular, was deposed, and Peter Stuyvesant (stī′ve-sant), the last and best of the Dutch governors in America, was appointed to the head of affairs in 1648. He administered with wisdom, but exercised almost absolute authority. Under his sway the settlements rapidly increased. The immigrants were characterized by industry and thrift. Their commerce was active and profitable.

The persecuted of every creed and clime were invited to Manhattan, whither flocked a most heterogeneous population, destined to found the cosmopolitan city of New York. As many as eighteen dialects were spoken in New Amsterdam. The laws were published in Dutch, English, and French. Notwithstanding Stuyvesant's monarchical ideas of government, the people claimed such liberties as were enjoyed in New England, and a popular convention was called to demand the right of representation for the taxed. The spirit of democracy rapidly gained ground. The Dutch Reformed Church was the established religion, though, as above stated, all sects were tolerated.*

III. NEW SWEDEN.

64. Gustavus Adolphus, Sweden's greatest king, cherished a vast design of colonizing the New World. His plans were not fulfilled; but, after his death, the Swedish court authorized Peter Minuet, formerly director of New Netherland, to conduct a colony of Swedes and Finns to

* See Brodhead's Hist. of New York, First Period; Irving's Knickerbocker's History of New York; also Paulding's Dutchman's Fireside, and Book of St. Nicholas.

What was Stuyvesant's character? What were the characteristics of the settlers? What languages were spoken in New Amsterdam? What was the established religion? What was the state of politics?

64. Who first led a colony of Swedes and Finns to America? Where did they settle? Where was Fort Christiana built? What was the character of the settlers? When was New Sweden conquered by the Dutch?

65. To whom did the British crown grant New Netherland? What change of name was made?

the shores of the Delaware. They built Fort Christiana in 1638, not far from the site of the Dutch fort Nassau. John Printz, governor of the colony, established himself in a fort of hemlock logs a few miles below the present site of Philadelphia. The Swedish settlements were very prosperous. The settlers were Protestants, industrious, and hardy, and of liberal politics. The Dutch claimed the Delaware region, named by its new occupants New Sweden, and in 1655 Governor Stuyvesant conquered it. The whole number of Swedes and Finns that had immigrated was but 700; their descendants, now scattered over the United States, constitute perhaps one two-hundredth of our entire population, and are excellent citizens.

65. New Netherland, having swallowed up her weak rival New Sweden, was herself destined soon to fall under the supremacy of a stronger power. In 1664 Charles II. granted to his brother, the Duke of York, the lands held by the Dutch in America, and the brave Stuyvesant, though reluctant, was obliged to yield to British arms. The name New Netherland was changed to New York.

GENERAL QUESTIONS AND DIRECTIONS.

When was St. Augustine founded? Port Royal? Jamestown? Plymouth? New Amsterdam? Fort Christiana? Who was the greatest man connected with the early history of New France? Name in chronological order the governors of New Amsterdam. Who was the greatest of these? What event distinguishes the years 1492, 1541, 1564, 1607? What events may be associated with the year 1620? What event distinguishes 1643? Prepare a chronological table of the events of Chapter Sixth.

New Amsterdam.

Map Questions and Geographical Review.

What state or states are wholly or partly embraced in the area once known as New France? In that once known as New Netherland? New Sweden? Virginia? Where was French Florida? Spanish Florida? What states now occupy nearly the same territory? What is the present name of Acadia? Of Port Royal in Acadia? What other Port Royal was there?

Did New England, as represented on this map, embrace more or less territory than New England now includes? On what river in Canada were the principal settlements? On what river were the chief settlements in New Netherland? What is the largest river in New England?

How did the boundaries of Canada in 1600 differ from the present boundaries? Where is the island of St. Croix? What towns did the French found on the St. Lawrence? For what is Mount Desert Island noted? What is the present name of Lake Iroquois? What lakes were discovered by Champlain? By what different names has the Hudson River been called? What is the present name of the South River? Locate Fort Nassau. Fort Orange. Fort Amsterdam. Fort Christiana.

What names given on the map were bestowed by the Spanish? The English? The French? The Dutch? The Swedes? The Indians? When was Lake Champlain discovered? What states now border on Lake Champlain? What Indians dwelt upon the St. Lawrence? Where, when, and by whom was the first permanent settlement made in the United States? The second? The third? The fourth? The fifth? The sixth? What bays have been mentioned thus far in this history? What capes? What lakes? What islands? What countries of Europe had colonies within the present limits of the United States? How many of these now have colonies in North America?

CHAPTER SEVENTH.

PROGRESS OF NEW ENGLAND AND VIRGINIA—SETTLEMENT OF MARYLAND.

1643—1660.

I. NEW ENGLAND.

Old First Church, Boston.

A FEW months before the union of the New England colonies, those civil wars had begun in the mother country which were followed by the execution of Charles I. and the elevation of Oliver Cromwell to the position of Protector of the British Commonwealth. The American provinces, left to themselves during this period, prospered beyond expectation. The common interests of New England were guarded by a board of federal commissioners. Their decisions were not binding on the several colonies; but each colony retained its separate government and officers as before.

67. Efforts for the amelioration of the Indians were not neglected. John Eliot, called the Apostle of the Indians,* translated the Bible into the Indian language, and he, Thomas Mayhew, Daniel Gookin, and others, seconded by the public authorities, devoted themselves to the conversion and civilization of the savages, but without very great

* See Sparks's Am. Biog., Vol. V., First Series.

QUESTIONS.—**66.** The events of how many years are recorded in Chapter Seventh? What was the condition of the colonies during this period?
67. Who besides Eliot were prominent Indian missionaries?

final success. The cause of their failure, as of that of the Jesuits, to elevate the Indians, seems to have been found in the incapacity of the latter to comprehend moral and religious truth. The savage nature could not be educated away. Many for a time professed Christianity, the number of "praying Indians" being estimated, when at the largest, at about 4,000.

68. In 1649 John Winthrop died, and John Endicott was elected governor. The austerity of the Puritan leaders, the despotic rigor of the laws, and the spirit of bigotry and persecution that manifested itself, especially in Massachusetts, did not fail to create dissatisfaction. Some ventured to petition the General Court for larger liberties; some even appealed to the British Parliament. Letters of remonstrance from prominent persons, both in England and America, were written to the magistrates against their extreme proceedings.

In 1656 the Quakers, then a new sect, lately founded in England by George Fox, first began to come to Massachusetts. Violent proceedings were taken against them as heretics and disturbers of the peace. Those who came to New England were fined, imprisoned, whipped, exiled; and, four were actually hanged at Boston.* But the boldness of the Quakers increased. They lived pure and unspotted lives, and though accused of fanaticism by the Puritans, they were not more fanatical than their accusers. Many sympathized with them, and popular sentiment at length checked ecclesiastical intolerance, and compelled a relaxation of the severity of law. Quaker constancy and courage established in Massachusetts the right of every man to worship God according to the dictates of his own conscience. The population of New England in **1660**, the date at which Charles II. became king of England, was probably 40,000.

* See Sewel's History of the Quakers: Penn's Writings; Marsh's and Janney's Life of Fox; Longfellow's tragedy, John Endicott.

How many "praying Indians" were there?

68. When did the Quakers first come to New England? How were they treated? Why? What was the effect of persecution? What was the population of New England in 1660?

II. VIRGINIA.

69. In 1644 the Indians made a second attempt to destroy the settlements of Virginia, and succeeded so far as to surprise and massacre 300 or 400 persons before they were repulsed. Opechancanough, now an old man, was taken and shot, and a treaty was made with his successor.

70. In October, 1650, the British Parliament promulgated the famous Navigation Act, by which foreign ships were forbidden to trade at Virginia. The object of this was to secure to England a monopoly of the tobacco trade. The act eventually proved very injurious to American commerce. The population of Virginia at the time of the Restoration was about 30,000.

III. MARYLAND.

71. Maryland, so named in honor of Henrietta Maria, wife of Charles I., was originally a part of Virginia. It was made a separate province in 1629, and granted by the crown to a Catholic nobleman, Sir George Calvert, Lord Baltimore. Before the patent was fully prepared Calvert died, but the grant was made good to his son Cecil, who also succeeded to his father's title.

In March, 1634, about 200 Catholics, headed by a brother of Cecil Calvert, laid the foundation of the town of St. Mary's, on the site of an Indian village purchased from the owners. The territory covered by Calvert's grant was already occupied by William Clayborne, who, acting under royal license and by permission of the governor of Virginia, had established trading stations on Kent Island and

---

69. Relate the second attempt made by the Indians to destroy the settlements of Virginia? When did the first occur?

70. What was the Navigation Act? What was the population of Virginia at the time of the Restoration?

71. Why was Maryland so named? To whom was Maryland granted? Where was the first settlement made?

72. What was the progress of St. Mary's? What was the character of Lord Baltimore's government?

at the mouth of the Susquehanna. A conflict occurred between the two claimants, and Clayborne's men were driven from Kent Island. Clayborne himself escaped, first to Virginia, then to England.

72. The settlement at St. Mary's flourished. "Within six months it had advanced more than Virginia had done in as many years." Civil affairs were conducted with mildness, prudence, and sagacity. The first statutes of Maryland, enacted in 1639, were just and liberal. Special provision was made for the protection of the Catholic Church. In **1660** the population of Maryland may have been 8,000.

GENERAL QUESTIONS AND DIRECTIONS.

Prepare a chronological table of the events given in Chapter Seventh. What was the established religion of Florida? Of New France? Of New England? Of Virginia? Of New Netherland? Of New Sweden? Of Maryland?

BIOGRAPHICAL REVIEW.

Give a sketch of the life of Columbus. Of De Soto. Of Menendez. Of Raleigh. Of Captain Smith. Of Champlain. Of Hudson. Of John Winthrop, Senior. Of Stuyvesant. Of Williams. Of the first Lord Baltimore. Of Pocahontas.

NOTE.—In preparing biographical sketches, the student should be encouraged to make all the research possible. The sketches may be written or oral.

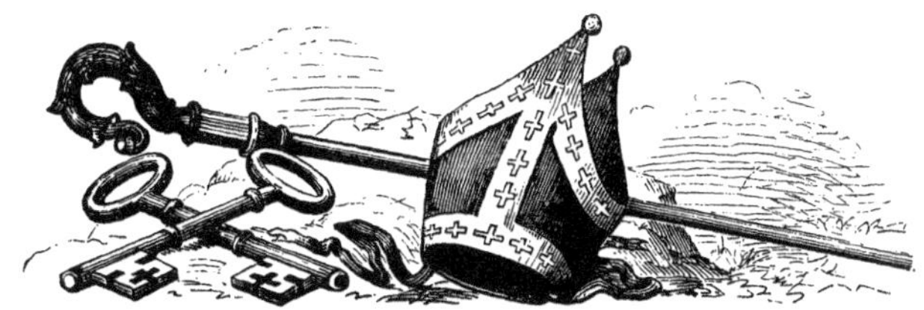

CHAPTER EIGHTH.

AMERICA UNDER CHARLES II. AND JAMES II.

1660—1689.

I. NEW ENGLAND.

CHARLES the Second was proclaimed in the colonies—reluctantly in Massachusetts, and not until almost a year after the Restoration. Soon was begun a series of royal interferences and oppressions, which may be regarded as the remote causes of the Revolution. The king required changes in the colonial laws, administration, and customs. He demanded an oath of allegiance to his royal person; toleration for the Church of England; the repeal of various statutes. All of the colonies, excepting Massachusetts, readily complied with his will. Royal commissioners were sent out to adjust local differences. These were well received, except in Massachusetts, where their authority was denied. Connecticut, through the efforts of her excellent governor, John Winthrop, Junior, obtained an ample charter, uniting in one state the colonies of Connecticut and New Haven. Rhode Island was favored with a charter still more liberal.

74. Massasoit died in **1660**, and to his son, Metacom, otherwise known as King Philip, fell the sachemship of

QUESTIONS.—**73.** When was Charles II. proclaimed in Massachusetts? What demands did this sovereign make? How were his demands received? Which of the New England colonies obtained charters?

the Pokanokets. With him a treaty was made, and peace reigned for more than ten years. Nevertheless, suspicions were entertained against Philip—he was frequently summoned before the colonial courts to answer charges made against him. Finally, he was accused of causing the secret murder of one Sausaman, a converted Indian, who had given information of the chief's supposed designs. The vexed savage at length resolved to assume openly the hostile character so persistently attributed to him. A war of stealth, ambush, and surprise was begun, and carried on with all the ferocity for which Indians are notorious. Canonchet, sachem of the Narragansetts, joined Philip against the common enemy.

The colonies made a vigorous defense. In December, 1675, the fort of the Narragansetts was captured, its wigwams were burned, and its occupants destroyed, as in the Pequot war. Canonchet was taken prisoner; the power of his tribe was broken. The Pokanokets were also defeated. King Philip himself was shot by a treacherous Indian of his own tribe. The war extended from Connecticut to Maine, and lasted for three years. The settlements suffered extremely. Twelve or thirteen villages were destroyed, and as many as 600 white men were slain. The number of Indians killed and taken was about 2,000. The captives were treated with extreme severity almost untempered with pity, being either executed or enslaved.*

75. Arbitrary and oppressive demands continued to come from the British parliament and king. A strict enforcement of the navigation laws, now more stringent than at first, was required. No merchandise could be imported, except under penalty of forfeiture, but in British vessels

* See Church's History of King Philip's War; Increase Mather's Brief History of the War; Irving's Philip of Pokanoket, in the Sketch Book; and R. C. Sands's Yamoyden, poem.

---

74. What Indian chief died in 1660? Who was his successor? What was the immediate cause of King Philip's animosity? Give a full account of the Indian war.

75. What course did the British take in reference to the navigation laws? What did these laws require?

navigated by British officers. Certain enumerated articles produced in America could be shipped only to English markets. Massachusetts, ever refractory, steadily refused to make the concessions required by the king. She resisted the laws which infringed commercial freedom. She held to her own statutes and customs, pointing to her charter as the safeguard of her liberties. The charter itself was vacated by legal decree in 1684, and Massachusetts, much against her will, became a royal province.

76. Charles II. died February 6, 1685, and his brother, the despotic James II., succeeded to the crown and scepter. The king appointed Edmund Andros governor of all New England. This arbitrary man, fit agent of his royal master, arrived in Boston, December, 1686, and assumed almost absolute dictatorial power. Unjust taxes were levied. Existing titles to land were pronounced invalid, and new patents for ownership were required. Private property was taken from individuals and given away to the governor's friends. The Puritan meeting-houses were forcibly occupied for the Episcopal service. The charters of Rhode Island and Connecticut were demanded.

Rhode Island was annexed to Andros's dominion in 1686, and Connecticut in 1687. In 1688 a royal grant extended this dominion so as to include New York and New Jersey. Oppressive legislation extended with the spread of the governor's jurisdiction. But the tyranny of Andros was not to continue long. James II. was deposed in 1688, and William, Prince of Orange, and his consort, Mary, were proclaimed king and queen of England. The people of Boston arose, seized and imprisoned Governor Andros, restored their old form of government, and elected the venerable Simon Bradstreet governor. Over all New England the new-crowned sovereigns were joyfully proclaimed.*

* See Neal's Hist. of N. England; Belknap's Hist. of N. Hampshire;

What state resisted the king? How did he retaliate?

76. Who was the successor of Charles II.? What was his character? Whom did he appoint as governor of New England? What provinces did he annex to New England? What brought his rule to an end?

II. VIRGINIA.

77. Virginia received no charter at the time of the Restoration. Sir William Berkeley—a man now remembered for having once said: "I thank God there are no free schools nor printing-presses in Virginia"—was appointed his majesty's governor, and a royalist assembly was elected. The navigation laws were peculiarly grievous in Virginia, since tobacco was included in the enumerated articles, the traffic in which was monopolized by the English. This staple fell in price to a penny a pound.

In 1662 the Virginia code was revised, and the first legislation in reference to slavery took place. The colonial government became oppressive. The governor, with a judiciary appointed by himself and an aristocratic assembly, ignored the rights of the common people. Burdensome taxes were imposed. Voting was restricted to "freeholders and housekeepers." In February, 1673, the whole of Virginia was assigned, by Charles II., to lords Culpepper and Arlington, for a term of thirty years. Under the exactions of these monopolists the people were in nowise relieved.

78. Again the lowering cloud of Indian war drifted along the colonial frontier, first in Maryland, then in Virginia. Nathaniel Bacon,† contrary to Berkeley's orders, but at the urgent desire of the settlers, led a force of volunteers against the Susquehannas. Bacon was arrested, but soon released. He raised a company of 300 or 400 men, and, appearing at Jamestown, demanded a commission to defend the colony from the Indians. Berkeley was obliged to comply with this demand; but Bacon had no sooner set out on

also Whittier's Margaret Smith's Journal; Hawthorne's Scarlet Letter; Mrs. Sedgwick's Redwood, Hope Leslie, and New England Tale; C. K. True's Shawmut; and R. Dawes's Nix's Mate, fictions.

† See Sparks's Am. Biog., Vol. III., Second Series.

---

77. Whom did Charles II. appoint royal governor of Virginia? What memorable saying of Berkeley's is quoted? What was the effect of the navigation laws in Virginia? What was the character of Berkeley's government?

his march than he was proclaimed a traitor, and Berkeley raised a military force to oppose him.

Bacon returned from a successful foray among the Indians, and moved against the governor, who retreated before him. Jamestown was burned by the insurgents. Radical changes might now have been effected in the government, had not Bacon suddenly died. The former administration was restored, and many of those who had engaged in Bacon's rebellion were hanged. Jamestown was not rebuilt, and Williamsburg was made the seat of government.

79. Berkeley returned to England, and Lord Culpepper was made governor of Virginia. Selfish and avaricious, Culpepper impoverished the people by the imposition of taxes and duties. The grant of Culpepper and Arlington was withdrawn in 1684, when Lord Effingham, a man distinguished alike for greedy exorbitance and petty despotism, succeeded to the governorship.

III. MARYLAND.

80. The history of Maryland, meanwhile, was similar to that of Virginia.* The same customs and commercial interests prevailed in both provinces. In both tobacco was the staple product. In both laws were enacted for the perpetuation of slavery and the importation of negroes. Maryland, though under a Catholic proprietary, was settled chiefly by Protestants. Few Catholics came there after the first migration. An anti-Catholic revolution in 1655 placed the political power temporarily in the hands of the Puritans. Charles II. restored the government to Cecil Calvert, who held it until his death, in 1676. He was succeeded by his

* See Bozman's and McSherry's Maryland.

---

78. Give an account of Bacon's rebellion. Who was probably most popular, Bacon or Berkeley?

79. What was Culpepper's character? What sort of governor was Effingham?

80. In what respects were Maryland and Virginia similar? What revolution occurred in Maryland in 1655?

son, Philip, known in American history as the second Lord Baltimore. The laws of Maryland tolerated every religious sect except Quakers, who received no better treatment from the Catholics than from the Puritans. It was lawful to apprehend and whip Quaker preachers as vagabonds.

IV. NEW YORK.

81. The Duke of York, to whom New Netherland had been granted, divided the province into two parts—New York and New Jersey. Richard Nicolls was appointed governor of New York, and by him a body of laws was published, similar in many respects to those of New England. It was Nicolls who compelled Stuyvesant to surrender New Amsterdam. Nicolls was followed in office by Francis Lovelace, whose exercise of arbitrary power caused popular discontent. In 1673, the Dutch being at war with the English, New York city was taken by a Dutch squadron. For fifteen months the province was held by its original proprietors. At the close of the war, British rule was restored, and New York fell under the general government of Andros as part of New England.

In 1683 Thomas Dongan, a Catholic, was sent out as governor of New York, and a Catholic collector of customs was also appointed. The anti-Catholic excitement prevailed in New York as in New England and Maryland. Jacob Leisler, professing to act for the preservation of Protestantism, put himself at the head of a mob and took forcible possession of the government. Two years later, Henry Sloughter was appointed governor of New York by King William. Leisler was arrested for high treason and hanged.*

* See Smith's, Macauley's, and Dunlap's History of New York; also, Cooper's Water Witch; Myer's First of the Knickerbockers, and Young Patroon, fictions.

---

81. How was New York divided? For what military service was Nicolls noted? What kind of laws did he proclaim? When was New York repossessed by the Dutch? Who was Thomas Dongan? What did Jacob Leisler do? What was Leisler's fate?

V. NEW JERSEY.

82. New Jersey was assigned to Lord Berkeley and Sir George Carteret, who immediately published "concessions," offering lands on liberal terms to settlers, and the promise of religious toleration. Influenced by prospects so favorable, a colony of Puritans from New England was induced to seek a location for a settlement. These founded Elizabethtown, August, 1665. Other settlements were soon made. Berkeley sold a portion of New Jersey to Quakers, and a company of those long persecuted people planted themselves at Salem. A colony of English Quakers, among whom was William Penn, purchased all that part of New Jersey lying south and west of a line drawn from Little Egg Harbor to the north-western corner of the provinces, and named West Jersey. Immigration was rapid to both East and West Jersey. They were united in 1702, forming a royal province.*

VI. PENNSYLVANIA.

83. The grant by Charles II. of the beautiful province of Pennsylvania, was confirmed to William Penn, March 5, 1681.† Penn entered into a treaty with the Indians, by which he gained their lasting friendship. His dealings with these savage people were uniformly just and kind, and during all the Indian wars no drop of Quaker blood was shed. The Quakers first settled Pennsylvania at Upland, or Chester. In the beginning of 1682 Penn laid out Phila-

* See S. Smith's and Whitehead's History of East New Jersey.

† See Weems's, Jacob Post's, Clarkson's, Janney's, and Dixon's Life of Wm. Penn.

---

82. To whom was New Jersey assigned? By whom settled? When was Elizabethtown founded? When did the Quakers first come to New Jersey? How was Jersey divided?

83. Who was William Penn? What province was granted to him? Where was Pennsylvania first settled? When was Philadelphia laid out? What was the character of Penn's government? What connection had Delaware with Pennsylvania?

delphia. By the end of the year eighty houses were erected. An admirable body of laws promoted the welfare of the Pennsylvanians. The government was democratic. The province was divided into six counties, and from each of these nine representatives were sent to the general council. The fame of Penn's colony spread far and wide, and population flocked to it from New England, Sweden, Holland, and all parts of Great Britain. Delaware was for twenty years a dependency of Pennsylvania, but became a separate province in 1702, though both colonies were subject to the same governor until the time of the Revolution.*

William Penn.

VII. THE CAROLINAS.

84. Lavish in his gifts, Charles II. bestowed upon eight noblemen, several of whom were favorite courtiers, the vast region between Albemarle Sound and the river St. John, and from the Atlantic to the Pacific. It was afterward extended southward to 29° and northward to 36° 30′, and named Carolina in honor of the king.

85. New Englanders had already planted a little colony

* See Watson's Annals of Philadelphia; Sypher's, Proud's and Gordon's History of Pennsylvania; also Bird's Hawks of Hawk Hollow, fiction.

84. To whom did Charles II. give Carolina?
85. When, where, and by whom was North Carolina first settled?

on the Cape Fear River, and adventurous Virginians had settled on the Chowan. William Drummond was appointed governor of these plantations, in 1664, and the district embracing them was called Albemarle. The next year Sir John Yeamans transferred a company of emigrants from Barbadoes to Albemarle, and formed the settlement of Clarendon. A considerable influx of Quakers increased the population of Albemarle.

86. The Carolina proprietors sent William Sayle from England with emigrants to settle the southern part of their province. A settlement was made at Port Royal, but it was soon removed to a point between the Ashley and the Cooper River, several miles above the site of the present city of Charleston, which was not founded until 1680. Emigrants came to South Carolina from Holland, Germany, England, Scotland, and Ireland. A number of French Huguenots also found refuge there.

87. It was the design of the lords to whom Carolina was granted, to establish an empire "agreeable to monarchy," founded upon old feudal systems, ignoring the rights of the common people. The Earl of Clarendon and the philosopher John Locke framed a complicated plan of government, called the Grand Model, according to which the new province was to be ruled. "But palatines, landgraves, and caciques, the nobility of the Carolina statute-book, were doomed to pass away." *

GENERAL REMARKS.

88. We have now traced the history of the settlement of those portions of our country out of which twelve of the

* See Williamson's and Martin's History of N. C.; Ramsay's History of S. C.; also, W. G. Simms's Cassique of Kiawah, fiction.

---

86. Where, and by whom was South Carolina settled?

87. What was the "Grand Model?" Who designed it?

88. How many states were formed from the colonies thus far mentioned? Name the states. What was the entire English population? What was the religion of the colonies? What nations had already yielded their territorial claims to the English?

United States were formed. The population of the whole region at the time of the accession of William III. and Mary, was about 200,000—in New England, 75,000; in the Middle Colonies, 40,000; in the South, 85,000. The New World afforded to immigrants a degree of civil liberty unknown in Europe. In every colony the tendency of government and institutions was toward republicanism. Royal interference might check, but it could not stay the strong current of the popular will. The religion of most of the people was Protestantism; of nearly all, Christianity.

The dominion of the Dutch and of the Swedes had come to an end. The Spanish in Florida were slowly gathering numbers and strength. The French, still more formidable, were soon to come in collision with the dominant power of the continent, the English. The work of exterminating the Indians had begun in Virginia and New England, and the hand of law had already fastened slavery upon the African.

GENERAL QUESTIONS AND DIRECTIONS.

Prepare a chronological table of the dated events given in Chapter Eighth. What Indian wars are mentioned? Name, in order, the British sovereigns from the time of the discovery of America to the year 1689. What was the general effect of the reign of Charles II. and James II. upon American industry and commerce? The effect upon the temper of the people? Was the accession of William and Mary considered favorable to the colonies?

CHAPTER NINTH.

OCCUPATION OF THE MISSISSIPPI VALLEY—INTER-COLONIAL WARS.

1689—1748.

THE destruction of the Hurons by the Iroquois, which was complete before 1670, obliged the Jesuits to seek new fields of enterprise. North of the great lakes they pushed westward. They established the mission of Saut Ste Marie (soo sěnt mă'ree); they built Fort Michillimacinac (mish'il-e-mak'in-aw). Other rival explorers ventured south of the lakes. La Salle (lå sål), a noted French adventurer, in 1671, discovered the Ohio River and the Illinois. Jacques Marquette (mår-kět') and Louis Joliet (zhō' le-ā') descended the Wisconsin in a canoe, discovered the Mississippi on the 17th of June, **1673**, and floated down its current as far as to the mouth of the Arkansas. The French soon afterward founded the first permanent settlement within the present state of Illinois at Kaskaskia. Louis Hennepin was the first to explore the upper Mississippi. La Salle, aided by the Italian Henry de Tonty, after incredible hardships and repeated failures, succeeded in navi-

QUESTIONS.—**89.** What missions did the Jesuits establish after the Hurons were destroyed? Who discovered the Ohio and the Illinois? When? What discovery was made by Marquette? How long after De Soto's discovery? Who accompanied Marquette? Where was Illinois first settled? What is said of Hennepin?

gating the Mississippi in canoes to its mouth, which was reached April 6, 1682. He took possession of the Mississippi Valley, under the name of Louisiana, for the French king Louis the Fourteenth.*

The brave and enterprising La Salle returned to his native France covered with the glory of his discovery. He was furnished with four vessels, on board of which embarked 280 persons, designed to plant a colony at the mouth of the Mississippi. In February, 1686, the squadron landed in Texas. La Salle missed the entrance of the Mississippi, nor could he find the river by inland exploration. The proposed colony came to naught. The gallant La Salle was assassinated in 1687 by two mutinous companions.

90. Commercial rivalry between England and France occasioned a war, called King William's war, in which the colonies were involved. Count Frontenac, governor of Canada, aided by Indian allies of the Algonquin family, came into conflict with both the English and the Iroquois. Frontenac's war parties made repeated stealthy descents upon the settlements of New England and New York, carrying with them midnight massacre, devastation, and dismay. Dover, Schenectady, Salmon Falls, Casco, and other villages, were attacked and destroyed. A band of French under Lemoine D'Iberville (de'bĕr-vēl') conquered all the English posts on Hudson Bay.

The English effected an easy conquest of Acadia which, however, was retaken by the French. Sir William Phipps,† commander of a squadron from Massachusetts, attempted to surprise Quebec, but signally failed, and returned inglorious to Boston. Frontenac encountered the Iroquois in a

* The story of the daring and romantic adventures of the French discoverers here mentioned is one of the most fascinating imaginable. See Parkman's Jesuits in North America, and Discovery of the Great West, works of authentic history quite as "entertaining as a novel."

† See Cotton Mather's Life of Sir Wm. Phipps.

Give an account of La Salle's further enterprise.

90. Give the history of King William's war. When was peace declared?

battle which resulted in their discomfiture. Peace having been declared between France and England, at Ryswick, in December, 1697, this intercolonial conflict came to an end.

91. It was during the progress of this war that the celebrated Salem witchcraft excitement prevailed in Massachusetts. This superstitious frenzy did not subside until twenty persons had been hung on charge of being leagued with the evil powers.*

92. A second war broke out in Europe, the war of the Spanish succession, in which England was arrayed against both France and Spain. The English colonies soon became involved in a conflict with both Florida and New France. Hostilities began in South Carolina in 1702. James Moore led some of the colonists against St. Augustine, but he was unable to take its fort, and was driven away by Spanish ships. In a second expedition, aided by Creek Indians, he reduced the Spanish settlements of the Appalachee country. In August, 1706, a French frigate landed at Charleston to subdue the place, but was itself captured.

In New England the barbarities of Indian warfare were renewed, Massachusetts suffering most severely. Deerfield and Haverill were surprised, and their inhabitants indiscriminately slaughtered. Hard beset, the colonists appealed to the mother country for aid, which was sent. Again Port Royal fell into English hands. A fleet was fitted out to go against Quebec, while the colonial forces and their Iroquois allies were to attack Montreal; but again a declaration of peace, April 11, 1713, interrupted warlike preparations. In America the English gained by this struggle, locally called Queen Anne's war, the whole of Acadia, Newfoundland, and the fur regions of Hudson Bay.

* See Mather's Wonders of the Invisible World; Upham's Lectures on Witchcraft; Whittier's Supernaturalism in New England; J. Neal's Rachel Dyer, fiction; and Longfellow's Giles Corey, of Salem Farms, tragedy.

---

91. Tell what you know about the Salem witchcraft.

92. How did the war of the Spanish succession involve the American colonies? What was the character of the war?

93. Meanwhile North Carolina suffered the depredations of a war waged by the Tuscaroras, and a combination of southern tribes harassed and desolated the plantations of South Carolina. Political discontents in those colonies led to a change in their government, which was at first proprietary. The latter became a royal province in 1720; the former, in 1729.

94. In 1732, June 9th, Georgia, the thirteenth Anglo-American colony, was chartered. Early the following year the first settlement was made at Savannah, under the auspices of James Edward Oglethorpe,* one of the patentees, and the first governor of the province. Oglethorpe has been much celebrated for the excellence of his character. He was one of the greatest philanthropists of the eighteenth century, and his virtues and talents were praised by Pope, Dr. Johnson, and other famous authors. The first settlers of Georgia were of a mixed character—English, Scotch Highlanders, Germans, Jews, and Moravians.†

95. Again the wave of European war rolled to America. England contested with Spain the privilege of commerce with the West Indies. Georgia bordered Florida, and Oglethorpe came in collision with the Spanish at St. Augustine. The Spanish invaded Georgia, but were gallantly repelled. At the close of this war the boundary of Georgia was pushed further south, and thus the Spanish domain in America was diminished.

96. French colonization went on in Louisiana. D'Iberville, in 1699, built a fort on Biloxi Bay. De Tonty, in 1700, built Fort Rosalie near the present site of Natchez; in 1701 Fort Detroit was erected; in 1702 the left bank of the Mobile was occupied; sixteen years later New Orleans was founded; the fort at Crown Point, famous in later

* See Robert Wright's Memoirs of James Oglethorpe.
† See Stevens's History of Georgia.

---

93. To what distress were the Carolinas subjected?
94. When and where was Georgia settled? Under whose direction?
95. How did the war with Spain affect the boundaries of Florida?

wars, was built in 1731; and Vincennes was settled by Canadians in 1735. The French of Louisiana were not exempt from the wrath of the red men. Three years of bloody conflict sufficed to destroy the hostile Natchez nation. The Chickasaws proved more formidable, and continued to harass the settlers for many years.

97. Still another intercolonial war vexed the exhausted settlements. Again England, at war with France, attempted the conquest of Canada, and with partial success. Ten armed vessels, furnished by Massachusetts, under command of William Pepperell, of Maine, and four British ships of war, under Captain Borlase Warren, besieged Louisburg in April, 1745. Louisburg was by far the strongest fort in America; but the garrison was feeble and poorly supplied. In June the French commander capitulated. The enterprise against Louisburg, according to Hildreth, assumed something of the character of an anti-Catholic crusade, since the besiegers were zealous Protestants and the French were mostly devoted Jesuits. This capitulation yielded as prisoners 650 regular soldiers and 1,300 citizens. No other very important event marked this war, which was terminated October, 1748, by the peace of Aix la Chapelle (åks lå shå'pell'). Louisburg was restored to the French.

98. In the period of fifty-nine years, the great events of which are very briefly related in this chapter, the progress of the colonies was rapid. All of the provinces out of which the original thirteen states of the Union were to be formed, were settled by the year 1743. The English population of the country had increased to more than one million. In 1710 more than 3,000 Germans came to New York; a still larger number settled in Pennsylvania; others came to North Carolina. This was the beginning of that influx of German population which has since become so vast. In 1729 nearly 6,000 Irish immigrants

---

96. What stations and settlements were made in America by the French between 1698 and 1736? What Indian wars occurred in Louisiana?

97. What were the leading events in America of the third war between the English and the French?

landed at the port of Philadelphia. Some of these went to Maryland; others, to Virginia.*

It is an interesting fact that many of the early settlers sought homes in America for the sake of religious liberty. This was the first motive of the Puritans. The Catholics found freedom in Maryland. The English Quakers, the French Huguenots, the Walloons of Belgium, and the Waldenses from Piedmont, emigrated to the New World to escape persecution in the Old. New England Puritanism had abated its asperity, and much controversy had resulted in the development of many Protestant sects.

Cotton Mather.

In 1738 Whitefield, one of the founders of Methodism, came to America and inaugurated the system of religious revivals. The cause of education made some advance. The College of William and Mary was founded in 1691; Yale College, in 1716. Printing-presses had been set up in Massachusetts, Connecticut, New York, and Virginia; but the freedom of the press was much restricted until 1755. The books read by the colonists were either historical, or religious and controversial. Increase Mather, one of the early presidents of Harvard College,

* See McGee's Hist. of Irish Settlers in North America.

---

98. The events of how many years are embraced in this chapter? Name the English colonies. What was their combined population? When did German and Irish emigration begin? Where did the Germans settle? What motive induced many Europeans to seek America?

and Cotton Mather, his son, both voluminous authors, may be said to have founded American literature. "Cotton Mather's Magnalia," says Emerson, "the first important book written by a native in this country, has a vitality still which makes it entertaining reading." The Magnalia is an ecclesiastical history of New England.

GENERAL QUESTIONS AND DIRECTIONS.

Prepare a chronological table of the dated events given in Chapter Ninth. Prepare a list of the forts and settlements founded between 1689 and 1748. What wars occurred within the same period? What noted persons figured in the colonies? What English sovereigns reigned during the time of the intercolonial wars? What French sovereign? What is meant by the expression *royal province?* What is a charter? Give a brief oral summary of Chapter First. Second. Third. Fourth. Fifth. Sixth. Seventh. Eighth. Ninth. How long was it from the settlement of Jamestown to the close of the fourth intercolonial war?

CHAPTER TENTH.

CONQUEST OF NEW FRANCE.

1748—1763.

AN association, known as the Ohio Company, obtained a grant of 500,000 acres of land on the northern margin of the Ohio River; and Christopher Gist, in 1751, carried the surveyor's chain almost as far westward as the falls of the Ohio. Anticipating English occupancy of regions claimed by themselves in virtue of La Salle's discoveries, the French made haste to fortify Presque Isle (prĕsk eel′), on Lake Erie, and, pushing southward, they established forts Le Bœuf (leh bĕf) and Venango on French Creek. This was in 1753. Robert Dinwiddie, lieutenant-governor of Virginia, sent George Washington,* a youth of twenty-one, to demand of the French an explanation of their encroachments.

Washington was politely received at Le Bœuf and Venango, but the French were in nowise disposed to relinquish their claims. In the spring of 1754 some of Dinwiddie's soldiers commenced building a fort at the head of the Ohio,

* See Irving's, Weems's, Marshall's, Sparks's, Paulding's, Headley's, Ramsay's, and Everett's Life of Washington.

QUESTIONS.—**99.** What grant did the Ohio Company obtain in 1749? What forts did the French erect in 1753, and why? What was George Washington's first embassy?

but they were driven away by the French, who completed the fort and named it Du Quesne (du kain′). Washington, leading a detachment of Virginia troops that had been enlisted to resist the French, surprised a scouting party, killed ten men and captured the rest. Having taken the precaution to erect, at Great Meadows, an imperfect stockade, which he called Fort Necessity, Washington moved toward Du Quesne. He was met by a superior force under M. De Villiers (dȧ ve′ye-ā′), and was obliged to fall back to his entrenchments, where, assailed furiously on the 3d of July, he made a gallant defense. Having kept up the fight all day against hope, Washington surrendered the fort on the agreement that his men should be allowed to retire with baggage and arms.

100. The final struggle of France and England, for dominion in America, was at hand. Early in 1755 both nations dispatched fleets across the sea in anticipation of war. In June two French ships were intercepted by the English off the foggy banks of Newfoundland, and captured. Before the end of the year, 300 French vessels fell a prey to British cruisers.

101. Edward Braddock was commander-in-chief of the English and American forces. His camp was formed at Fort Cumberland, on the Virginia border. Early in June his army, consisting of British regulars and colonial volunteers, moved westward through the unbroken wilderness. The march was slow and toilsome. On the 8th of July the Monongahela River was reached by the advanced lines of a chosen force of 1,200. Scouts had already apprised Contrecœur, the commander at Du Quesne, of the enemy's approach. Braddock disdained to take precautions against foes whom he held in contempt, and, contrary to the advice of Washington, he pressed recklessly on, sending a few scouts ahead to reconnoiter. "At about nine miles from

---

When and by whom was Fort Du Quesne built? Give an account of Washington's first military operations.

100. What naval operations took place in 1755?

101. Recount the story of Braddock's march and defeat.

the fort, they reached a spot where the narrow road descended to the river through deep and gloomy woods, and where two ravines, concealed by trees and bushes, seemed formed by nature for an ambuscade."

Hidden in these ravines, the French and their stealthy Indian allies crouched, awaiting the British, who moved proudly on, unconscious of danger. Suddenly the concealed foe, raising a terrific yell, fired upon the advancing grenadiers. A dreadful scene of carnage and confusion ensued. For three hours the battle raged. More than 700 British soldiers were killed, and over forty officers. Braddock fell. The command then devolved upon Washington, who rode among the panic-stricken soldiers endeavoring to rally them. Two horses were shot under him; four times his clothes were pierced by bullets. In spite of his cool demeanor and strong personal effort to reform the broken ranks, dismay prevailed, and those of the English that escaped death and capture fled with precipitation. Nor could order be restored until all had reached Philadelphia. The Indians who witnessed the defeat and panic of Braddock's army, began to doubt the bravery of the English. On the other hand, they conceived a high opinion of the prowess of the French, with whom they readily formed an alliance. They at once began to ravage the unprotected frontier of Pennsylvania and Virginia.

102. A force of over 2,000, commanded by Col. Monckton, found little difficulty in overcoming the French in Acadia. The forts on the Bay of Fundy were surprised and captured in June. A cruel outrage was perpetrated upon the peaceful farmers who dwelt in rustic simplicity about Beau Bassin. The English demanded that these inoffensive people should take an oath of allegiance to Great Britain. This they would not do, and their refusal was made a pretext by the English for the execution of their inhuman scheme. The Acadians were treacherously kidnapped, hurried on

---

What was the British loss? What effect had this battle upon the Indians?

102. Relate the conquest of Acadia. What was the fate of the people of Beau Bassin?

board of ships, and transported, some to every British colony in America. "Wives separated from their husbands in the confusion of embarking, and children from their parents, were carried off to distant colonies, never again to see each other!"*

103. An expedition under William Johnson,† destined to attack Crown Point, had encamped near Lake George. A detachment under Colonel Williams was sent out by Johnson to intercept Dieskau (dees'-kŏw), a German officer in the French service, who was marching to attack Fort Edward, on the Hudson. Williams was slain, and his small force was driven back with slaughter. Dieskau, following up his advantage, attacked Johnson's camp, and a hot engagement ensued, in which the English came off victorious. The French were repulsed with the loss of 1,000 men. Dieskau received a fatal wound. The English loss was 300. In this battle the backwoodsmen of America first proved their mettle in coping with the disciplined soldiers of Europe. Johnson did not proceed against Crown Point, and the French were allowed to establish themselves at Ticonderoga.

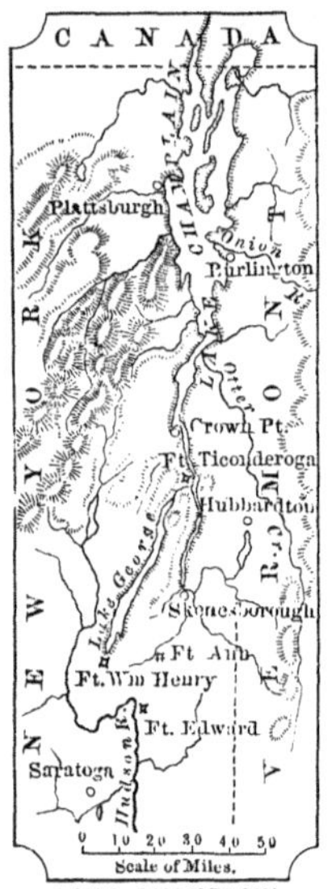

LAKE CHAMPLAIN

104. War was not formally declared between France and England until May, 1756. In the following August, Louis Joseph de Montcalm (mŏnt-kăm'), successor of Dieskau,

*See Longfellow's Evangeline, a Tale of Acadia,—Poem.
†See W. L. Stone's Life of Sir Wm. Johnson.

103. What forts were on or near Lake Champlain? Give the particulars of the encounter between the forces of Johnson and Dieskau near Lake George. How did the colonial soldiers behave in this fight?

104. When was war formally declared? What was the first achievement of Montcalm?

captured Fort Oswego, on Lake Ontario, taking 1,000 prisoners. The English army met with no success in the campaign of 1756.

105. Montcalm, with a force of 8,000, laid siege to Fort William Henry, on the southern shore of Lake George. The fort was garrisoned by only 2,000 men under Colonel Monro. After a brave resistance of six days, Monro was obliged to capitulate, August 9, 1757. It was stipulated that the garrison should march out with the honors of war, and be secured from attack until they reached Fort Edward, fourteen miles distant; but Montcalm's Indian allies, fierce for English blood, fell upon the retreating unarmed troops and butchered more than twenty of them.*

106. The vigorous ministry of William Pitt, premier of England, changed the aspect of the war in America. General Amherst was put in command of an expedition against Cape Breton. Aided by Admiral Edward Boscawen, Amherst invested Louisburg with thirty-eight ships of war. After a long siege, memorable in history and tale, the strong fortress was taken. With Louisburg, Cape Breton and Prince Edward Island fell into the hands of the conquerors. Meanwhile General James Abercrombie, who had moved against Ticonderoga with a force of 15,000 British was repulsed with a heavy loss, and his army retreated in disorder.† In August Fort Frontenac, on Lake Ontario, was captured by General John Bradstreet. In November the French abandoned Fort Du Quesne, which was immediately occupied by the English, who changed its name to Fort Pitt, in honor of the great commoner.

107. The next year's campaign continued the successes of the English. Sir William Johnson advanced to Fort Niagara, and encountered a French army of 1,700, which

* See Cooper's Last of the Mohicans.

† See C. W. Hall's Twice Taken, and G. P. R. James's Ticonderoga.

---

105. Who besieged Fort William Henry? With what result?

106. By whom was Louisburg besieged? What was the result? Who took Fort Frontenac? When did Du Quesne fall into English hands? To what was the name changed?

he defeated, taking many prisoners (July 23, 1759). On the next day he occupied the surrendered fort. Ticonderoga was taken by Amherst.

108. Early in June, 1759, General James Wolfe* sailed up the St. Lawrence with 8,000 men, and encamped on the island of Orleans. Quebec, the French stronghold, was garrisoned with about 14,000 soldiers, under the command of Montcalm. The French army lay encamped on the north bank of the St. Lawrence, below the city. On the 31st of July a strong English force crossed the river in boats and made a desperate attempt to storm the French just above the mouth of the Montmorenci. They were repulsed with a loss of 400. Wolfe now formed the bold design of a direct attack upon Quebec. Embarking the greater part of his army, he sailed up the St. Lawrence and landed several miles above the city. On the night of the 12th of August, the whole British army, being provided with small boats, floated down the tide toward Quebec. "As they approached the landing place, the boats edged closer in toward the

General James Wolfe.

* See Robert Wright's Life of Major-General James Wolfe.

---

107. What military successes did Johnson gain in 1759? By whom was Ticonderoga captured?

108. Who commanded at Quebec? What was the strength of his garrison? What number of men had General Wolfe? Describe the battle of July 31.

northern shore, and the woody precipices rose high on their left like a wall of undistinguished blackness. 'Qui vive?' shouted a French sentinel from out the impervious gloom. 'La France!' answered a captain from the foremost boat." Assured by this prompt response in his own tongue, the French sentinel allowed the boat to land and himself to be captured. The British were soon ashore. Ascending the steep acclivity swiftly but silently, they were hastily marshaled on the plains of Abraham.

Montcalm was soon apprised of Wolfe's position. The French troops were quickly brought into the field. They moved forward to repulse the enemy. A terrific battle raged; but it was of short duration. The French lost 1,500 men; the English, 600. Montcalm received a mortal wound; the heroic Wolfe, pierced by three balls, died upon the field of his victory.

Five days later, and without further fighting, Quebec surrendered, and was garrisoned by 5,000 British soldiers.

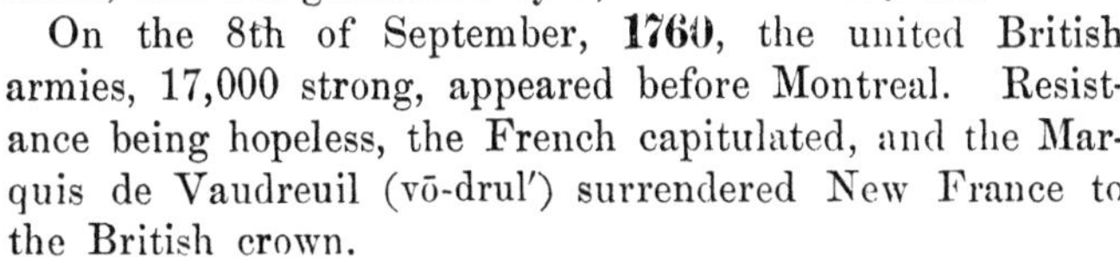

On the 8th of September, **1760**, the united British armies, 17,000 strong, appeared before Montreal. Resistance being hopeless, the French capitulated, and the Marquis de Vaudreuil (vō-drul') surrendered New France to the British crown.

109. The conclusion of the war did not bring peace to the colonies. Provoked by the rash severity of the governor of South Carolina, the Cherokees had begun a war, in 1760, on the southern frontiers, which was not brought to a close

---

Narrate the particulars of the capture of Quebec. When and where did the French surrender Canada?

without a vigorous campaign. In the west a formidable conspiracy of many tribes, headed by Pontiac,* principal chief of the Ottawas, concerted an attack upon the whole English frontier. In 1763 all the western posts were surprised and taken except four, and three of these were beleaguered and long kept in great peril. Desolating incursions were made along the borders of Virginia, Maryland, and Pennsylvania. Hundreds fell victims to the tomahawk and scalping-knife. So extreme grew the excitement in Pennsylvania that a number of backwoodsmen (the Paxton men) formed themselves into an avenging band, and in their rage massacred a number of peaceable Indians.

Two expeditions, one led by Henry Bouquet† (boo-kā′), and one by William Bradstreet, through the Ohio and the lake regions, succeeded, to a great extent, in subduing the belligerent tribes. But it was long before hostilities were brought to an end. Indeed, Indian war, like fire in dry stubble, was ever ready to break out anew, and for two hundred years was the scourge and dread of the frontier. In these early French and Indian wars, 30,000 colonial soldiers perished, and $16,000,000 were expended.

110. By treaty in 1763, France ceded to England her territory lying east of the Mississippi, and to Spain that lying west. Spain also ceded to England the whole of Florida;‡ so that now the British possessions in America extended from the Gulf of Mexico to the Polar Sea, and from the Mississippi to the Atlantic.

111. At the close of the French war, emigration from Europe revived; and from the old colonies it began to flow

* See Parkman's Conspiracy of Pontiac.
† See Bouquet's Expedition against the Ohio Indians in 1764.
‡ Spain re-conquered Florida in 1781.

---

109. What war broke out in Carolina in 1760? Tell what you know of Pontiac and his conspiracy. Who conducted expeditions against the Indians? What loss of life did the colonists suffer in the war? What expense of money?

110. What were the boundaries of the English possessions in America after the war?

westward over the Alleghanies and south to Florida. New settlements multiplied. "This was the golden age of Virginia, Maryland, and South Carolina; their population and productions were now increasing at a rate never equaled at any other period of their history." The population of the colonies was probably not far from two millions. Boston and Philadelphia had each about 20,000 inhabitants. New York had a third less. The effect of the war upon the colonies was to produce greater self-reliance and closer political union. The power of the Indians had greatly declined. Of those ill-fated people, more had perished from small-pox and rum than from all other destructive agencies introduced by the white men.

Jonathan Edwards

Agriculture continued to be the chief employment of the people, especially in the south. In addition to the products mentioned in a former chapter, potatoes, rice, indigo, and cotton were cultivated. In North Carolina turpentine was made. Clothing, shoes, paper, axes, and hats were manufactured in New England. Iron, hides, and hats were exported. Ship-building made progress; cod-fishing was carried on; and whale-fishing was begun. The facilities for travel were

---

111. What effect had the restoration of peace on migration? Which of the colonies were especially prosperous? What was now the total population? What was the chief cause of the decline of the Indians? What progress was made in agriculture? In manufactures? In education? In law? In medicine? In science? In art?

very poor; the first stage-coach was not built until 1772, and but few of the rivers were crossed by bridges.

Six colonial colleges had already been established. The practice of law had risen to the dignity of a profession. In 1674 a medical college was started in Philadelphia. Franklin's famous discoveries in electricity won for American science the applause of the world. American art found a worthy votary in Copley, the only native artist of real merit before the Revolution. In literature, the notable men of the period were Franklin, who began his career as a writer in general literature, politics, and science; and Jonathan Edwards, a great American metaphysician.

GENERAL QUESTIONS AND DIRECTIONS.

Prepare a chronological table of the dated events mentioned in Chapter Tenth. Prepare a list of the battles and sieges of the French war. Name the British sovereigns in whose reign the events of Chapters Ninth and Tenth occurred. What nations held possessions in America when the conquest of New France was completed?

BIOGRAPHICAL REVIEW.

Prepare a biographical sketch of Charles II. Of Edmund Andros. Of Cotton Mather. Of La Salle. Of William Penn. Of James Oglethorpe. Of General James Wolfe. Of King Philip. Of Pontiac. Of Jonathan Edwards.

NOTE.—The American Cyclopedia and Dr. Thomas's Biographical Dictionary will be found useful in compiling these sketches.

Map Questions and Geographical Review.

When, where, and by whom was Maryland colonized? New Jersey? Pennsylvania? Delaware? The Carolinas? Georgia? When, and by whom was the Mississippi Valley claimed for France? Why was it named Louisiana?

Why was Baltimore so named? When did Williamsburg become the capital of Virginia? What was the original name of New York City? What city was founded in 1682? What territory did the English gain by Queen Anne's War?

What rivers were discovered by La Salle? Who explored the Upper Mississippi? What missions did the Jesuits establish on the lakes? Where, and by whom was Indiana first settled? Illinois? When was New Orleans founded? Who built Fort Rosalie? Where? What fort was built in 1701?

Locate Sault Ste. Marie. Michillimacinac. Fort Frontenac. Fort St. Joseph. Fort Miamis. Fort Niagara. Fort George. Fort Edward. By whom, and why were forts Presq' Isle, Le Bœuf, and Venango built? Where was Fort Pitt located? What was it first named? What city now covers its site?

What were the boundaries of the British possessions in America before the conquest of New France? After the conquest? In the year 1763?

What Indian tribes had been destroyed before the year 1740? Locate the Cherokees. The Creeks. The Choctaws. The Chickasaws. The Delawares. The Ottawas. The Sacs. The Wyandottes. What tribe was south of Lake Michigan? West of the Wabash?

See page 82. Locate Fort Ticonderoga. Fort William Henry. Crown Point. Lake George. Fort Ann. What is the length of Lake Champlain?

See page 85. In what direction from Quebec is Point Levi? Beauport? Orleans Island? Wolf's Cove? The plains of Abraham? What streams flow into the St. Lawrence not far from Quebec?

CHAPTER ELEVENTH.

THE REVOLUTION.

1763—1783.

THE isolated position of America, the tendency of her governments and anti-monarchical institutions, the prevailing customs and opinions of her self-reliant people, inevitably destined her for a separate national existence. Causes less natural hastened severance from the mother country. Among these causes were unjust legislation in England, and the despotic administration of British officials in the colonies.

113. George III.* had ascended the British throne. An exacting ministry, seconded by an aristocratic parliament, were in power; and the Americans, subjected to multiplied oppressions, were moving faster than they or their tyrants dreamed toward revolution and independence.

114. Notwithstanding the impoverished condition of the colonies and the local distress caused by the late wars, England proposed to lighten her own heavy debt by raising a revenue in America. A vigorous attempt was made to enforce the odious Navigation laws in their utmost strin-

* See Macfarlane's History of George III.; Jesse's Memoirs of Life and Reign of George III.; Thackeray's Lectures on the Four Georges.

QUESTIONS.—**112.** What were the causes of the Revolutionary War?

113. What was the character of the king, ministry, and parliament in power?

114. Why did England wish to tax the colonists?

gency. Writs of Assistance were granted, empowering the holder to invade any one's premises and search for contraband goods. The eloquent logic of James Otis* proved the illegality of such writs, and compelled their disuse.

115. On the 27th of February, 1765, Parliament passed the famous Stamp act, by which no written instrument, such as bill, bond, note, or lease, could be held valid in law unless it was inscribed on stamped paper upon which an impost was to be paid. The passage of the Stamp act aroused the indignation of the colonists, who held that Parliament had no right to tax them without their consent. They declared that taxation without representation is tyranny. Patrick Henry,† in the Virginia Assembly, made a thrilling denunciatory speech, which secured the passage of strong resolutions against the action of Parliament. These resolutions met with general approval in the colonies. Newspapers, pamphlets, speeches, and sermons against the Stamp act increased the popular excitement.

Patrick Henry.

In Boston a mob assaulted the houses of some of the

* See Wm. Tudor's Life of James Otis; Sparks's Am. Biog., Vol. II.

† See Wirt's and A. H. Everett's Life of Patrick Henry.

What were the Writs of Assistance?

115. What was the Stamp act? How did the colonists receive it? Why did they object to it? What was Patrick Henry's action? How was popular disapprobation expressed?

king's officers whose duty it was to distribute the stamped paper. In New York the merchants resolved to import no goods from England until the Stamp act was repealed. Non-importation associations sprang up in many other places. A convention of delegates from nine colonies met at New York, and prepared a declaration of rights and grievances, in which they claimed all the privileges that Englishmen anywhere enjoyed. They forwarded a petition to the crown and memorials to Parliament. The Stamp act never went into effect, and it was repealed in 1767.

116. Still Parliament claimed the *right* to tax the Americans, and an act was passed imposing a duty upon tea, paints, lead, glass, and paper. This indirect tax was not less objectionable than a direct one, and, to evade it, the colonists bought none of the articles enumerated. The duty was now taken from every thing except tea, and on that it was reduced to three pence a pound; but the right to impose *any tax at all* was denied, and no tea was imported.

117. Several regiments had been stationed at Boston to intimidate the people of that independent and patriotic city. The bitterest animosity was engendered between the irritated populace and the soldiers. On the night of March 5, 1770, a picket guard of eight men, infuriated by an abusive mob, fired into a crowd, killing three persons and wounding several others. Upon the peremptory demand of the town authorities, the troops were now removed to an island in the harbor; but the excitement produced by the so-called Boston Massacre was intense and lasting.

118. For nearly ten years popular discontents had been growing. The murmurs of Massachusetts were repeated in all the other colonies. The general longing for liberty found new voices every-where, and they grew bolder every

---

What was done in Boston? In New York? What was done in the convention of October, 1765? When was the Stamp act repealed?

116. What was the next unjust act of Parliament? What effect had it in America? How were the tax laws finally amended? Why did the Americans refuse to pay three pence a pound on tea?

117. Give the facts concerning the Boston Massacre.

day. Benjamin Franklin, John Adams,* Patrick Henry, and other wise and bold patriots, were educating the people for the great Revolution.

119. In 1773 the East India Company sent several ships laden with tea to the American cities. The vessels for New York and Philadelphia were not allowed to unload, and they soon returned to England; the cargo sent to Charleston was stored in damp cellars where it spoiled; at Boston forty or fifty men, disguised as Indians, boarded the tea ships on a moonlight night and emptied the 342 chests with which they were freighted into the waters of the bay. The audacity of this proceeding provoked the British ministry to precipitate measures that were the direct cause of war. By act of Parliament, the port of Boston was closed. The charter of Massachusetts was virtually abrogated. The seat of government was removed to Salem. Four more regiments were forwarded to Boston. "The penal acts of 1774 dissolved the moral connection between the

Benjamin Franklin.

* See Sparks's and Parton's Life of Franklin, and especially Bigelow's edition of Franklin's Autobiography; also Charles F. Adams's Life of John Adams.

---

118. What three men were most influential in educating the people for independence?

119. What was done with the tea shipped in 1773 to American cities? What was the consequence of the "Boston tea party?"

two countries." These acts passed in Parliament by a vote of four to one.

120. The fate of Boston elicited sympathy in all quarters. New York proposed a congress of colonial delegates. The desire for such a congress was general. Accordingly, at the call of Massachusetts, fifty-three delegates from twelve colonies, Georgia alone not being represented, assembled at Philadelphia on the 5th of September, 1774. This Congress, while acknowledging allegiance to England, asserted with dignity the colonial rights which it denied the authority of Parliament to abrogate; appealed to the sense of justice of the people in both countries; humbly petitioned the king to restore lost liberties and abate growing grievances.

But reconciliation was not to be. Neither the moderation of the Continental Congress, nor the statesmanship of Pitt, nor the diplomacy of Franklin, could avert a conflict of arms. Parliament was determined to coerce the Americans; the king spurned their petitions. Meanwhile, preparations for war were going on. In the Virginia Assembly, Henry fired his auditors by a memorable speech, closing with the words, "Give me liberty or give me death!" The Assembly of Massachusetts met, contrary to the orders of General Thomas Gage, the royal governor, a man "neither fit to reconcile nor subdue." They appointed a committee of safety, and elected John Hancock* provisional governor. A volunteer militia of minute-men was enrolled. Both the British and the Americans were diligent in collecting arms and stores.

121. It was near midnight on April 18, 1775, that a body of 800 soldiers, secretly prepared by Gage, set out from Boston to destroy some military stores that were collected

* See Goodrich's Lives of the Signers of the Declaration of Independence.

---

120. How was the closing of Boston port regarded by the Americans. What state proposed a colonial congress? What was the action of this body? How did the British government receive the petitions and arguments of the Americans? What was the feeling in Virginia? What preparations for war were made in Massachusetts?

at Concord. The design was anticipated, the plan discovered, and by ten o'clock fleet messengers on horseback had been dispatched, who rode all night rousing the minute-men at almost every village and farm-house for miles around. A beacon raised in the belfry of the old North Church shot afar its signal light of alarm.* At Lexington the British troops found collected on the green a party of sixty men armed with firelocks. "Disperse, ye rebels!" cried the leader of the British, and, no one moving, he immediately ordered his grenadiers to fire. Seven of the patriots fell dead and nine were wounded. The minute-men returned some scattering shots without effect, and the red-coats marched on with music and cheers.

At Concord a much larger body of minute-men had assembled. Another short encounter took place. The British fired first. Two men were killed on each side. The British, without having found any valuable stores, presently began a hasty retreat. The retreat soon became a disorderly flight. The road to Boston was lined with minute-men. Each was his own commander, and fought for himself and his invaded soil.

New England blood was up. From behind trees, fences, and walls the defenders fired upon the running foe. At Lexington the British were re-enforced by 900 men, but the retreat was not checked, nor was the hot chase given over until the panting grenadiers found refuge in Boston. On that memorable day the American loss was about 85, while nearly 300 British soldiers fell. And so the Revolutionary War began. "Other wars, before and since, have been waged *for* the people, but this was the first war actually waged *by* the people that is recorded in history." The tidings of war flew through the colonies. Within a few days Boston was besieged by an army of 16,000 volunteers.†

* See Longfellow's Paul Reviere's Ride.

† See Bryant's Seventy-Six and Street's Concord, poems.

---

121. Who was General Gage? What expedition did he send out on the night of April 18, 1775? How was the alarm spread abroad? What took place at Lexington? At Concord? On the road to Boston? How many were killed? What effect had this day's work on the Americans?

122. On the 10th of May, Ethan Allen* surprised Ticonderoga with a handful of Green Mountain boys, and demanded its surrender "in the name of the great Jehovah and the Continental Congress." The fortress yielded. Seth Warner captured Crown Point on the same day, and two hundred pieces of artillery and a supply of powder were obtained from the two forts.

123. On the night of June 16, about 1,000 men, under the command of Colonel William Prescott, threw up an entrenchment below Bunker's Hill, Charlestown. In the morning, the British ships in the harbor, aided by a battery on Copp's Hill, began to fire upon the half-finished redoubt. At noon 3,000 troops, led by Sir William Howe, crossed from Boston to take the American works by assault. Prescott had been re-enforced by some 500 men, and the British were driven back. The village of Charlestown was now set on fire by the British, and they again charged bravely up the hill. Met by deadly volleys, they were again repulsed with heavy loss. A third time they advanced, and, after a sharp conflict, gained the redoubt. Prescott's ammunition was spent, and the Americans were forced to retreat. More than 1,000 of the British fell at the battle of Bunker's Hill. The Americans lost 145, the lamented General Joseph Warren being of the number.†

* See H. W. DePuy's Ethan Allen and Sparks's Am. Biog.

† See Everett's Life of Warren; also Cooper's Lionel Lincoln, fiction.

---

122. What did Ethan Allen and Seth Warner do? When?

123. Describe the battle of Bunker's Hill. When was it fought? With what loss on each side? What American general fell?

124. The people of the colonies were neither unanimous in opinion nor harmonious in action. Two parties had arisen, Whigs and Tories, the latter friendly to Parliament and the king. The Tories were numerous in New York, Pennsylvania, Maryland, South Carolina, and Georgia. The majority of the people strongly inclined to independence. British arrogance and despotism were fast alienating even the most loyal. Boston was under martial law. Gage had proscribed John Hancock and Samuel Adams* as traitors and rebels. Ten thousand British troops were already at Boston, and more were on the way thither.

125. The second Continental Congress met at Philadelphia on the 10th of May. Hope of reconciliation was not yet extinct, and committees were once more appointed to petition the king and appeal to the British people. At the same time articles of war were agreed to, and continental bills of credit were ordered to meet prospective expenses. George Washington was unanimously chosen commander-in-chief of the American army. A post-office system was established, with Franklin at its head.

126. Washington assumed command of the army before Boston, July 2, 1775. He made Cambridge his headquarters, and at once began the organization of the troops. Want of ammunition for a time prevented any renewal of hostilities. An expedition had been projected against Canada, and in August General Philip Schuyler (skī'-ler) † proceeded with a small force down Lake Champlain and the Sorel River. Falling sick, he returned, and General Richard Montgomery ‡ assumed the command. He succeeded in taking Fort Chambly, St. Johns, and Montreal before winter. By these successes seasonable supplies of military

* See W. V. Wells's Life and Public Services of Samuel Adams.

† See B. J. Lossing's Life and Times of Philip Schuyler.

‡ See Sparks's Am. Biog., Vol. I., First Series.

---

124. What parties existed in America? What warlike preparations did the British make? Whom did Gage proscribe?

125. When did the second Congress meet? What was its action?

126. Give an account of the operations against Canada.

stores and clothing fell to the use of the needy invaders. Montgomery pushed on to Quebec, whither Colonel Benedict Arnold* had preceded him with a detachment from Boston, which, with difficulty, reached its destination by way of the Kennebec and the wilderness of Maine.

The united armies, numbering less than 1,000 men, on December 31, attempted to take Quebec by assault in the midst of a snow storm. A gallant and well-nigh successful charge was made; but Montgomery fell, Arnold was severely wounded, and, with a loss of 400 in killed and prisoners, the assailants withdrew. Within six months a large body of British troops arrived at Quebec, and the American army was ejected from Canada with the loss of all the points that had been gained.

127. The winter passed. Fifty pieces of artillery had been dragged on sleds from Ticonderoga to Boston. On the dark night of the 4th of March, **1776**, Washington sent out a strong detachment to occupy Dorchester Heights. On this commanding elevation, south of Boston, fortifications were erected. A furious storm prevented the British from a prompt attack, and the works were so strengthened that Howe, now commander-in-chief, thought best to evacuate the city, which he accordingly did on the 17th. Ten days later Washington entered Boston in triumph amid the rejoicings of the people.

128. Howe sailed to Halifax, where he remained for three months. He then proceeded to New York. The British army had been re-enforced by 17,000 hired Hessians, Waldeneckers, and Hanoverians, and numbered, in all, 40,000 men. Washington, leaving five regiments at Boston, went immediately to New York, and employed his raw army, only 8,000 strong, in putting that city in such a state of defense as his means would allow.

* See Sparks's Am. Biog., Vol. III., First Series.

---

127. How did Washington get artillery to Boston? What was done on the night of March 4, 1776? What occurred on the 17th of March?

128. Whither did Howe sail? How was his army re-enforced? Why did Washington go to New York?

129. In June General Howe sent a detachment of his army by sea, under Sir Henry Clinton, against Charleston, South Carolina. The principal defense of Charleston was a fortress of palmetto logs hastily erected on Sullivan's Island, commanding the harbor. On the 28th, Clinton's well-appointed squadron made its attack. A protracted bombardment ensued, but the British were finally repulsed with a loss of about 300. The American loss was but 35. To Colonel William Moultrie belongs the chief glory of defending the fort, upon which his name was bestowed by universal consent.

130. In the Continental Congress, on the 7th of June, **1776**, Richard Henry Lee* of Virginia, introduced what John Adams pronounced "the greatest question ever debated in America, and as great as ever was or will be debated among men." He moved "that the United Colonies are, and ought to be, free and independent states, and that their connection with Great Britain is, and ought to be, dissolved." On the 2d of July this resolution passed unanimously; and on the FOURTH, the Declaration of Independence, penned by Thomas Jefferson,† was adopted, and the United States began a separate national existence. The ringing of the State House bell announced the final action of Congress, and the welcome tidings went forth to gladden and strengthen the heart of citizen and soldier.

131. During the years 1776 and 1777 all of the states either established new constitutions, or altered their charters so as to adapt them to the necessities of a free and independent people. Massachusetts was the first to remodel her government. Rhode Island and Connecticut made no

* See R. H. Lee's Life of R. H. Lee.

† See Smucker's, F. Dwight's, B. L. Rayner's, G. Tucker's, and H. S. Randall's Life of Jefferson. Read the Declaration of Independence.

---

129. Relate the particulars of Clinton's expedition against Charleston.

130. What famous resolution was passed in Congress on the 2d of July, 1776? Who wrote the Declaration of Independence?

131. What effect had the change of government upon state constitutions?

change in their charters except to substitute in those instruments the word people instead of king. New York established a new constitution last of all the thirteen states, but framed it most liberally of all. The new constitutions did not greatly differ from one another, nor did they widely depart from the spirit of the English organic law. The right of suffrage was restricted in several of the states. Excepting in Pennsylvania, none but property holders were eligible to the principal offices.

132. It required all of Washington's ability to conduct the war in which his ill-prepared country was involved. Sectional jealousies existed. The army officers, many of whom were incompetent, wrangled about precedence in rank. Privates, mistaking insubordination for independence, hindered operations which it was their duty to hasten. Provisions, equipments, arms, and ammunition were scarce. Volunteers went home without leave at the expiration of the short time for which they had enlisted, and the army seemed on the point of dissolution. Congress but feebly seconded the military measures of the commander-in-chief, and but partially heeded his wise advice. In the face of so many obstacles, Washington calmly controlled events with an eye single to the nation's good.

133. The British army was under perfect discipline. It was well officered, and supplied with all that is needful in a military campaign. Admiral Richard Howe,* brother of Sir William, had recently arrived at New York with re-enforcements, and the land forces were now supported by 400 ships and transports, 10 ships of the line, and 20 frigates. As yet the United States possessed no navy worthy of the name, though American privateers had already done considerable service, having captured 350 British vessels during the first year of the war.

* See Campbell's Lives of the British Admirals.

---

132. What difficulties did Washington encounter?

133. What was the character and condition of the British army? Which of the Howes was general? What was the position of the other? What service was done by American privateers?

134. All things being in readiness, the Howes determined to attack the American forces at Long Island. On the 27th of August, 1776, a battle took place, in which 5,000 Americans were engaged against five times that number of the enemy. This battle was disastrous to the Americans, who, though they fought desperately, had no well-concerted plans, and were driven behind their defenses at Brooklyn, with a loss of 3,000, three-fourths of whom were prisoners.

The British loss was 380 killed and wounded. The brunt of the battle of Long Island was borne by a few southern regiments from Maryland and Delaware, commanded by Lord Stirling. Many hireling Hessians were engaged in this fight, and they gained hateful notoriety for deeds disgraceful to the soldier's profession. Neither the disarmed nor the dying found mercy at their cruel hands. Petitions for quarter were answered by the Hessian bayonet thrust to the suppliant's heart.

135. Relinquishing the hope of holding Long Island, Washington drew off his troops, with great secrecy and celerity, during the night of August 29, and retired in safety to New York. This retreat, pronounced by Nathaniel Greene* the best effected, considering its difficulties, of any retreat of which he had ever read or heard, probably saved the American army from capture. Still in danger

* See Geo. W. Greene's Life of General Greene.

134. When was the battle of Long Island fought? Where? By what forces? Led by whom? With what losses? With what results?

of being surrounded by overwhelming numbers, the Americans retired to the Heights of Harlem. From Harlem the army was soon removed to White Plains, where, on the 28th of October, a part of Howe's forces made an attack. A severe but short action ensued, with a loss of over 300 on each side. The Americans were driven behind their entrenchments, and the British retired to camp.

136. Under cover of night, Washington again shifted his position, and now lodged among the rocky hills of Northcastle. Leaving there a portion of the army under General Charles Lee, he proceeded with the rest to cross the Hudson and re-enforce Fort Lee, situated on the right bank of the river. Nearly opposite this fort, on the northern end of Manhattan Island, stood Fort Washington, garrisoned by about 2,000 brave men under command of Colonel Magaw. The British assaulted this post on the 16th of November, and succeeded in capturing it, with the loss of 1,000 men. Washington, powerless to rescue, witnessed with deep distress the fate of the garrison.

Hastening to remove the stores and ammunition from the now imperiled Fort Lee, the ill-starred patriots once more resumed their retreat. A large and well-appointed detachment, under Lord Charles Cornwallis,* the ablest British general who took part in the war, crossed the Hudson in eager pursuit. Washington, having sent word for the troops at Northcastle to join him with all speed, marched to the neighborhood of Newark; thence to Brunswick; thence to Trenton, where he crossed the Delaware, having first secured all the boats for seventy miles up and down stream. This dismal retreat of nearly a hundred miles was protracted for two-thirds of a month. Lee, disre-

* See J. W. Kaye's Lives of Indian Officers.

---

135. What did Greene say of Washington's retreat from Long Island? Whither did Washington go from New York? When did the army remove to White Plains? Why this continual retreat? What battle was fought on the 28th of October? Who gained?

136. Where did the Americans next take refuge? Where was Fort Lee? What did Washington witness from Fort Lee? What was Washington's route from Fort Lee to the Delaware?

garding Washington's repeated urgent messages, delayed to send forward his troops, though they were sorely needed to strengthen the retreating army, which was too feeble to risk an engagement with the enemy.

At length the disobedient general slowly moved. A humiliating experience awaited him. Having one night taken lodgings three miles away from his main camp, he was taken prisoner by a band of dashing dragoons. His army was conducted without mishap to Washington's camp. Cornwallis, unable to cross the Delaware for lack of boats, distributed his men in small divisions at Trenton, Burlington, and other points, to wait for the freezing of the river. He himself returned to New York, and joined the Howes in their comfortable winter quarters.

Lord Cornwallis.

137. Congress prudently resolved that the commander-in-chief should be possessed of power to order and direct all things relative to the department, and to the operations of war. His little army being consolidated and somewhat re-enforced, Washington meditated a *coup-de-main*, which was thus executed: On Christmas night troops to the number of 2,400 re-crossed the Delaware. The weather was intensely cold, and the December wind blew roughly. It was four o'clock in the morning before all the men were ferried across the dark stream, obstructed as it was with drifting

---

Who pursued him? What happened to Lee? What disposition did Cornwallis make of his troops?

137. What power did Congress confer upon Washington?

ice. Twenty small cannon were carried over. These the soldiers dragged after them, marching as rapidly as possible toward Trenton, nine miles distant. At Trenton, Cornwallis had stationed Colonel Rahl with a force largely composed of Hessians. It was Washington's purpose to surprise the enemy. The venture was well-nigh desperate. The Americans, with amazing fortitude,

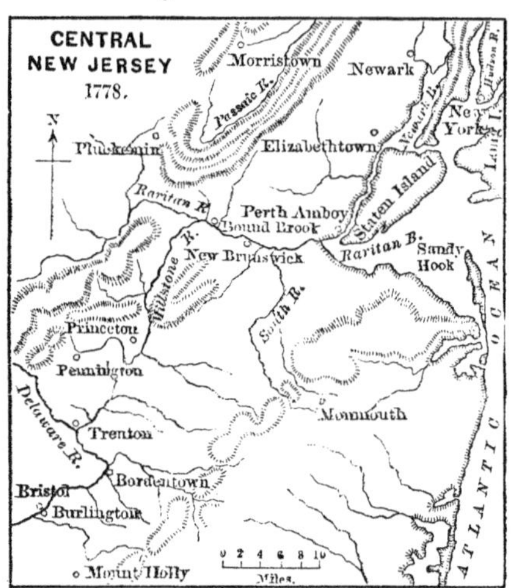

pushed on, facing a storm of hail and snow. It was daylight before they reached Trenton; but their approach was not discovered, and the surprise was complete. "Der feind! der feind! heraus! heraus!" was the cry of the attacked Hessians as they rushed confusedly to arms or to flight. Rahl, with great personal courage, rallied a part of his men and led a brave defense, but he received a mortal wound, and one of his officers struck the British colors and surrendered. Washington immediately recrossed the Delaware with nearly a thousand prisoners, thirty-five of whom were officers. Having sent his prisoners to a place of safety, he once more crossed into New Jersey and encamped near Trenton.

When Howe heard of Washington's movements, he at once ordered Cornwallis to return in person to New Jersey, to direct military operations. Cornwallis accordingly proceeded to Trenton with a large force, and on the night of January 2, 1777, encamped within eight miles of the

---

Relate the particulars of Washington's *coup-de-main* against Trenton. Who was in command at Trenton?

American army. "In the morning we will bag the fox," said Cornwallis to his officers. In the morning Washington's camp was found to be deserted. By a second bold maneuver, Washington had not only rescued his army from destruction, but had also added glory to American arms. He withdrew his troops from the camp and led them by a circuitous route toward Princeton, where some regiments of British, intending to join Cornwallis, were lodging for the night. On the bright frosty morning of the 3d, Washington encountered a detachment of troops already on the march from Princeton. A battle was fought in which the Americans were the victors, killing 100 and taking 300 prisoners, with a loss on their part of only 30. Washington continued his march to Morristown, where he intrenched himself. The out-generaled Cornwallis, giving up the chase, retired into winter quarters at Brunswick.

138. Thus, with a gleam of hope, closed the most critical campaign of the war. The condition of military affairs was still disheartening. The loss of Lee, the petulant ambition of General Horatio Gates, the discontents of Arnold and others, all tended to disorganize and weaken the army. In the American camp the small-pox prevailed. The political aspect of events, however, was brightening. A thriving commerce was opened with France, Spain, and Holland. Through the commissionership of Franklin, secret aid in the form of loans and war stores was obtained from France, which nation was hostile to England. A number of foreign patriots volunteered their services to aid the cause of American independence. Among those that, during the war, rendered valuable services as officers were the German barons John De Kalb and Frederick Steuben, the Poles Thaddeus Kosciusko (kos-se-ŭs'ko) and Count Casimir Pulaski (pū-las'ke), and especially the French Marquis de La Fayette.*

* See Wm. Cutter's and P. C. Headley's Life of La Fayette.

Narrate the operations of Cornwallis and Washington subsequently to the affair at Trenton. Where did Washington take up winter quarters?

138. How did Washington's success influence the Americans? The British? What famous foreigners came to assist the Americans?

139. No important military movement occurred during the winter. With the opening of spring, General Howe employed various stratagems to induce the Americans to quit their secure camp and risk an open battle; but Washington's characteristic caution, a quality which won for him the appellation of the American Fabius, prevented such an event, and the British at length evacuated Jersey. Leaving New York well protected, Admiral Howe embarked a numerous force on transports and put to sea. Washington could not ascertain the design of this movement. On the 14th of June, 1777, Congress adopted, as the national emblem, the flag of stripes and stars.*

Marquis de La Fayette.

140. A large army, composed of British regulars, German mercenaries, and Canadians, under the command of the brave and generous General John Burgoyne, set forth from Canada to destroy the American defenses in the north. To this army a large body of Iroquois warriors was added, under the leadership of the noted war chief, Brant. A number of American loyalists also joined in the expedition. Burgoyne conducted his forces up Lake Champlain to Ticonderoga. This stronghold, although garrisoned by 3,500

* See Drake's American Flag; Cutter's Flag of our Union; S. Hamilton's History of the American Flag.

139. When did Howe evacuate Jersey? When did Congress adopt a national flag?

men, was presently evacuated by General St. Clair, with prodigious loss of ammunition and stores. The Americans made a hasty and inglorious retreat, pursued by the enemy. They effected a junction with the rest of the northern army at Fort Edward, on the Hudson. Here assembled in all about 5,000 men, of whom Schuyler had the command. Burgoyne advanced and Schuyler fell back to Stillwater, and then to the mouth of the Mohawk. See p. 109.

Burgoyne, being much in need of horses, oxen, and vehicles to transport supplies from Ticonderoga, sent out Colonel Baum, at the head of 500 select men, toward Bennington, to procure what was wanted. Apprised of the enemy's design, a force of 800 or 900 volunteers, led by General John Stark,* marched out to meet the marauders. On the morning of August 10, the battle of Bennington was fought. "Now, my men, there are the red coats," said the American colonel: "by night they must be ours, or Molly Stark will be a widow." A sharp conflict ensued, in which the Americans were the gainers. In the afternoon both sides were re-enforced, and a second encounter took place. The fighting continued until dark, and resulted in the total defeat of Baum, with the loss of four brass field pieces, 900 swords, 1,000 stands of arms, and nearly 600 prisoners. Stark lost but 100 men.†

141. A strong detachment of Burgoyne's army had been sent against Fort Stanwix, on the Mohawk, the most western military post in New York. A division of militia under General Herkimer, advancing to the relief of the fort, fell into an ambush at Oriskany, and a ferocious conflict ensued. Red Jacket and Joseph Brant both figured in this sanguinary struggle, in which 400 Americans were

* See Sparks's Am. Biog., Vol. I., Second Series.

† See A. B. Street's Bennington, poem; also Green Mt. Boys, fiction.

---

140. Of what was General Burgoyne's army composed? What was Burgoyne's design? Who commanded at Ticonderoga? What did he do? Where was Schuyler's army assembled? Give Schuyler's movements. Describe the battle of Bennington.

141. Describe the battle of Oriskany.

slain. The besieged fortress held out resolutely for several weeks, when the besiegers, alarmed at rumors of an overwhelming force coming against them, decamped precipitately. Their tents and baggage fell into the hands of General Arnold, who had been sent to the rescue of the garrison with a small force. Arnold was distinguished for shrewd cunning. He had spread exaggerated reports of his numbers to excite the fears of the British.

142. Burgoyne, alarmed at the course affairs were taking, determined to push on as fast as practicable toward Albany, hoping to form a junction with Howe. His situation was growing perilous. His Indian allies, whose atrocities had excited strong feelings of revenge in the Americans, were daily deserting him. His losses in battles and skirmishes, and by sickness, were great. His men were poorly supplied and in low spirits. On the other hand, the American army was in excellent condition, and was rapidly increasing in numbers. Harvest was over, and the farmer volunteers flocked to camp bearing their own provisions, and impatient to defend their invaded land. The patriotism of Concord and Bunker Hill again blazed high. Every thing seemed to promise a successful issue to the year's campaign. Just at this juncture Schuyler was superseded in the command of the northern army by his ambitious rival, General Gates. No sufficient reason can be given why Congress should displace so good an officer as Schuyler, especially at a time when all his plans seemed working toward a glorious consummation.

The British army, having crossed the Hudson, moved first to Saratoga, and then slowly southward toward the American camp at Bemis's Heights. On the 19th of September Burgoyne offered battle, which Gates promptly accepted, and a general engagement took place. The field was stubbornly contested, and both armies claimed the victory. Night put an end to the battle. The British encamped on

---

What was Arnold's stratagem to get possession of Fort Stanwix?

142. What was now Burgoyne's situation? How was the American army re-enforced? Who superseded Schuyler?

the field, and the Americans retired behind the works. A second battle was fought near the same ground on the 7th of October. In this the British were repulsed, though they fought bravely and against superior numbers. The victors slept on their arms, prepared to renew the attack next day. The next day proved rainy and dismal, and was spent in skirmishing. Foiled and dejected, Burgoyne at night effected a gloomy retreat. He returned to Saratoga. His communication with Ticonderoga was cut off, and that stronghold was invested by Americans. The road to Fort Edward was guarded by the enemy. In adversity, the British were deserted not only by the Iroquois, but also by the Canadians and loyalists. Courageous to the last, Burgoyne took a position south of the Fishkill River, hoping to keep Gates at bay until the arrival of Sir Henry Clinton, who was expected to bring re-enforcements by way of the Hudson River.

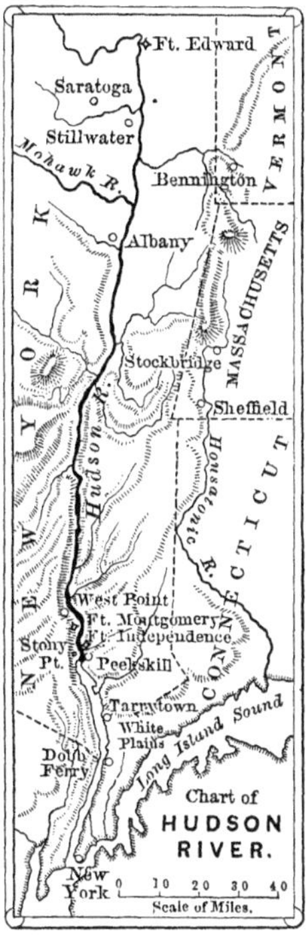

Chart of HUDSON RIVER.

Despairing at length of succor, he called a council of war, and it was resolved to capitulate. On the 16th of October, 1777, his whole army was surrendered on condition that the men should be allowed to return to England, under promise not to take up arms again during the war. The number of prisoners was 5,642. The previous losses of the army were about 4,000. By this capitulation the Americans gained 7,000 stand of arms, a fine train of artillery, and a good supply of tents, clothing, and general military stores. Too late, Sir Henry

---

Describe the battles of Bemis's Heights. The subsequent movements of Burgoyne. When did Burgoyne capitulate? Where? How many prison ers were surrendered?

Clinton made his appearance after a successful expedition against the forts on the Hudson. Nothing remained but for him to dismantle the forts he had captured, and to return to New York. Ticonderoga was speedily abandoned, and again the Americans took possession of it.*

143. How fared it, meanwhile, with the southern army? Upon Howe's departure from Jersey, Washington removed his camp to the vicinity of Philadelphia; thence to Wilmington. On the 25th of August, Howe began to land a large force at the upper end of Chesapeake Bay, with the evident intention of proceeding against Philadelphia. Every possible preparation was made to oppose the threatened invasion. Washington determined to meet the enemy in open field, and to check its progress. Howe moved on without opposition until within twenty-six miles of Philadelphia, when he encountered the Americans at Brandywine Creek, and after a hard fight defeated them. This was on the 11th of September, 1777. Soon afterwards Cornwallis pushed forward at the head of a large detachment, and entered the capital in triumph. Congress had retired to York, beyond the Susquehanna, where, before the close of the year, they adopted articles of Confederation and perpetual Union.

144. The British main army, under Howe, was stationed at Germantown, a straggling village near Philadelphia. Washington and his officers resolved to try the chances of battle once again. This time it was decided to act on the offensive. At dusk on the 3d of October, the Americans left their camp near the Schuylkill, and, marching fourteen miles, reached Germantown at break of day. A heavy fog rendered the morning almost as dark as night. General

* See Halleck's Field of the Grounded Arms, poem; D. P. Thompson's Rangers, fiction; and Hawthorne's Ticonderoga, in Twice Told Tales.

What, meantime, were Clinton's movements?

143. Where had Washington encamped? What was Howe's design? When was the battle of Brandywine fought? When did Cornwallis enter Philadelphia? To what place did the Congress retire? What did they do there?

144. Where was Howe stationed after the fight at the Brandywine?

Anthony Wayne* led the attack. The fighting was fierce. The Americans gained a vast advantage, though not aware of the fact, and were on the point of carrying the whole British encampment, when, for some unknown cause, a panic seized them, and they fled from their own victory. Other misfortunes followed the retreat from Germantown. Forts Mifflin and Mercer, important defenses on the Delaware, were besieged, and, after a protracted and heroic resistance, reduced. The enemy now had water communication from Philadelphia to the sea.

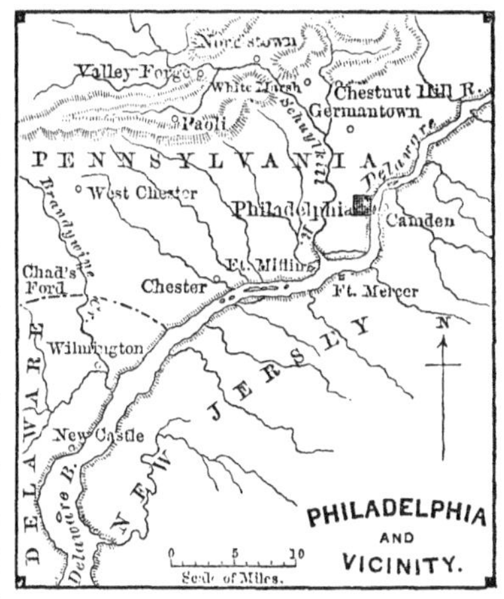

145. The campaign of 1777 was closed. To the northern army it brought victory and glory; to the southern, failure and humiliation. In the middle of December, Washington conducted his discouraged troops to Valley Forge, on the Schuylkill, about twenty miles from Philadelphia. Some eleven hundred arrived in camp and built huts for the winter. Their distresses were many and great. They had not been paid. Supplies of all kinds were wanting. The weather was cold. The men's clothes were in rags. So great was the destitution of shoes that the frozen ground over which the soldiers marched was stained by their bleeding feet. Such were the hardships endured by those who won for themselves and their posterity the blessings of American independence.

* See Sparks's Am. Biog., Vol. IV.

Describe the battle of Germantown. Who led the attack? What disasters followed the battle of Germantown?

145. Where is Valley Forge? When did Washington encamp there? With how many soldiers? Relate their sufferings.

Notwithstanding the gloomy aspect of affairs, the military condition of the country was evidently more hopeful than it had been a year before, and the patriots were in tolerable spirits. Washington, with his usual energy, set to work to re-organize the army. General Greene was appointed quartermaster, and more efficient means were taken to obtain provisions and clothing. Baron Steuben was made inspector-general. Under his direction, the men were drilled according to approved European tactics.

146. Burgoyne's surrender had a marked effect upon Parliament. Conciliatory bills were introduced pledging the repeal of the tax laws, and appointing commissioners to negotiate for peace. But it was too late to talk of peace. The day of reconciliation had passed. America, having drawn the sword, was disposed to fight until freedom was securely won or utterly lost. Congress asserted the entire independence of the United States. While the continental soldiers were in huts at Valley Forge, the cheering intelligence came across the ocean that France had openly acknowledged the new republic, and it was presently rumored that a French fleet, commanded by Count D'Estaing (dĕs-tăn′), was under sail to aid the Americans.

Clinton, who had superseded General Howe in command, saw the necessity of removing his forces to New York. He evacuated Philadelphia about the middle of June, crossed the Delaware, and slowly retreated through the Jerseys. Washington broke up his camp and followed in pursuit. On the morning of June 28, an advanced portion of the American army, commanded by Lee (who had been exchanged for a British prisoner of equal rank), attacked the enemy, then at Monmouth. See p. 104. Finding his situation extremely hazardous, Lee, contrary to instructions, ordered a retreat, and was falling back on the main army, when Washington rode up. The latter, exas-

---

Who was appointed quartermaster? Who inspector?

146. What effect had Burgoyne's surrender on Parliament? What action did the French nation take? Who superseded General Howe? When was Philadelphia evacuated?

perated at what he saw, reprimanded Lee severely, and ordered him to renew the attack. Lee gallantly led his division to the field again. Re-enforcements came up, and the fighting continued until nightfall, with a loss of 200 Americans to 300 British. Under cover of darkness, Clinton resumed his retreat, and further pursuit was abandoned. The British army finally reached the vicinity of New York. Clinton's entire loss by deaths and desertions, in the march from Philadelphia, was two thousand.

For violation of orders at the battle of Monmouth, and for subsequent disrespectful language to the commander-in-chief, General Lee was tried by a court-martial, and suspended from duty for one year. At the expiration of this time, he was dismissed from the service on account of an insolent note which he sent to the president of Congress. The unmanageable disposition of Lee, Gates, and some other of the leading American officers, was in striking contrast with the opposite character of such men as Nathaniel Greene and Henry Knox, both of whom were distinguished for respectful obedience and great military ability. General Knox rendered efficient service at Monmouth, as he had also done at Trenton, Princeton, and Germantown.

147. Early in July, D'Estaing arrived off New York with twelve ships of the line, six frigates, and a land force of four thousand French regulars. A combined attack was now planned upon the British stationed at Newport. Washington moved his army to White Plains. General John Sullivan led the land forces, while D'Estaing was to coöperate with his squadron. But a severe storm disabled both the French and the English war vessels. D'Estaing put into port at Boston to refit, and Sullivan, after some destructive skirmishing, drew off his army. D'Estaing, when he had put his ships in order, sailed for the West Indies, whither the British fleet followed him.

Describe the battle of Monmouth. What was Lee's conduct? What the result of it? What is said of Knox?

147. What naval force did D'Estaing bring from France? What plan of operations was decided upon? How was this executed?

148. The overtures of the peace commissioners being rejected, the British adopted a relentless policy as to the conduct of the war. A system of petty onslaughts and predatory raids was inaugurated, often attended by shocking barbarities. Clinton sent out parties in various directions to ravage and destroy. Devastating expeditions under lawless leaders visited the coast of New England, desolating fields, burning houses and ships, and treating the inhabitants with brutal violence. Whenever, on midnight foray, a feeble American garrison could be surprised, or a detached handful of militia surrounded, the rule was to cut them down without quarter. The most atrocious proceedings of the war were set in operation at Fort Niagara. This was "the common rallying place of tories, refugees, savage warriors, and other desperadoes of the frontier." In July, a body of eleven hundred savages, both red and white, sent out by Colonel John Butler and the Iroquois chief, Joseph Brant, made a descent upon the valley of Wyoming, along the Susquehanna. This fierce horde easily defeated the inadequate force stationed to defend the peaceful valley, and the whole settlement was laid waste. Conflagration, rapine, and murder marked the career of the invaders. Four hundred of the defenseless settlers were slain.*

General Knox.

* See Campbell's Gertrude of Wyoming, and Halleck's Wyoming, poems; Grace Greenwood's Forest Tragedy, tale.

148. What barbarous features characterized the war in the North?

The Massacre of Wyoming was followed by an incursion into Cherry Valley, New York, attended by like terrible scenes. Washington took vigorous measures to retaliate upon the Indians such bloody vengeance as alone could intimidate them. General Sullivan was sent to carry their mode of warfare into their own territory; and his success was such as to check for a time the course of savage hostility.

149. In the winter of 1778, Washington distributed his army in a line of cantonments, reaching from Long Island Sound to the Delaware, his own headquarters being at Middlebrook. The year's campaign closed with a successful expedition of the British by sea and land, against Savannah, which was taken in December. By the middle of January the whole of Georgia was reduced.

150. The depredations of marauding parties were renewed with the opening of a new campaign. An expedition sent up the Chesapeake succeeded in destroying much valuable property along the James River and the Elizabeth. Sir Henry Clinton himself went on a cruise up the Hudson, with six thousand men, and captured the yet unfinished fort of Stony Point, just below the Highlands, and the opposite fort, Lafayette, on Verplanck's Point. General William Tryon, formerly royal governor of New York, with twenty-six hundred men, ravaged the coast of Connecticut, plundered New Haven, and burnt the villages of Fairfield and Norwalk. Tryon's brutal soldiery every-where committed atrocities of the most shocking description.

151. While these movements of the enemy went on, the Americans were not inactive. Washington planned the recapture of Stony Point; and General Wayne, sometimes called Mad Anthony on account of his dauntless courage, was intrusted with the execution of the plan. At about one o'clock on the night of the 16th of July, Wayne envi-

---

Give an account of the Massacre of Wyoming. What similar incursion was made in New York?

149. How did the campaign of 1778 close?

150. What depredations were committed by the British in 1779?

roned the fortress without being discovered, effected a sudden entrance, and captured the garrison at the point of the bayonet, without firing a gun. Only fifteen Americans were killed. Of the garrison, sixty-three were killed and five hundred and fifty-three taken prisoners. "The storming of Stony Point," says Irving, "stands out in high relief as one of the most brilliant achievements of the war."

Wayne made ready to recapture Fort Lafayette; but, an overpowering force of British came up the river, and he was obliged to evacuate the post he had so gallantly won, in order to save his prisoners. Emulating the heroism of Wayne, Major Henry Lee, popularly known as Light-horse Harry, at the head of three hundred gallant fellows, surprised the British post at Paulus Hook, just opposite New York, and carried off a number of prisoners, with a loss of but two men.

152. The year was distinguished by brilliant enterprises at sea, as well as on land. Commodore Paul Jones,* during the summer and autumn conducted a most daring and extraordinary cruise on the coast of Britain, creating much local alarm and capturing many rich prizes. The most signal exploit of the expedition was an audacious encounter of his own flagship, named in honor of Franklin, the Bon Homme Richard, with a powerful British man-of-war, the Serapis. The action took place on a moonlight night in September. It lasted for several hours, and resulted in the capture of the Serapis. This bloody sea-fight is one of the most celebrated in American history. The Richard was so much injured that it became necessary to abandon her, and she sunk.

153. A naval expedition sent out by the people of Boston, against a British post near the mouth of the Penob-

* See W. G. Simms's, J. Hamilton's, and J. H. Sherbourne's Life of J. P. Jones, and Cooper's History of the Navy; also Cooper's Pilot, and S. Mugge's Paul Jones, fictions.

---

151. Describe the storming of Stony Point. Did the Americans retain the fort? What exploit did Harry Lee execute?

152. Relate the gallant operations of Paul Jones.

scot, met with a fortune quite the reverse of that which favored Jones. The besieging armament of more than a dozen vessels, instead of reducing the post, was driven up the river by the enemy's ships. The men, to the number of three thousand, disembarked in the wilderness, and, after destroying their flotilla, made their way homeward on foot. The Boston people were much chagrined at this result.

154. Hostilities had been renewed in the South, which was destined to be the principal theater of the war for the next two years. There a sort of guerrilla warfare had been inaugurated of a most peculiar character. Numerous conflicts occurred between comparatively small opposing parties. These encounters were often extremely fierce and bloody, more so than any of the conflicts at the North, excepting those with the savages. The alliance of tories with the British aggravated mutual animosities. Intense partisan feelings existed. Resolute, impetuous, and sometimes reckless officers were found to lead belligerent bands.

Thomas Sumter, the intrepid patriot of the Carolina wilderness, Francis Marion,* the Bayard of the South, Light-horse Harry Lee, and others of like fame, with their fearless followers, were the terror of the British and the tories. On the other side, Banaster Tarleton† and his merciless dragoons, Patrick Ferguson and his formidable riflemen, and other bold marauders scoured the country to plunder and harass the patriots.

The scene of these irregular and exciting hostilities was a territory vast and wild, abounding with swamps, morasses, and tangled woods, cut up by streams, and bordered on the west by a mountainous frontier. Rapid marches, startling surprises, hair-breadth escapes, unaccountable successes and

* See P. Horry's, M. L. Weems's, and W. G. Simms's Life of Marion; also Duyckinck's Cyclopedia of American Literature, and H. Lee's Memoirs of the War in the Southern States.

† See Tarleton's Campaigns of 1780-81, in the Southern Provinces.

---

153. What expedition was sent to the Penobscot? With what result?

154. What were the peculiarities of the war in the South? Who were the chief partisan officers?

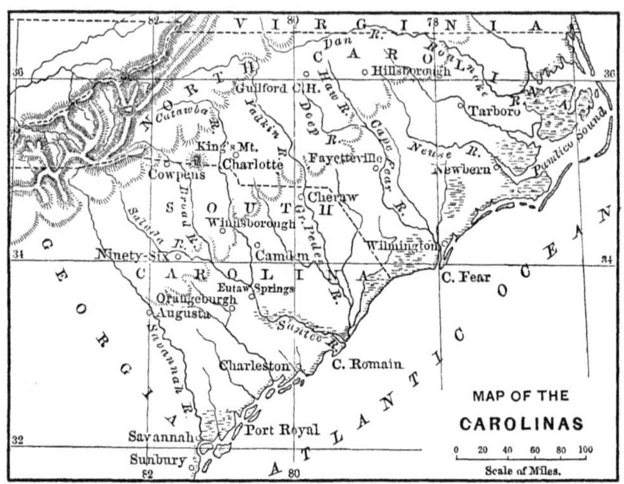

reverses, characterized this strange warfare. Bush-fighting was reduced to an exact art. Much of the dark and stirring romance of war is connected with the history of the Revolution in the South.*

155. In October, 1779, a strenuous attempt was made to recover Savannah. The town was attacked with spirit, on the 6th, by General Benjamin Lincoln, farmer, soldier, and statesman, with the aid of D'Estaing's fleet and six thousand French soldiers. The besiegers were driven back with heavy loss, the brave Count Pulaski was slain, and the enterprise was abandoned. D'Estaing presently sailed for France.

156. Having concentrated his forces by calling in the troops from Newport and the forts on the Hudson, Sir Henry Clinton sailed southward with an army of seven

* See W. G. Simms's The Partisan, Mellichampe, The Scout, Katherine Walton, Woodcraft, The Forayers, and Eutaw, tales.

What was the topography of the scene of the Southern war?

155. Describe the siege of Savannah. Was it successful? What noted officer was killed?

156. To what point did Clinton sail? With what force?

thousand, leaving Baron Knyphausen (knip'hŏw'zen), a German general, in command at New York.

157. Washington's troops were now in huts among the hills of Morristown. Their suffering was excessive, even greater than it had been at Valley Forge. The winter, as in the year before, was so cold that New York harbor was covered with thick ice. There was extreme scarcity of food and clothing. Complaints, and murmurs of sedition began to be heard. Some Connecticut troops actually mutinied. To meet pressing wants, supplies were collected from the country round about. Counties were called upon to furnish stated quantities of meat and flour. The cause of this destitution in the army was the deranged state of finances. So much continental currency had been issued, that its value had depreciated alarmingly. Bills were out to the nominal value of $160,000,000; but forty dollars currency were not worth so much as one dollar in specie. The decline in the value of continental bills paralyzed business, and embarrassed both military and civil affairs.

158. The object of Clinton's southern expedition was the subjection of the Carolinas. He proceeded, in connection with Admiral Mariot Arbuthnot, to lay siege to Charleston, whence he had been repulsed in 1776. A powerful armament blockaded the harbor, and the bombardment was begun. General Lincoln, whose entire forces numbered seven thousand, held the city as long as possible; but the defenses were not strong enough to withstand the battering of heavy balls, and were at length almost demolished. The siege lasted forty-two days. On the 6th of May, Fort Moultrie yielded; and on the 12th, Charleston surrendered, Lincoln and his forces becoming prisoners of war.

159. Its stronghold being thus captured, the whole state of South Carolina was overrun and subdued, many of the

---

Whom did he leave in command at New York?

157. How did Washington's troops fare at Morristown in the winter of 1779? What revolt occurred? Why were the troops so dissatisfied? What was the financial condition of the country?

158. Describe the siege of Charleston.

inhabitants taking the oath of allegiance to King George. Clinton returned to New York, leaving Cornwallis in command at Charleston, with instructions to push the war into North Carolina and Virginia. Some of the British troops remained at Charleston, but the main body was stationed near Camden.*

160. Early in June, Knyphausen crossed to the Jersey side of the Hudson with a force five thousand strong. Moving toward Washington's camp, he proceeded a few miles beyond Elizabethtown, where, vigorously opposed by volunteer militia gathered from all directions, he retreated, burning a village on the way. Clinton himself now joined Knyphausen with re-enforcements, and on the 23d, the British advanced again with the view of attacking the camp at Morristown. Again they were foiled. A detachment of fourteen hundred regulars checked their advance in a sharp skirmish at Rahway, and the roused farmers, like angry bees, swarmed out to chase the invaders back. The British, after burning a village near Newark, fled and recrossed the river to New York.

161. Congress appointed Gates to the command of the Southern army, and he set off for Carolina full of self-confidence, notwithstanding the ominous warning of Charles Lee: "Take care that your northern laurels do not change to southern willows." Gates had taken the credit of the victory over Burgoyne to himself, though, in fact, it was the result of the foresight and planning of the commander-in-chief, aided by Schuyler. Washington, before he heard of the fall of Charleston, had sent De Kalb south with re-enforcements. De Kalb had encamped at Deep River, a

* See Ramsay's History of the Revolution in South Carolina, and Moultrie's Memoirs of the Revolution in N. C. and S. C.

---

159. What followed the capture of Charleston? Who was put in command of the British troops? Where were the troops stationed? What did Clinton do?

160. Narrate the proceedings of Knyphausen in New Jersey.

161. Why was Gates appointed to the command of the Southern army? Whom had Washington already dispatched to the South with troops?

branch of the Cape Fear, where Gates joined him, July 25, 1780. Gates immediately put the army in motion toward Camden.

His design was, by a rapid and brilliant movement, to carry the British encampment. Contrary to prudent advice, the impatient commander led his army "through a region of pine barrens, sand hills, and swamps, with few habitations, and these mostly deserted." Unwholesome food, and exhausting marches in a hot climate, produced much sickness.

The army, having been increased by the accession of raw militia, numbered about three thousand, only one-third of whom were regulars. The enemy's forces were also about three thousand strong, though Gates supposed their numbers to be fewer. Indeed, Gates's knowledge of the foe was exceedingly scanty. He did not even know that the wary Cornwallis was in command at Camden. With headstrong precipitancy, he pushed forward. Unaware of his near approach, the British were marching to intercept him, when, to their mutual astonishment, the two armies came together. There was no alternative but to fight, and the British gave battle at break of day, August 16.

Hardly had the firing more than begun, when a panic seized the dismayed militia, and they fled in confusion, leaving the regulars to bear the brunt of battle. The regulars stood their ground courageously, until, overborne by numbers and deprived of their gallant leader, De Kalb, who fell pierced by eleven wounds, they too were forced to retreat. All attempts to rally the militia failed. In the battle and rout of Camden, 900 Americans were killed. It was with the utmost difficulty, after this defeat, that Gates collected at Hillsborough, 180 miles from Camden, as many as 1,000 men.

Cornwallis presently pushed forward into North Carolina in prosecution of his plan of conquest. Just previous to the action at Camden, Sumter had captured a convoy and

---

When and where did Gates join him? Describe Gates's march toward Camden. Describe the battle of Camden. To what point did Gates retreat?

200 prisoners; but he was soon afterward surprised by Tarleton, and his entire force was taken with much loss of life. Sumter himself escaped by galloping away hatless and coatless, bullets whistling about his head. He collected a new force. Marion also gathered fresh recruits from the swamps of the Pedee.* These two, now commissioned as generals, by incessant activity, kept up the credit of American arms in the distracted South.

But the event most encouraging to the patriots, and which, indeed, turned the tide of war, and brought a disastrous campaign to a successful close, was the battle of King's Mountain, which occurred near the northern border of South Carolina, on the 9th of October, and in which the dreaded Ferguson fell, and his fellow forayers, numbering about a thousand, were nearly all captured or killed.

The victors in this renowned fight were hardy mountaineers from the frontier of Georgia and Carolina, Kentucky hunters, and Virginia backwoodsmen, hastily summoned together, and led by half a dozen militia colonels, each acting from a patriotic impulse to repel invasion. Having accomplished their object, these minute-men of the South dispersed to their homes. Disconcerted at the belligerence of the North Carolina people, whom he expected to find loyal, Cornwallis deemed it prudent to return toward Charleston, and to send for re-enforcements.

162. During the year La Fayette had visited his native country and obtained the promise of further aid. In July, 1780, a French fleet arrived in the harbor of Newport, with an army of six thousand men under Marshal Jean Baptiste de Rochambeau (ro-shôn-bō′). To offset this fleet, a British squadron came also, and the French vessels were blockaded. Washington, meditating an attack on New

* See Bryant's Song of Marion's Men.

What did Cornwallis do? Relate the exploits of Sumter and Marion. Describe the battle of King's Mountain. What effect had this victory in changing the plan of Cornwallis?

162. When did Rochambeau's force reach America? By whose efforts had this been procured? What befell this French fleet?

York by the combined American and French land forces, went to Hartford to consult Rochambeau on a plan of operations. In his absence came to light the startling facts which we have now to relate.

163. General Benedict Arnold had been carrying on a secret correspondence with Sir Henry Clinton, in which he proposed to betray into the enemy's hands West Point and the other fortified posts on the Hudson. The recompense that Arnold asked of the British was money—money to extricate himself from deep debt, and to maintain him in extravagant and dissolute habits, to which he was wedded. He was also impelled to his base procedure out of spite to Congress, which had authorized a court-martial to try him for alleged fraudulence in the use of public money while he was military governor of Philadelphia. In accordance with the sentence of the court-martial, he was reprimanded by Washington. To gratify revenge, he was willing to sell himself and his bleeding country.

Major John André,* Clinton's aid-de-camp, volunteered his personal services to meet the traitor and settle the terms of the nefarious bargain. From a British ship anchored in the Hudson, André was rowed to the west bank of the river, a little after midnight on the 25th of September, by one Smith, a dupe of Arnold's. The parties held an interview "at the foot of a shadowy mountain called the Long Clove, a solitary place, the haunt of the owl and the whippoorwill, and well fitted for a treasonable conference." The next day was spent in negotiation at Smith's house. Furnished with plans of the Highland fortresses, and with written explanations, André set off on his return to New York. Crossing the Hudson at King's Ferry, he hastened southward. He rode disguised. About six miles below the Croton River, he was intercepted by a man, who stepped from the side of the road with a leveled gun and ordered him to halt. This

* See Winthrop Sargent's Life and Career of Andre; also Sparks's Am. Biog.

---

163. Relate in detail the story of Arnold's treason and Andre's capture.

man's name was John Paulding. He was presently joined by two companions likewise armed. André was searched. The papers were found concealed in his boots. "He is a spy!" exclaimed Paulding. In due time, the unfortunate captive suffered death on the gallows as a spy, according to the stern requirements of military law. His sad fate was lamented even in America; in England it excited the strongest feelings of revenge. Arnold, informed of André's capture, escaped to the enemy and received ten thousand pounds and a generalship in the British army. Another and juster reward he also received—the condemnation of the civilized world. The shining record of his gallant deeds under the American flag was blotted forever. His name is fixed in language, like that of Judas, as the synonym of Treachery.*

164. The projected attack on New York was abandoned. The Northern army went into winter quarters at and above Morristown, and once more the soldiers, unpaid and ill-supplied, were forced to endure hardship and privations. Again arose clamors and complaints against the government. In January, a number of Pennsylvania regiments revolted, and Congress was obliged to grant them a general discharge. Later some of the New Jersey troops became insurgent, but their mutiny was quelled by military force.

165. The scene of war now shifts again to the South. At the beginning of the year 1781, the renegade Arnold, with an armament which he boasted would shake the continent, made a buccaneering cruise to Virginia. His operations were similar to those of Tryon in Connecticut. He plundered and laid waste the country on Chesapeake Bay and James River, burnt the public buildings of Richmond and other places, causing much misery and alarm. Every effort

* See N. P. Willis's poem entitled Andre's Request to Washington; Lord's Andre, a drama; and Calvert's Arnold and Andre, a dramatic poem.

What was the fate of Andre? What reward did Arnold receive?

164. What insurrections took place in Washington's camp, at Morristown, in the winter of 1780-81?

was made to repulse him. After a few months, he was joined by the haughty and irritable General William Phillips, with two thousand British troops. Phillips took the chief command, and kept up the devastating warfare inaugurated by Arnold. The field of decisive military operations, however, was not Virginia, but Carolina.

166. Gates had been recalled by Congress from the South, and, at Washington's suggestion, his place had been given to General Nathaniel Greene. This efficient officer joined the army at Charlotte, in December, and immediately began aggressive action. He sent General Daniel Morgan* westward with 1,000 troops, to the river Pacolet. Cornwallis, having dispatched Tarleton with 1,100 light troops against Morgan, left his camp at Winnsborough and moved northward. Tarleton encountered Morgan on the 17th of January, at a place called the Cowpens, thirty miles west of King's Mountain. A battle was fought, in which Morgan was victorious. Tarleton's men were put to rout with a loss, in killed and prisoners,

General Nathaniel Greene.

* See James Graham's Life of Daniel Morgan.

---

165. Describe the operations of Arnold and Phillips on Chesapeake Bay and James River.

166. Who succeeded Gates in the South? When, where, and between what forces was the battle of Cowpens fought? Was it decisive? What was the force of each army?

of over six hundred. Only twelve continentals were killed. Tarleton and a few of his dragoons escaped and joined Cornwallis.

Just at this time General Leslie arrived with British re-enforcements, sent by Clinton from New York by way of Charleston. Cornwallis immediately set off to capture Morgan; but the latter, by adroit movements, baffled pursuit. He managed to cross the Catawba River on the evening of the 19th of January, just two hours before the enemy came up. In the night, the river rose so as to become impassable; and before it fell Morgan had ample time to send his prisoners to a place of safety. The American forces were presently united under Greene. They numbered about 2,000 men fit for duty. The British numbered about 3,000, all seasoned veterans. Cornwallis pressed forward, desiring to bring his adversary to an engagement. Greene, ever cautious, aware of the enemy's superior force, made a rapid retreat toward Virginia, over a rough country, cut up by streams, and obstructed by woods. The enemy followed in hot chase.

On the night of February 2, 1781, the British arrived at the banks of the Yadkin, in time to capture a few delayed wagons belonging to the American supply train. Greene's army had crossed the river and secured the boats. A sudden rise in the stream hindered the advance of the British while the retreating army hurried toward the River Dan. Cornwallis crossed the Yadkin within a few days, and made almost superhuman efforts to overtake the Americans. But Greene conducted the retreat in a masterly manner. He gained the banks of the Dan on the morning of the 15th, having marched all the preceding night. In the course of the day, his men were all ferried across into Virginia. The British arrived at the ford just in time to behold the last boat loads of the Americans in the act of crossing. The river was so swollen that it was impossible to cross it without boats. The vexed pur-

---

Describe the retreat of Greene. How was Cornwallis foiled?

suers were brought to a provoking stand-still. All their exertions had been vain, and all their hopes were frustrated. Cornwallis now moved southward, and Greene, having been re-enforced, recrossed the Dan, and, in his turn, became the pursuer.

At Guilford Court-house, near the head waters of the Cape Fear, Cornwallis stood at bay. There, on the 15th of March, the armies came in bloody collision. A hard-fought battle took place, resulting in the defeat of the Americans, with a loss of nearly 500 in killed and 900 missing. About 500 of the British were lost. The effect of the battle was to discourage the British, who could ill afford to lose even a few men out of so small an army. Cornwallis, though victorious, continued his retreat, and Greene, with renewed hope, resumed the exciting chase.

Changing his plan suddenly, Greene discharged his militia, and led the remnant of his gallant army toward Camden, where, on the 25th of April, he boldly attacked the British forces under Lord Francis Rawdon. He was again defeated; but he so crippled the enemy that they set fire to Camden and retired to Charleston.

Positive successes now began to reward the struggling patriots. Post after post was reconquered. Nearly the whole of Georgia and the Carolinas was speedily restored to its rightful masters. The last great event of the Southern war was the battle of Eutaw Springs, on the Santee. In this battle, fought on the 8th of September, the American loss was 500; that of the British, 700. Both sides claimed the victory, but the benefits were all on the American side. The enemy retreated to Charleston, which city and Savannah were now the only places in the South held by the British.

167. The story of the Revolutionary War now rapidly draws to a close. Cornwallis, when apprised of Greene's

---

Describe the battle of Guilford Court-house. What was the moral effect of this fight? What were the subsequent movements of Greene? When did he join battle with Rawdon? With what results? What was the last great battle of the war in the South?

bold advance into the South, resolved, with equal daring, to invade the North. He marched into Virginia, effected a junction with Phillips, and took post at Petersburg. His first endeavor was to dislodge La Fayette, who was encamped with a small force at Richmond. La Fayette retired toward the Rappahannock, and was joined early in June by Wayne with troops from the North, and by Steuben, who also brought re-enforcements. Both of the belligerent armies were alert. Skirmishes were frequent. Tarleton and others renewed their raids. The American force under La Fayette was increased to four thousand, and Cornwallis was obliged to retreat.

He first retired to Portsmouth. From Portsmouth he removed with his whole army to Yorktown, on the south side of York River. Meantime Rochambeau's troops had left Newport and joined Washington's forces in the Highlands. About this time three thousand Hessians arrived at New York, where Clinton remained, expecting an attack. It was known that a powerful French fleet, under Francis Grasse-Tilly, commonly known as Count de Grasse (grâs), was on its way to the Chesapeake; and the design of Washington was to concentrate all his forces against Yorktown. The expected fleet, comprising twenty-eight ships of the line, arrived and sailed up the Chesapeake, together with the French squadron heretofore blockaded at Newport, but now relieved. The combined American and French land forces were rapidly concentrated about Yorktown. Sixteen thousand besiegers in all invested that last retreat of Cornwallis.

---

167. How did Cornwallis expect to counteract Greene's success? Where did he join Phillips? What were his further movements?

Yorktown had been fortified as strongly as possible. The British and their brave commander displayed admirable fortitude. On the 6th of October, a regular siege was commenced. Day after day the constant discharge of artillery wrought increasing havoc. Redoubts were stormed. Ramparts crumbled away. To avert a final assault upon his inner works, Cornwallis, on the 17th, proposed to capitulate. Two days thereafter the entire British garrison, numbering seven thousand men, surrendered as prisoners of war.

168. A cessation of hostilities was proclaimed April 19, **1783**, and a final treaty of peace was signed at Paris, September 3. The American army was disbanded. Washington resigned his commission to Congress, and retired to his home at Mount Vernon. "The scene is at last closed," wrote he; "I feel myself eased of a load of public care. I hope to spend the remainder of my days in cultivating the affections of good men, and in the practice of the domestic virtues."

169. During the war, immigration was confined chiefly to Kentucky and Tennessee.* In 1722 a settlement was begun on the Holston River, and in 1780 Nashville was founded. From 1777 to 1784 Tennessee was part of North Carolina. Daniel Boone, great prototype of pioneer heroes of the West, penetrated the wilds of Kentucky in 1769. In 1774 Harrodsburg was founded, and Boonesborough was begun the following year. A record of the adventures of the settlers with the Indians would fill volumes. These settlers were from Virginia and North Carolina. They lived lives of hardship, danger, and privation. Their habi-

* See Marshall's, Butler's, and Collins's History of Kentucky; also Haywood's Histories of Tennessee.

Describe the siege and capture of Yorktown. Why did not Clinton come to the relief of Cornwallis?

168. When was peace concluded? What was done with the army? What did Washington do? What were his words?

169. When, by whom, and at what points was Tennessee settled? Kentucky? Tell something of pioneer life.

tations were log cabins, protected by block-houses. Their garments were usually of deer-skin; their beds were the shaggy coat of the buffalo or the bear. Their labor was to clear the land and cultivate such articles of food as necessity demanded; to hunt wild game; to fight the Indians.

Irving thus describes some of the backwoods soldiers who figured in the battle of King's Mountain: "Some were on foot; but the greater part on horseback. Some were in homespun garb; but the most part in hunting-shirts, occasionally decorated with colored fringe and tassels. Each man had his long rifle and hunting-knife, his wallet or knapsack, and blanket, and either a buck's tail or a sprig of evergreen in his hat."

In 1778, George Rogers Clark, a Kentuckian, acting under the authority of Virginia, proceeded down the Ohio, founded Louisville, and, with a small force of backwoodsmen, marched to the north-west and took Kaskaskia, Cahokia, and the other posts of the far West. Had it not been for this important conquest, the western boundary of the United States might have been fixed at the Alleghanies.* The vast region north of the Ohio, now divided into six states, was formed by Virginia into one immense county, called Illinois, which, in 1784, was ceded to the general government.

The entire population of the United States at the close of the Revolution was about four millions. Slavery existed in all the states, though several had taken measures for its abolition. Every state in turn had been the seat of war, and of course industry was greatly disorganized. National independence made no sudden nor violent change in the laws or political institutions of America. State legislation was based on the English common law. It was not until

* See Colonel George Rogers Clark's Sketch of his Campaign in Illinois, one of the volumes of Robert Clarke & Co.'s invaluable Ohio Valley Historical Series.

Repeat Irving's description of the pioneer soldiers of the West. When did George Rogers Clark conquer the great West? To what region was the name Illinois first given? What was the population of the United States at the close of the war? Where did slavery exist?

1781 that the Articles of Confederation, adopted by the Continental Congress in 1777, were ratified by all the states, and when ratified they were of little force.

Churches rapidly multiplied. Several new sects sprang up, among which were Methodists and Universalists. Congregationalism continued to be, by sanction of custom and support of law, the established religion of New England; and Episcopacy still held sway in the South. A high degree of religious liberty prevailed in Rhode Island, Pennsylvania, and Delaware. No less than nine leading American colleges were established—three Congregational, three Episcopal, one Presbyterian, one Baptist, and one Dutch Reformed.

Benjamin West.

Only four states (Massachusetts, Connecticut, New Hampshire, and Maryland) could boast of a system of common schools. Private and parochial schools were encouraged in the South. The fine arts were cultivated with distinguished success. John Trumbull, one of Washington's aids-de-camp, was the painter of Revolutionary scenes, the best of which now adorn the rotunda of the Capitol. Benjamin West, many of whose pictures are in the Academy of Fine Arts at Philadelphia, and his pupils, C. W. Peale and G. C. Stuart, the latter famous for his excellent por-

---

Upon what was American legislation based? What progress had been made in religion? What colleges existed? In what states was the common school system established? Name the prominent artists of the period. Name the principal writers of Revolutionary times.

trait of Washington, were all in their early prime at the time of the war. In 1791 West was chosen President of the Royal Academy of Art, London. The valuable literature of the Revolutionary period consists chiefly of writings on legal and constitutional principles. Among the authors whose works survive are Franklin, Otis, Jefferson, Adams, Hamilton, Madison, Jay, Dickinson, and Washington. Dr. David Ramsay, the earliest American historian, must not be omitted from the list.

GENERAL QUESTIONS AND DIRECTIONS.

Prepare a chronological table of the dated events given in Chapter Eleventh. Give a list of the battles of the Revolutionary War by land and sea. Which were the decisive battles of the war, and why were they so? What memorable retreats took place? What led the French to aid the Americans? What induced the Hessians and other German allies to join the British? What part did the Indians take in the struggle? Who were the Tories? Did the war extend west of the Alleghanies? Give a history of the Continental Congress. What is a royal governor? A provisional governor? An act of Parliament? A state constitution? A revenue? Define the terms, militia, volunteer, grenadier, assault, skirmish, ambuscade, redoubt, garrison, cantonment, *coup-de-main*, regiment, squadron.

BIOGRAPHICAL REVIEW.

Prepare a sketch of the life and services of Patrick Henry, John Hancock, Benjamin Franklin, Ethan Allen, Philip Schuyler, Benedict Arnold, Israel Putnam, General Cornwallis, Casimir Pulaski, La Fayette, General Burgoyne, John Knox, Nathaniel Greene, General Wayne, Paul Jones, Thomas Sumter, Francis Marion, George Washington, Benjamin West.

Map Questions and Geographical Review.

What were the boundaries of the United States at the close of the Revolutionary War? To what nation did Canada belong? Florida? Louisiana? What states were comprised in the United States in the year 1783? Of what state was Tennessee then a part? Of what was Kentucky a part? What settlements had been made west of the Alleghanies before the year 1783? Locate Detroit. Kaskaskia. Louisville. New Orleans.

What streams were of advantage or of disadvantage to the armies in the Revolutionary War? What mountains or hills were important? What lakes? What bays and harbors? What islands?

Locate Quebec. Montreal. Oswego. Presque Isle. Baltimore. Norfolk. Charleston. Charlestown. Savannah. Pensacola. At what different places did the Continental Congress meet?

See page 96. In what direction from Boston is Concord? Charlestown? Dorchester Heights? Cambridge?

See page 101. In what direction from New York is Brooklyn? Paulus Hook? Staten Island? Where is New York Bay? Newark Bay? Raritan Bay? The Narrows? Where is White Plains? Dobb's Ferry? Newark?

See page 104. How far is it from Newark to Trenton? From Trenton to New Brunswick? From Monmouth to New York? Locate Morristown. Princeton. Burlington.

See page 109. How far is it from New York to Stony Point? From Stony Point to Saratoga? Locate Fort Edward. Where are the Hudson Highlands? What direction and how far from Albany is Bennington?

See page 111. How far is Germantown from Philadelphia? Locate forts Mifflin and Mercer. Valley Forge. White Marsh. Norristown. Brandywine Creek. Newcastle.

See page 118. Name the chief rivers in the Carolinas. Locate Charleston. Hillsborough. Guilford Court-house. Kings Mountain. Cowpens. Winnsborough. Camden. Eutaw Springs. Savannah.

CHAPTER TWELFTH.

FROM THE CLOSE OF THE REVOLUTION TO THE END OF THE WAR OF 1812.

1783—1815.

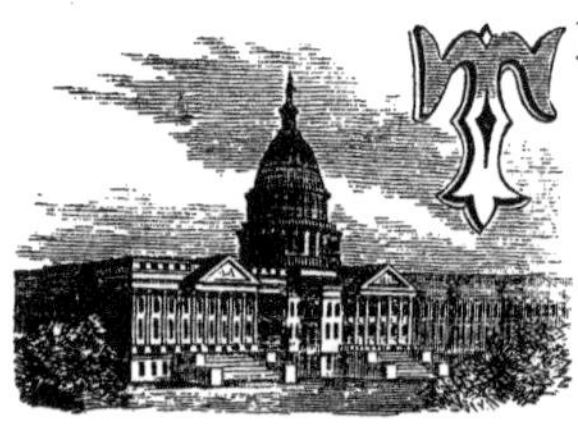

THE close of the Revolutionary War found the United States treasury empty. In order to create a revenue, Congress levied immoderate taxes, and called upon the respective states to collect their proportion. But Congress was powerless to enforce its own measures, and the requisitions on the states were not met. Indeed, the states looked upon the authority of the general government with jealousy and mistrust. A strong repugnance to taxation manifested itself among the people at large. In Massachusetts armed mobs closed the courts of law, and a wide-spread insurrection threatened to involve the country in anarchy. Several regiments of militia were called into the field to quell these disturbances. It was obvious to the thoughtful, who witnessed with alarm any tendency of the people to throw off allegiance to the general government, that some means must be employed to secure the co-operation of the several states in matters relating to the common good.

The Articles of Confederation were barely sufficient for the exigencies of war, when considerations of public safety alone could have almost held the states together. Danger

---

QUESTIONS.—**170.** What was the financial condition of the United States at the close of the war? Why did the people object to taxation? What were the Articles of Confederation?

cements union. The purposes of a nation in time of peace can only be accomplished by wise and prudent laws. It seemed to many that the formation of a strong central government was absolutely necessary for the preservation of the precious institutions for which the battles of the Revolution had been fought. On the other hand, many held out for *state sovereignty*, and deprecated centralization as restrictive of popular freedom and promotive of monarchical tendencies. Opinion divided the people into two political parties —Federalists and anti-Federalists, or Republicans. The former advocated a constitutional government; the latter were committed to the doctrine of state sovereignty.

171. The subject of reorganizing the government was much agitated. At length a convention was called for the purpose of devising such a fundamental system as would meet with general approval. The convention assembled in May, 1787, at Philadelphia. It was composed of delegates from all the states but Rhode Island, and represented the best intelligence of America. Washington presided over its deliberations, and Franklin was one of its members. It continued in session four months, and the result of its discussions was the adoption of the Constitution which still continues to be the organic law of the United States.

The Federal Constitution may be regarded as a series of compromises between the two great political parties, and among men representing conflicting interests.* The accession of nine states was necessary before it could go into operation. In some sections it met with the most determined opposition. The Federalists were strongly in its favor. Indeed, they were sometimes called the Constitutional party. The accomplished statesman, Alexander

* Read the Constitution in connection with some explanatory text-book, such as Towle's or Alden's.

What two parties were now originated? What is meant by centralization? By state sovereignty?

171. How was the convention of 1787 composed? Who was chairman? What state was unrepresented? What did the convention accomplish? Was the Constitution universally popular?

George Washington.

Hamilton, was the ablest advocate of a centralized government. In conjunction with James Madison and John Jay, he wrote a series of "profound and luminous" articles in favor of the adoption of the Constitution. These essays first appeared in the New York Gazette, and were afterward published in several volumes, called the *Federalist*, which had an extensive circulation, and were generally read.*

By the end of 1788, eleven states had ratified the Constitution, which thereupon went into effect. In accordance

* See Renwick's and J. C. Hamilton's Life of Hamilton; Adams's and Rives's Life of Madison; and William Jay's Life of John Jay.

When did the Constitution go into effect?

with its provisions, an election of legislative and executive officers was held. George Washington was chosen President of the United States for a term of four years. His journey from Mount Vernon to New York, the capital, was a continual ovation. At Trenton, his reception was very beautiful and touching. A triumphal arch was there erected, supported by thirteen columns decorated with evergreens. Upon this arch were inscribed the words, "The Defender of the Mothers will be the Protector of the Daughters." As the President rode up to the arch, he was met by a throng of matrons and young girls dressed in white, who, while they sang an ode of welcome, scattered flowers in their hero's way.

The inauguration took place in the presence of a large concourse of people, on the 30th of April, 1789. Standing on the balcony of Federal Hall, attended by the senators and representatives, the illustrious man who had so lately laid aside his burden of military cares, pledged himself to discharge the equally severe duties of the great office which he was the first to fill. Washington's wisdom, moderation, and executive ability eminently fitted him for the chief magistracy, and his administration gave general satisfaction. At the end of his first term, he was re-elected. He was not universally popular. There were not wanting critics to condemn his policy, and enemies to censure his motives. Though a Federalist himself, Washington selected his cabinet from men of both parties. Thomas Jefferson, the leader of the Republicans, was chosen Secretary of State; General Knox was retained at the head of the War Department; Hamilton was appointed Secretary of the Treasury.

172. While the Federal convention was in session at Philadelphia, the Continental Congress, at New York, passed an ordinance fraught with benefit to posterity, and

---

Under its provisions, what elections took place? Where did Congress meet? Whom did Washington appoint to his cabinet? What is meant by the cabinet? What are the duties of the judiciary officers? Of the chief executive? Of the Legislature? Of what politics was Washington? Jefferson?

famous in our political annals. It was fitting that a body with which so many good and great movements had originated, should signalize the close of its career by an act of prudent and liberal statesmanship. The Ordinance of 1787 was for the government of the vast and rich territory northwest of the Ohio. It provides, in the most generous way, for the perpetual welfare of the inhabitants of the territory named. It secures to them entire religious liberty, ample political rights, and the means of common school education. Under the beneficent provisions of this wise ordinance, how many noble institutions have been fostered, how many thousands of people have enjoyed the highest blessings of modern civilization!

173. The new Congress naturally gave its first attention to financial matters and the regulation of commerce. An act was passed imposing duties on imports and tonnage, and protecting home manufactures. The executive and judiciary departments were next organized. Washington assigned the position of Chief Justice to John Jay. The national debt early became the subject of discussion in Congress. Hamilton advised that the general government assume the debts of the several states. His recommendation was acted upon. The whole debt was funded, and taxes were imposed for its liquidation. By Hamilton's influence, a United States Bank was chartered, the charter being limited to twenty years. Financial theories had become the main issue of political parties. Hamilton and the Federalists advocated a protective tariff and a national bank; Jefferson and the Republicans opposed both of these.

During the first session of Congress, the subject of slavery came up, and caused an exciting debate. This was the beginning of a contention to be settled after long years

---

172. What was the last important act of the Continental Congress? When was the Continental Congress first organized? What were its chief acts?

173. What acts were passed by the first Congress? What scheme was adopted for disposing of the national debt? Who was the great financier of the time? On what questions did the political parties now divide? Why was the tariff opposed? Why was a national bank opposed?

only by the stern arbitration of the sword. As yet, all of the states, Massachusetts alone excepted, held slaves, though several had taken steps toward abolition. The financial measures adopted by Congress had a magical effect in reviving commerce. A trade with India, China, and the north-western coast of America sprung up; and, indeed, the flag of American merchantmen was soon flying on every sea.

174. The Indian tribes on the Ohio, the Wabash, and the Maumee were extremely hostile, and dread of them long retarded immigration to the North-western Territory. All attempts at peaceful negotiation having failed, the government resolved to employ military power. In the autumn of 1790, General Harmar, at the head of eleven hundred militia, moved against the tribes on the Maumee; but the result of his expedition was disastrous, and he was obliged to retreat in disgrace.

Alexander Hamilton.

General Arthur Saint Clair, governor of the North-western Territory, next undertook to subdue the Indians. He set out from Fort Washington, Cincinnati, in September, 1791, and marched to the head waters of the Wabash with an army of two thousand men. The expedition was singularly unfortunate. The army, too confident of success, heedlessly

---

What is said of the slavery question?

174. Narrate the events of the Indian war in the north-west.

marched into danger, and was surprised by the wily savages under Little Turtle, a Miami chief. Half of the soldiers became the ghastly victims of the scalping-knife. The rest found safety in disorderly flight.

Washington's parting words to Saint Clair, when the latter was about to set forth on this campaign, were: "You know how the Indians fight; beware of a surprise!" It was reserved for the veteran Wayne to accomplish what Harmar and Saint Clair had undertaken in vain. The hero of Stony Point, having collected a force of 2,600 regulars and 400 mounted Kentucky volunteers, penetrated into the heart of the Indian country and dealt the hostile nations a blow from the effect of which they did not soon recover. He destroyed many of their villages and desolated their fields. The campaign lasted for ninety days in the summer and autumn of 1794. A decisive battle was fought near the Maumee rapids, at a place known as the Fallen Timbers.

In 1795, a general treaty of peace was made at Greenville, Ohio, where eleven hundred Indian warriors met Wayne at his headquarters. An exchange of prisoners took place, and a large number of white people who had long lived in captivity were restored to their friends. The meeting of kindred who had abandoned the hope of reunion upon earth, was in many instances very affecting. It is difficult for those who now dwell upon the peaceful farms or in the thriving villages of Ohio, to imagine the anxieties, dangers, and vicissitudes of life in the West three quarters of a century ago.

175. The foreign relations of the United States during the latter part of Washington's administration, were complicated and threatening. The terms of the treaty of Paris had not been strictly complied with by either the Americans or the English. In France a mighty revolution had overthrown monarchy, and erected in its place a republican form of government. Many of the Americans, particularly

---

What part did Saint Clair take in the war against the Indians? Wayne? When was peace made with the Indians?

the Republicans (or Democrats, as they now began to be called), ardently sympathized with the French revolutionists. Their sympathy was the more active because associated with the sentiment of gratitude. The Marquis de La Fayette was a prominent revolutionist, and his great popularity in America won for the new government many enthusiastic friends.

The Federalists, representing, as they did, commercial and manufacturing interests, were desirous of preserving and promoting amicable relations with Great Britain. John Jay was sent to London to accommodate matters in dispute between America and England, and by him a treaty was negotiated which, though unsatisfactory to the Democrats, was ratified in Congress by a majority of two. France being at war with England, the heads of the new French government, called collectively the Directory, considered Jay's treaty as unfair and unfriendly, considering the services the French had rendered the Americans in the struggle for independence.

Washington, wishing to avoid any entangling alliance with foreign powers, issued a proclamation of neutrality. This proclamation the French revolutionists put to nought, confidently assuming that the American people would cooperate with them even against the policy of the government as announced by the chief executive. Washington, on the 4th of March, 1797, retired from office, having previously published his Farewell Address to his fellow-citizens. This document was universally read, and its value has scarcely diminished with the lapse of time.*

At the presidential election in the fall of 1796, each of the political parties put forward a candidate for the chief magistracy. John Adams, the nominee of the Federalists,

* Read Washington's Farewell Address in this connection.

175. What change of government had been made in France? How were the American parties affected toward the French? Why were the Federalists disposed to conciliate England? What did the French Directory think of Jay's treaty? What policy did Washington adopt? What predisposed the Americans to favor France?

was elected over his opponent, Thomas Jefferson. Adams was a native of Massachusetts. He was distinguished for his sturdy patriotism. One of his cotemporaries calls him the colossus of the Continental Congress. He was an able lawyer and a good writer. During Washington's administration he had been Vice President. When he became chief executive, the French difficulties were increasing. In his speech to Congress, Adams sustained Washington's policy, and gave renewed offense to the French Directory. That body had refused to receive the United States minister appointed by Washington. Three special envoys were now sent to Paris; but an official reception was denied them also, unless they would pledge their country to a loan, and bribe the individual members of the Directory.

John Adams.

Disdaining these proposals, the envoys at length returned to America. War with France now seemed inevitable. "Millions for defense, not a cent for tribute," words first used by Charles Cotesworth Pinckney, one of the insulted envoys, became the rallying cry of the party opposed to the French. Congress, yielding to the popular demand, passed bills for raising a provisional army and organizing a navy. Washington was appointed commander-in-chief. Yet war was not formally declared, and, though hostilities had begun upon the sea, Adams again unexpectedly dispatched ministers to Paris.

Who was chosen President after Washington? What do you know about him? What course did he take relative to foreign affairs?

On their arrival, the brief career of the republic had closed, and Napoleon Bonaparte was at the head of affairs in France. With him satisfactory terms were made, and the *quasi war*, as it was called, terminated abruptly. The tidings of peace came to a people sorely afflicted. On the 14th of December, 1799, George Washington died at Mount Vernon. He was mourned by all, for, as even his rival and political enemy said, "He was, indeed, in every sense of the word, a wise, a good, and a great man." And the world indorses the well-considered assertion of Irving, that "Washington's fame stands apart from every other in history, shining with a truer luster and a more benignant glory." In the year of Washington's decease, Patrick Henry also died; the venerated Franklin had closed his mortal career nine years before. Thus the founders of American liberty were, one by one, passing away.

176. In 1800, the national capital was removed from Philadelphia to the new city of Washington, where suitable public buildings had been erected. The exercise, by Congress and the President, of extraordinary powers during the time of threatened war, gave the Democrats grounds for bitter opposition to the Federal rule, and rendered the re-election of Adams impossible.

The Democrats were now greatly in the ascendancy, and Jefferson, their candidate, was elected President. Like Washington, he was re-elected at the end of his first term, and so held office for eight years, or until March, 1809. He was a Virginian by birth, a ripe scholar, a bold reformer, the author of the Declaration of Independence, and the founder of the Democratic party. Perhaps, the most important event of his administration was the purchase of Louisiana. This vast territory had been ceded by Spain to France, and Bonaparte disposed of it to the United

---

How was the *quasi war* ended? When and where did Washington's death occur? Repeat, *verbatim*, the quotations relating to him. What other distinguished American died the same year? When did Franklin die?

176. When was the capital removed to Washington City? What causes had made Adams unpopular? Who was chosen third President? How long did he continue in office? What was the Louisiana purchase?

States, in April, 1803, for twelve million dollars. In 1804, Jefferson sent an overland exploring expedition to the Pacific, under Captains Lewis and Clarke. These enthusiastic travelers ascended the Missouri to its sources, and followed the Columbia to its mouth.*

177. Jefferson's administration was not one of unbroken peace. The Barbary States had long maintained a sort of lawless supremacy upon the Mediterranean, preying upon the commerce of other countries and defying all opposition. They made captives of persons from all climes, and either enslaved them or exacted heavy ransom for their release. Strange as it now seems, the principal powers of Europe bought exemption from the piratical attacks of these fierce little states, by the regular payment of tribute. The United States participated for a time in this humiliating custom. But the demands of the Bashaw of Tripoli grew exorbitant, and compliance with them was refused.

Thomas Jefferson.

The Bashaw declared war, and Congress, as the brave Captain Bainbridge† had suggested, determined to deliver tribute only at the cannon's mouth. The naval operations conducted on the African coast, by the American commo-

* See Lewis & Clarke's Journal.

† See Thomas Harris's Life of Commodore William Bainbridge.

What expedition was sent to the Pacific by the United States in 1804?

177. Where are the Barbary States?

dores Charles Morris and Edward Preble,* were brilliant and exciting. Many deeds of heroic daring are recorded of the American seamen during the Tripolitan war. Before the city of Tripoli, Lieutenant Stephen Decatur, at great hazard and with extraordinary bravery, recaptured the Philadelphia, a vessel that had been taken by the enemy, carried into port, and moored within a quarter of a mile of the Bashaw's castle. Decatur, with one vessel, the Intrepid, and a small ketch, manned by a select crew, surprised and boarded the Philadelphia by night, and in less than ten minutes was master of his prize. This exploit, perfect in its plan and execution, was the basis of Decatur's after-fame, and secured for him, from Congress, a captain's commission and the gift of a sword.

Tripoli was repeatedly bombarded by United States blockading ships. Military operations against the Bashaw were at length begun upon land. Hostilities were prolonged for four years. In June, 1805, a treaty of peace was signed. The war was of great benefit to America in affording excellent training to her young navy. "Perhaps no service," says Cooper, "either in the way of ships or officers, ever had so large a proportion of what was excellent in it, and so small a proportion of what was defective, as the navy of the United States the day peace was signed with Tripoli." †

178. Toward the close of Jefferson's last term, two important bills passed in Congress; one abolished the foreign slave trade; the other authorized the survey of the United States coast, a vast enterprise which has already been more than half a century in progress.

179. In July, 1804, Alexander Hamilton, a man whom Washington thought "no one exceeded in probity and ster-

* See Sparks's Am. Biog.; also S. P. Waldo's Life of Decatur.

† See Cooper's History of the U. S. Navy.

Narrate the events of the Tripolitan war. How long did it continue? In what way did it benefit America?

178. What important acts of Congress marked the close of Jefferson's administration?

ling virtue," and whose equal Talleyrand once declared he had never known, was killed in a duel, at Weehawken, by Aaron Burr.* The cause of the duel was political animosity on the part of Burr, the challenger, a man afterwards notorious for his connection with the romantic Harman Blennerhas'set in treasonable schemes to found a monarchy in the West.

180. James Madison, already mentioned in connection with Hamilton and Jay as a leading advocate of the Federal Constitution, was elected fourth President of the United States. He was sent to Congress in 1789 from his native state, Virginia, and acted with the Republican party. In 1801, he was appointed Secretary of State, an office which he retained during the whole of Jefferson's administration. He was inaugurated March 4, 1809, and re-elected to the Presidency in **1812** over his competitor, DeWitt Clinton, the Federalist candidate. Madison's administration was distracted by political contests and shaken by war.

James Madison.

Indian depredations had been renewed on the frontier. A treaty was made with the southern tribes; but the restless warriors of the north-west, having partially recovered from the effects of Wayne's destructive incursion, were

* See Parton's Life of Aaron Burr; also W. H. Safford's Life of Harman Blennerhasset.

---

179. Tell what you know about Burr, and his duel with Hamilton.

180. Who was the fourth President? What disturbed his administration? Narrate the events of the Tecumseh war.

again on the war path. The celebrated Shawnee chief, Tecumseh, made powerful efforts to unite the western Indians in a general conspiracy to exterminate the whites. William Henry Harrison,* governor of the territory of Indiana, after several fruitless attempts to treat with Tecumseh, marched with a force of about eight hundred militia, from Vincennes to the vicinity of a large Indian village, the Prophet's Town, a few miles north of the present city of La Fayette, and near the river Tippecanoe. On the morning of November 7, 1811, he was attacked in his camp. A battle was fought, and Harrison came off victorious. He was thenceforward famous in the West as the hero of Tippecanoe.

The Indians did not renew hostilities until, as allies of the British, they participated in the War of **1812–15**. This war, sometimes called the second struggle for Independence, now claims our attention.

181. The violation of American commercial rights was the principal one of several causes which led to the War of 1812. England and France were at war. England forbade all neutral ships to trade with France, excepting such as paid tribute to the British. Napoleon decreed that all ships which paid such tribute should be liable to confiscation by the French. Between these extraordinary measures, the commerce of the United States was likely to be crushed. Congress, with a view to retaliation, laid an embargo on all ships in American ports. This almost entirely stopped commerce, and created great dissatisfaction in the manufacturing states. The embargo was now limited to non-intercourse with the offending nations.

Napoleon's decree was finally withdrawn, with the view of precipitating the United States into war with England. Nearly a thousand American vessels had fallen prey to the British since the year 1803. Besides violating the principle

* See M. Dawson's, James Hall's, and S. J. Burr's Life of William H. Harrison.

---

181. State in detail the causes of the War of 1812.

of neutrality, England offered other insults to America. She claimed and exercised the privilege of impressing American sailors on the open sea, on the suspicion that they had once been British subjects. It was alleged that six thousand men had been unjustly impressed. She claimed and exercised the privilege of searching American vessels for deserters. In June, 1807, the frigate Chesapeake was attacked by the British ship Leopard. After a short fight, the Chesapeake hauled down her colors. The officers of the Leopard came aboard and carried away three American citizens, who had escaped from a British vessel upon which they had been forcibly impressed.

This flagrant outrage was of a nature to fan into a blaze the "still glowing embers of ancient hate." The popular mind was further inflamed by the charge made against the British, that they had secretly instigated the Indians to rise against the whites on the western frontier. In view of all their provocations, a large proportion of the American people clamored for war. The Federalists opposed the war from first to last; but the majority prevailed. Congress made provision for increasing the army, which at the beginning of the war numbered but ten thousand. The navy also was somewhat strengthened. Henry Dearborn, of New Hampshire, an officer who had served at Bunker Hill, Saratoga, and Yorktown, was appointed commander-in-chief. On the 18th of June, **1812**, war was formally declared.*

182. The first object of the army was to invade and conquer Canada, a difficult enterprise too confidently undertaken. General William Hull,† an old revolutionary officer, governor of Michigan Territory, with a force of eighteen hundred, mostly Ohio militia, in July, crossed from Detroit to move against a British fort at Malden. Having waited in camp so long that the British had time

* See Lossing's Field Book of the War of 1812.

† See Life and Services of Gen. Hull, by his daughter, Maria Campbell.

Relate the affair of the Chesapeake and Leopard. When was war declared? Who was appointed to the head of the army?

to obtain re-enforcements, Hull gave up his first design and returned to Detroit, whither the British, under General Isaac Brock, followed him. Brock demanded the surrender of Fort Detroit, which was at first refused. An attack was ordered, but scarcely had the firing begun when, to the surprise and chagrin of the Americans, Hull caused the white flag to be raised, and yielded up his garrison and stores to the enemy. This was equivalent to the surrender of the whole of the territory of Michigan. A month before the capitulation of Detroit, Fort Michillimacinac, had surrendered to the British.

The north-western frontier, thus wrested from its protectors, was exposed to the ravages of Tecumseh and his savage hordes, now the avowed allies of the British. Tecumseh was appointed to the rank of brigadier-general. Another invasion of Canada was attempted, in October, by General Stephen Van Rensselaer, *the Patroon*, who sent about one thousand New York volunteers across the Niagara to take Queenstown. The whole force fell into the hands of the British. General Alexander Smyth, and, later, General Dearborn, also made futile attempts to carry the war into Canada. Upon the whole, the American army operations of the year 1812 resulted in failure and humiliation.

183. The navy, or rather the privateer service, redeemed the glory that was lost by the land forces. It has been truly said that the American navy fought itself into popularity during this war. The lessons learned upon the Mediterranean were now put to good use on the broad Atlantic.

---

182. Give the particulars of Hull's invasion, retreat, and surrender. How did this disaster affect the Indians? Describe the military operations of Van Rensselaer, Smyth, and Dearborn on the Canada frontier.

In August, 1812, the frigate Constitution, commanded by Captain Isaac Hull, after a close action of thirty minutes, captured the British war ship Guerriere, Captain Dacres, with a loss of fourteen to seventy-nine, disabling the Guerriere so that she had to be destroyed.

In October, two brilliant sea fights occurred, both terminating in favor of the Americans. The sloop Wasp, Captain Jones, after a brief but furious engagement, captured the brig Frolic, with a loss of five to eighty. The frigate United States, Commodore Decatur, with trifling injury to herself, took the British ship Macedonian, killing and wounding a third of her crew of three hundred. In December, the Constitution, Captain Bainbridge, captured the frigate Java, after a bloody conflict, the British loss amounting to nearly five times that of the Americans. This succession of victories by American vessels gave a somewhat ironical meaning to the sounding boast "Britannia rules the wave!"

184. The campaign of 1813 opened with renewed endeavors to invade Canada. It was the ambition of the Western army, now under command of Harrison, to recover Detroit, and thus wipe out the disgrace of Hull's surrender. Harrison's headquarters were at Franklinton, now Columbus, Ohio. In January, General James Winchester, with a small force, advanced to the river Raisin. Having dispersed a party of British at Frenchtown, he encamped near that village. Here, on the 22d, he was surprised by a body of British and Indians, commanded by Colonel Henry Proctor and the Indian chiefs Roundhead and Splitlog. Winchester was taken prisoner and his men were induced to surrender, trusting in Proctor's promise that they should be protected as prisoners of war. After they had given up their arms, many of them were tomahawked by the Indians, and some of the wounded were tortured in the flames of the village, which the savages set

---

183. Describe the naval victory of Captain Hull. Of Jones. Of Decatur. Of Bainbridge.

184. Relate the events of the campaign of 1813 in the West.

on fire. About three hundred were slain during and after the battle, and six hundred were taken prisoners.

When Harrison heard of this disaster, he gathered his forces together at Maumee Rapids, where he garrisoned Fort Meigs. Here he was besieged by Proctor until May, when a fresh force of twelve hundred Kentucky volunteers came to his relief. More than half of these brave fellows were drawn into an ambuscade by the cunning Tecumseh, and were compelled to surrender. Proctor, however, gave up the siege of Fort Meigs and retired to Malden.

185. Commodore Isaac Chauncey had equipped, for service on Lake Ontario, a small flotilla, consisting of the sloop Madison of twenty-four guns, one brig, and eleven armed schooners. Embarking seventeen hundred soldiers at Sackett's Harbor, he sailed for York, now Toronto, the capital of Upper Canada, where the troops landed April 27. A descent was promptly made upon the British under General Roger Sheaffe. A half hour's sharp fighting gave the victory to the Americans. The enemy fled. Several ships of war were taken, and a quantity of naval stores was destroyed. After victory was assured, two hundred of the assailants were killed or wounded by an appalling accident, the explosion of a powder magazine.

The Americans evacuated York early in May, and proceeded, under Dearborn, against the posts on the Niagara. On the 27th of May, a large force was landed near Fort George, which post was attacked. Lieutenant-colonel Winfield Scott* led the assault. After a brave defense, the enemy retreated, with a loss of three hundred. Fort George being lost, the other British posts on the Niagara were evacuated. Detachments sent out after the fall of Fort George, against the British at Stony Creek and at Beaver Dams, met with signal disaster. They suffered an aggregate loss, by capture, of seven hundred men, includ-

* See Mansfield's Life of Scott; also the Autobiography of Lieutenant-general Scott.

185. Describe Chauncey's fleet on Ontario. Describe the battle of York. The battle of Fort George.

ing two officers of rank. Sir James Yeo, commander of a British fleet on Lake Ontario, made an effort to get possession of Sackett's Harbor, which important point was admirably defended by General Jacob Brown, a fine officer, who, in 1815, became commander-in-chief.

186. It is a relief to turn from the minor and indecisive military operations just recorded, to the splendid achievement of Oliver Hazard Perry, on Lake Erie. This young naval officer had constructed two large brigs, the Niagara and the Lawrence, besides which he procured seven smaller vessels. With this small squadron, mounting in all fifty-five guns, he attacked the British fleet on Lake Erie, consisting of six ships carrying sixty-three guns, and commanded by Commodore Barclay. The opposing crews were about equal, each numbering some five hundred men. The engagement took place September 10, 1813, not far from Put-in-bay, and is known in history as the battle of Lake Erie, or Perry's Victory. After a furious combat of three hours, attended with the loss of one hundred and fifty men on each side, the whole British squadron surrendered. "We have met the enemy, and they are ours," was the laconic report which Perry made in writing to his superior officer, Harrison, commander of the Western army.

Commodore Perry.

187. The enemy being swept from Lake Erie, Harrison

What disasters followed the capture of the British posts on the Niagara?

186. Describe Perry's Victory. Quote Perry's official report of it.

made use of Perry's ships to transport troops to Canada, to operate against Proctor. The latter left Malden and retreated to the Moravian town on the Thames, where, overtaken by Harrison, he was attacked on the 5th of October. The British were totally defeated, with a loss of six hundred prisoners. Proctor sought personal safety by dishonorable flight. The renowned and truly heroic Tecumseh was killed.* The army on the Niagara, under General James Wilkinson, made an abortive effort to take Montreal. An expedition begun in boasting met with a humiliating check, and a loss of three hundred and fifty men in the battle of Crysler's Farm, and was abandoned.

188. The series of brilliant naval triumphs was also interrupted by the loss, near Boston, of the frigate Chesapeake, which, having accepted the challenge of the Shannon, a British frigate, to single combat, was captured, with dreadful slaughter, June 1, 1813. The battle lasted altogether not more than fifteen minutes, and yet, says Cooper, "both ships were charnel houses." Captain James Lawrence, mortally wounded in the fight and delirious from pain, continued to cry out, "Do n't give up the ship!"

189. In the year 1813, the South became the scene of Indian war. The Creeks of Alabama and Georgia had, in August, attacked Fort Mims, situated on the left bank of the Alabama River, and massacred nearly four hundred persons of both sexes, who had flocked to that stockade for safety. The vengeance which followed was swift and bloody. General Andrew Jackson,† the commander of the expedition against the Creeks, expressed himself as resolved to exterminate them. A large force of Southern militia, aided by Choctaw and Cherokee allies, carried havoc from village to village; and, finally, having cooped up about one

* See G. H. Colton's Tecumseh, or the West Thirty Years Since, poem.
† See James Parton's Life of Andrew Jackson.

---

187. Describe the battle of the Thames. What failure did Wilkinson make in Canada?

188. Give an account of the capture of the Chesapeake.

189. Narrate in full Jackson's operations against the Southern Indians.

thousand of the Creeks at Horseshoe Bend, on the Tallapoosa River, charged upon them with such effect as to kill or drown six hundred and capture the rest. Nothing was now left for the remnant of the broken nation but to sue for peace.

190. At this stage of the war the British sent large re-enforcements across the ocean, and military operations on the part of the Americans became almost entirely defensive. Attempts at invasion were not abandoned, however, until after General Brown's army, in two pitched battles on Canadian soil, had proven beyond all question the personal valor of the average American soldier. In the battle of Chippewa, fought July 5, 1814, between Brown's forces, three thousand strong, and about an equal number of British, commanded by General Riall, the British were routed after a furious conflict attended with great loss on both sides. It was just before the final charge at Chippewa that General Scott uttered the words: "The enemy say that the Americans are good at a long shot, but can not stand the cold iron. I call upon you instantly to give the lie to the slander. Charge!"

On the 25th, another obstinately contested battle was fought, known as the battle of Niagara, or Lundy's Lane. The fight raged till midnight, with indecisive results. The American loss was 745; the British, 878. Riall was captured; Brown and Scott were badly wounded. The Americans, though in possession of the field, retired to Fort Erie, where General Edmund Gaines took command. In the middle of August, General Drummond, with four thousand troops, moved against Fort Erie. On the 15th, a midnight attack was made; but Gaines repulsed the assailants, 962 of whom were killed and wounded. The American loss was but eighty-four.

The Americans had a camp at Plattsburg, on Lake Champlain. There General Macomb was left in command

---

190. Describe the battle of Chippewa. Repeat Scott's speech. Describe the battle of Lundy's Lane. Where did Gaines establish himself? What occurred on the night of August 15, 1814?

with a small force, most of the troops having been drawn away to the northern border. Sir George Prevost, governor of Canada, in conjunction with the British Commodore Downie, planned a combined attack, by land and water, upon this comparatively feeble encampment. Prevost, in person, conducted an army of twelve thousand men toward the threatened point, while Downie sailed up the lake with a squadron of sixteen vessels, carrying ninety-five guns and one thousand seamen. Fortunately, there was a small American fleet lying at Plattsburg, commanded by Commodore McDonough. It comprised four vessels and several gunboats, carrying in all eighty-six guns and about eight hundred men. The British made their proposed attack on the 11th of September. That part of the battle which took place on the lake was short, but brilliant and decisive. McDonough's squadron obtained a complete and glorious victory. Within three hours, every one of Downie's vessels was compelled to strike its flag. The attack by land also failed, and Prevost only waited the coming of night to begin a hasty retreat to Canada.

191. These American successes were counterbalanced by disasters of the most alarming kind. From near the beginning of the war, the sea-port towns had been in a state of blockade. War vessels swarmed along the coast, and crowded every important harbor. A squadron, bearing General Ross and five thousand troops, sailed up the Patuxent, and landed at Bene-

Describe the engagement at Plattsburg.

191. What was the condition of the sea-port towns?

dict. From this point Ross marched to Washington, meeting on the way the feeble opposition of General Winder at Bladensburg, on August 24, where, as Hildreth ironically remarks, "very few Americans had the honor to be either killed or wounded." Arriving at Washington, the British burnt the capitol, and all the other public buildings except the post-office and the patent-office, and then retreated.

Ross next appeared before Baltimore with his fleet, and opened a cannonade upon Fort McHenry. A land attack was also attempted on September 12th, in which Ross was killed. The fortifications of Baltimore proving stronger than they had anticipated, the enemy presently retreated without effecting their purpose. While the bombardment of Fort McHenry was going on, Francis S. Key, an eye-witness of "the rocket's red glare, the bomb bursting in air," composed the Star Spangled Banner.

192. The closing event of the war was the battle of New Orleans, the glorious issue of which established the military fame of Jackson. British troops to the number of eight thousand, under the command of General Edward Pakenham, a brother-in-law of the Duke of Wellington, approached New Orleans by way of Lake Borgne, and encamped about fifteen miles south of the city. "Booty and beauty" was the watchword of the British soldiers, who were confident of

MAP OF NEW ORLEANS.

Describe the movements of General Ross. When was the battle of Bladensburg fought? What buildings did the British destroy at Washington? When was Baltimore besieged? With what result?

192. What British forces menaced New Orleans?

easy victory. Jackson had five thousand men, most of them volunteer militia. With a large detachment of these, he made an attack on the British camp, on the night of December 28, 1814. He inflicted severe injury upon the enemy, and retreated in safety with a loss of two hundred and twenty men.

Andrew Jackson.

On the 8th of January, 1815, Pakenham led his veterans in force to the grand attack. By this time the Americans were strongly intrenched behind a deep ditch and impregnable bulwarks of spongy soil. They had also been re-enforced by two thousand Kentucky riflemen. The British moved resolutely to the assault, and the storm of battle burst upon them. After an hour's struggle, in which the British lost two thousand men, General Pakenham being among the slain, General Lambert, who succeeded to the British command, withdrew the army and retreated to Lake Borgne. The British soon afterwards re-embarked. The American loss in the battle was only seventy-one.

Thus terminated a war replete with disasters to the United States, destructive to her commerce, and extremely unpopular with a large number of her people, especially in New England. It must not be thought that Jackson's successful campaign was the means of bringing England to

---

What occurred on the night of December 28, 1814? Describe the battle of New Orleans. When and where was peace negotiated? How was the news of peace received in the United States? Was the war productive of much good?

terms. A treaty had been negotiated at Ghent, by commissioners from the belligerent nations, before the battle of New Orleans was fought; and on February 11, 1815, messengers arrived at New York bearing the welcome tidings of peace. The whole country was filled with rejoicing. Even the friends of the war were glad of its termination. In Boston the people were especially jubilant. There was a simultaneous ringing of all the bells, and a general cessation of business; the streets were filled with delighted throngs; the schools were treated to an extra holiday.

193. For the first twenty years after the Revolutionary War, the average foreign immigration was about six thousand annually; then for ten years, owing to the hostile relations of England, France, and America, the stream of immigration was pent up at its fountain. The entire population of the United States in 1810 was more than seven millions, of whom over one million were slaves. After the overthrow of the Indian confederacies of the West and South, settlement went rapidly on. Exploration, stimulated by the fur trade, was pushed to the far north-west. The enterprise of John Jacob Astor established a trading post near the mouth of the Columbia, early in 1811. Vermont and Kentucky were admitted into the Union in 1791; Tennessee, in 1796; Ohio, in 1803. Ohio was first settled at Marietta, in 1788, by New Englanders. Cincinnati was founded a year later. Louisiana, a state whose history is extremely interesting, was admitted in 1812.*

The subject of internal improvements first received attention while Jefferson was President. Provision was made for the construction of canals and turnpikes. The famous

* See Irving's Astoria; also Howe's Ohio Historical Collections, Walker's History of Athens County, Ohio; Martin's History of Franklin County, Ohio; S. P. Hildreth's Lives of the Early Settlers of Ohio; Gayarre's History of Louisiana.

---

193. What is the history of migration to America during the period of time embraced in this chapter? What was the population of the United States in 1810? What progress was made in exploration and settlement? What states were admitted into the union, and in what years? What internal improvements were made?

National Road from Cumberland, Maryland, to Wheeling, Virginia, was begun early. Eli Whitney, of Connecticut, invented the cotton-gin in 1793, and from that date the cultivation of cotton rapidly increased in the South. In 1807, the first steamboat was completed, at Albany, by its inventor, Robert Fulton.* Before the close of the war, steamboats were in use on the Ohio and the Mississippi.

Robert Fulton.

The animosity between the two political parties continued violent. The debates in Congress upon the issues of the times developed a school of polemic orators famous for fiery eloquence.† Among these were John Randolph, of Virginia; and, later, John C. Calhoun, of South Carolina, and Henry Clay, of Kentucky. Daniel Webster, afterwards so renowned as statesman and orator, made his first speech in Congress, in 1814. Celebrated among the politicians of the period were Josiah Quincy, distinguished for his legal attainments; DeWitt Clinton, whose perseverence and patriotism secured the construction of the Erie Canal; and John

* See Colden's and Reigart's Life of Fulton; also J. C. Hauck's Robert Fulton, historical romance.

† See Garland's Life of Randolph, Jenkins's Life of Calhoun, Sargent's Life of Clay, Curtis's Life of Webster, E. Quincy's Life of Josiah Quincy, and Seward's Life of Adams.

When, and by whom was the cotton-gin invented? The steamboat? What is said of the congressional debates of this period? Of the oratory? What great politicians were prominent?

Quincy Adams, sixth President of the United States. "In the half century from 1765 to 1816, the peculiar literature of America is to be found in a series of newspaper essays, some of them of distinguished ability. Rich jewels now and then glitter in the general mass; but the editorial portion of the papers, and no small part of the communications also, consist of declamatory calumnies, expressed in a style of vulgar ferocity."

Besides the effusions of the hour here referred to, other and more ambitious labors of the pen were accomplished. Several literary men of marked ability flourished. Philip Frenau, the political editor and poet; Joel Barlow, author of the Columbiad; John Marshall, author of an excellent Life of Washington; the accomplished Fisher Ames; Noah Webster, the lexicographer; Richard Alsop; William Wirt; and Charles Brockden Brown, the first American novelist, may all be considered as belonging to this period. The leading artists of the time were Malebone, Sully, Morse, J. W. Jarvis, Vanderlyn, and especially Washington Allston, who was noted also as a writer.* Vanderlyn's portrait of Washington hangs in the hall of the United States House of Representatives, and one of his paintings fills a panel in the rotunda of the Capitol. Allston is considered the greatest historical painter that America has produced.

Education had made such progress that it was said by a competent judge, that the ratio of knowledge in the United States was as one hundred to one compared with what it was before the Revolution. Near the close of the eighteenth century was begun in New England a theological conflict between the orthodox and the liberal churches, into which the ancient Congregational body had divided.

* See Tuckerman's Book of the Artists; also Duyckinck's Cyclopedia of American Literature.

What was the form and style of the prevailing literature? What advance had been made in education? Mention the chief literary men of the period. The leading artists. What religious controversy took place in New England at about the close of the eighteenth century?

Harvard College became the headquarters of the Liberal sect, who found their exponent and champion in William E. Channing, perhaps the greatest ethical writer America has produced.

GENERAL QUESTIONS AND DIRECTIONS.

Prepare a chronological table of the dated events given in Chapter Twelfth. Prepare a table of the battles of the War of 1812. What was the cause and what the effect of the old French war? Of the Revolutionary War? The Tripolitan war? The War of 1812–15? What was the origin of party divisions in New England, in Colonial times? When and why were the people classed as Whigs and Tories? As Federalists and Republicans? Why was tariff advocated in New England, and free trade in the South? What effect had the invention of the cotton-gin on Southern interests? Why, at the close of the War of 1812, was migration to the West greatly accelerated? What influence did the invention of the steamboat exert in the development of the West? Why did emigrants go West?

BIOGRAPHICAL REVIEW.

Who were the great men of the period of American Discovery? Who were noted as founders of settlements or states? Who were the leading men of the South in Colonial times? Of New England? Of the Middle States? Name the celebrated characters that figured in the old French war. In the Revolution. Name the successive kings and queens to whom the English colonies in America gave allegiance. How many in all? Who was the last? Name the first four Presidents of the United States in the order of their succession. Prepare a sketch of the life of John Adams, Thomas Jefferson, John Jay, Alexander Hamilton, James Madison, General Saint Clair, Edward Preble, William Bainbridge, Stephen Decatur, Aaron Burr, Tecumseh, Oliver Perry, Isaac Chauncey, Robert Fulton, John Randolph, Philip Frenau, Washington Allston, William E. Channing.

Map Questions and Geographical Review.

What were the boundaries of the United States in 1812? When, and of whom was Louisiana purchased? What were its boundaries? To whom did Florida still belong? How many states were in the Union in 1812? Which of these were admitted since the Revolution? In what years? What states were formed out of the North-west Territory? What territories are named on the map? When did Washington City become the national capital? What was the capital before that time? What towns and cities are marked on this map that are not found on the map opposite page 133?

What Indian tribes remained in Georgia? In Alabama? In Mississippi and Tennessee? In Florida? Were there any other tribes east of the Mississippi in 1812?

Locate Ogdensburg. Kingston. York. What is the present name of York? Locate Mackinaw. Oswego. Buffalo. Erie. Cleveland. Chicago. Cincinnati. Alton. Mobile. Nashville. Augusta. French Town. New Orleans. Which of these places are in Canada? At or near what cities and towns were battles fought during the war of 1812? Was the scene of hostilities the same in any instances as in the Revolutionary War? What naval engagements took place on Lake Erie? On Lake Ontario? On Lake Champlain? How many, and what states were the seat of war? What bays and rivers were entered by British ships? Near what rivers were battles fought?

When was the National Road begun? Between what points? When were steamboats first used on the Ohio and Mississippi? What was the first great canal constructed in the United States? When, and by whom were the Missouri and the Columbia rivers explored? Who discovered the Ohio River? What was the population of the United States in 1810? How much had it increased since the close of the Revolutionary War? What motives induced migration to the Ohio Valley?

CHAPTER THIRTEENTH.

FROM THE CLOSE OF THE WAR OF 1812 TO THE END OF THE MEXICAN WAR.

1815—1848.

FOR a period of thirty years the republic was undisturbed by foreign wars. With the return of peace, the tide of migration resumed its flow from the Old World to the New. During the year 1817, not less than twenty-two thousand four hundred and forty persons arrived at ports of the United States from foreign countries; twice as many as had emigrated in any previous year. The whole number of passengers arriving at our shores, within the period of time embraced by this chapter, was over two millions.

Manufactures suffered with the renewal of exportation from Europe, but agriculture assumed a magnitude and importance hitherto unknown. An endless procession of pioneers poured into the fertile valley of the Ohio and Mississippi. Along the National road toiled the long train of emigrant wagons, and the cry was, Westward ho! Down

---

QUESTIONS.—**194.** How many foreign emigrants came to the United States between 1815 and 1848?

the beautiful Ohio, on rafts and barges, floated the sons of toil with their families and household goods, to settle the ever receding frontier, to subdue nature, and transform the savage wilderness into smiling fields and busy thoroughfares.

The marvelous development of the West is without parallel in history. It is like a tale of magic. Let the student who reads this page try to conceive that eighty years ago most of the territory north of the Ohio River was covered by the primeval forest. St. Louis, then as now the largest town of the West, had a motley population of three or four hundred Creoles, Yankee traders, Kentucky adventurers, Indians, half-breeds, and boatmen of the Mississippi. Cincinnati was but a village of log huts protected by the stockades of Fort Washington. Chicago was a small trading post on the edge of a wet prairie; and Louisville a rude hamlet in the shadow of dense woods.

The region west of the Mississippi was almost a *terra incognita.* The time is within the recollection of many now living, when Tennessee, Kentucky, and Ohio had few or no roads, and no home markets; when cattle and hogs were driven across the mountains to Baltimore; when a whole neighborhood would join together and build a flat-boat, and ship their united produce—pork, feathers, ginseng, and whisky—to New Orleans, and perhaps walk home again. As late as 1828, the chief mode of transporting goods was by the great Conestoga wagons with three, four, or six-horse bell teams. To the present generation, the Conestoga wagon, like the distaff and wheel, is a curiosity of the past. Many of the words most familiar to our grandfathers, such as chimney-lug, hominy-block, hunting-shirt, bee-coursing, log-rolling, and latch-string, have become obsolete, or else are used only in a figurative sense.

195. Within ten years from the date of the Treaty of Ghent, six new states had been formed and admitted into the Union—Indiana in 1816, Mississippi in 1817, Illinois

---

By what routes and conveyances did pioneers reach the West? Draw a contrast between the West of to-day and of eighty years ago.

in 1818, Alabama in 1819, Maine in 1820, and Missouri in 1821.* These states were settled by emigrants from all parts of the Union, and from Germany, Ireland, England, Scotland, and Canada. The germ of the population on the upper Mississippi, as at New Orleans, was French. Of late years, many Scandinavians have found their way to the northern states. It is an interesting fact that migration moves as a rule on the same parallels of latitude. The states of Michigan, Wisconsin, and Minnesota, and the northern parts of Ohio, Indiana, Illinois, Iowa, and Missouri, were settled mainly by people from New England and New York; Tennessee, Kentucky, and the southern part of Ohio, Indiana, Illinois, and Missouri, by people from Virginia and the Carolinas. Alabama, Mississippi, Arkansas, and Texas were settled by emigrants from the Carolinas and Georgia. In a very literal sense, "westward the course of empire takes its way."

196. It will be observed that of the first six states admitted to the Union after the War of 1812, three were northern, and three southern, and that the North and the South alternately acquired a state. In the southern states slavery was allowed; from the northern, it was excluded. For years, indeed ever since the formation of the Federal Constitution, the troublesome question of slavery had been agitated in Congress. Latterly, it had become the main subject of debate. When the bill for the admission of Missouri came before Congress, a memorable discussion arose—a debate long protracted and violent, in which the northern members opposed, on moral and political grounds, the addition to the Union of another slave state. The southern members, whose interests were involved with slave

* See Dillon's History of Indiana; O. H. Smith's Early Indiana Trials; Edwards's History of Illinois; and Parker's Missouri as it is.

---

195. Name the first six states admitted to the Union after the War of 1812. By whom were the Western states settled? What law governs migration?

196. What exciting question agitated the councils of our nation after the War of 1812?

labor, holding the doctrine of state sovereignty, denied the constitutional right of the general government to interfere with the institutions of the particular states. They held that the people of the respective commonwealths should decide whether slavery should or should not exist within their borders.

The controversy was for a time set at rest, in 1820, by the adoption of the Missouri Compromise, which provided that Missouri should come in as a slave state, and that thereafter slavery should be forever prohibited north of 36° 30′. The territory south of that line was to be open to slavery or freedom, as the people should choose.

197. At the expiration of Madison's second term of office, James Monroe, of Virginia, was elected to the Presidency, which office he held eight years—from March 4, 1817, to March 4, 1825. Monroe had been a Revolutionary officer, a foreign minister, governor of Virginia, and a member of Madison's cabinet. In politics he was a moderate Republican. During his administration, the issues of war-time having naturally died, a complete amalgamation of the old political parties was effected, and an "era of good feeling" prevailed. Causes were at work, however, which soon divided the people into two other great parties, known as Whigs and Democrats.

The questions upon which these parties held opposing views were, as before the war, commercial and financial. American manufactures languished, and to stimulate and protect them the Whigs advocated a high tariff upon foreign imports. The Democrats favored free trade. The Whigs advocated and the Democrats opposed the establishment of a National Bank. The Whigs gained the ascendancy, and in 1816 a protective tariff was imposed and a National Bank chartered, the charter of Hamilton's United States Bank having expired. After the settlement of the Missouri

---

What was the Missouri Compromise?

197. When did Monroe become President? How long did he serve? What was the state of parties during his administration? What new organizations were presently formed? On what principles were they based? Which party at first triumphed?

question, commerce and finance were the engrossing themes of congressional debate and legislation.

The closing year of Monroe's last term is commemorated in our annals as dating a visit to this country of the venerated La Fayette, then an old man. Tenderly associated in the minds of the people with Washington, La Fayette was received as the nation's guest, and honored with every attention that gratitude and patriotism could bestow.

198. John Quincy Adams, a Whig, and the son of John Adams, was the sixth President of the United States. He was a scholar, an orator, a diplomatist, and a model legislator. His administration, embracing but a single term, was prosperous, though much distracted by party strife. In 1828, the friends of protection amended the tariff laws so as to increase the duty on several articles of import that competed with home manufactures. The amended bill gave great offense to the South, since it interfered with the cotton trade.

199. The next presidential campaign, an exciting one, resulted in the defeat of the Whig candidate, Adams, and the election, by a very large majority, of Andrew Jackson, the hero of New Orleans, a stanch Democrat. So popular was Jackson, that he was re-elected in 1833. He was a man of strong will and energetic action. His executive ability was soon called into exercise at a very critical juncture. The discontent of the South with the tariff legislation had greatly increased. On the 19th of November, 1832, the state rights people of South Carolina held a convention at Columbia. They issued an ordinance declaring that the action of Congress was unconstitutional; that the tariff laws should be considered null and void; and that, in case the national government attempted to enforce those

---

What interesting event occurred in Monroe's last term?

198. Which party elected John Quincy Adams President? When? What was the character of his administration? What important bill did Congress pass in 1828?

199. Who was elected the seventh President? How long was Jackson in office? What transpired in South Carolina in 1832?

laws, the people of South Carolina would form an independent government. The great leader of the *nullifiers* was John C. Calhoun, Vice President of the United States. Jackson issued a proclamation in which he declared the procedure of the convention treasonable, and announced his determination to execute the laws at whatever cost.

Preparations were promptly but quietly made for military operations against South Carolina. The forts about Charleston were put in order, and General Scott was placed in command. The known firmness of Jackson and the prudence of Scott were the means of averting civil war. In 1833, the South was conciliated by the passage, in Congress, of Henry Clay's celebrated Compromise bill, providing for the gradual reduction of duties on certain articles, and limiting the operation of the existing tariff laws to ten years.

John C. Calhoun.

200. Before the troubles in South Carolina, an Indian war had commenced in Illinois. The Sacs and Foxes had sold their lands on the Rock River, and agreed to move west of the Mississippi; but Black Hawk, their chief, claimed that the treaty was informal, and resisted all efforts to force his people from their homes. In 1832, he attacked the settlers who had established themselves on the

---

Who was Calhoun? What was the President's action? What was the compromise of 1833? Who introduced it in Congress?

disputed lands, but was soon pursued by a force under General Atkinson. The Indians were defeated, and Black Hawk was captured. The tribes were afterwards quietly removed.

The Chocktaws and Chickasaws had been removed by the United States, to Indian Territory, in 1831. In 1838, the Cherokees were removed from the beautiful country they had long occupied in North Carolina, Georgia, Alabama, and Tennessee. General Scott, whose troops conducted these peaceful tribes into exile, declares that they were an interesting people, and that many of them were quite as civilized as their neighbors of the white race. They were very reluctant to leave their homes. When brought into camp by military authority, preparatory to their removal, they manifested great dejection of mind, and, though half starved, some refused the food that was offered them. Scott says that he never witnessed a scene of deeper pathos than was the departure of these simple people to the territory provided for them.

Henry Clay.

201. The design of the government to remove the Seminole Indians westward was not so easily accomplished. The Seminoles were originally Creek Indians, who had

---

200. Tell all about the Black Hawk war. About the removal of the Cherokees.

migrated as early as 1750, and taken up their residence in Florida. There, also, numbers of negroes, fugitive slaves from Georgia and Carolina, found refuge. These black exiles, called Maroons, and the Seminoles formed an intimate alliance for mutual aid and protection. They had a fort, which, notwithstanding its location on Spanish territory, General Jackson caused to be taken in 1816.

In this fort were three hundred Maroons of both sexes and thirty-four Indians. Of these, two hundred and seventy were instantly killed, July 27, by the explosion of a magazine, into which a hot ball was fired by a party sent to blow up the fort. This wanton destruction of life seems to have been unprovoked. The next year a boat ascending the Apalachicola, with supplies for Fort Scott, was intercepted by the negroes and Indians. On board were forty men, and a number of women and children. All but seven of these were massacred.

In retaliation, Jackson collected three thousand troops and carried a destructive campaign into the Seminole country. In 1819, the United States purchased Florida of Spain for five million dollars. Strong efforts were now made to induce the Seminoles to remove beyond the Mississippi. To this they were little inclined, and the negroes, fearful of being carried into slavery if their protectors should depart, used every means to induce them to remain. A treaty, however, was made with some of the Seminole chiefs, by which they agreed that their people should remove in the years 1833–4. When the time came, the greater number refused to leave their Floridian homes, and denied the validity of the treaty.

It was now deemed best by the government to employ military force. Expedition after expedition was sent to Florida, under command of the ablest officers in the army. Generals Scott and Taylor both served in the Floridian war. The expenditure of blood and treasure was enor-

201. Who were the Seminoles? The Maroons? What transpired, in 1816, in Florida? To whom did Florida then belong? How did the negroes and Indians retaliate? When, and on what terms did the United States obtain Florida? Why did not the Seminoles willingly migrate?

mous. In miasmatic wilds, among swamps and everglades, the war raged at intervals until 1842, a period of seven years, and even then its object was not gained. In this obstinate struggle, the counterpart of which is not to be found in history, the celebrated Osceola was a leading figure. Osceola, a young Seminole warrior, had married a beautiful Maroon, who, while on a visit to Fort King with her husband, was seized as a slave. Osceola became frantic with rage, but was instantly placed in irons while his wife was hurried away. He was released, but revenge was henceforth the consuming passion of his bosom. The record of his fierce and terrible deeds furnishes material not unfit for dramatic poetry.*

202. The eighth occupant of the presidential chair was Martin Van Buren, who succeeded Jackson March 4, 1837. Van Buren was associated with Jackson four years as Vice President, and held the usual democratic views upon the tariff and a National Bank. He was a citizen of New York, and had been governor of that state. He had also held the positions of United States senator and Secretary of State. His administration is chiefly memorable for a financial crisis—the "panic of '37"—during which the banks suspended payment, business was interrupted, and general hard times prevailed. These monetary difficulties, growing out of reckless speculation and other abuses of capital, were felt in every part of the country, and were of long continuance.

Van Buren, being considered in some measure responsible for the troubles of the country, lost popular confidence, and at the next election was defeated by the Whig candidate, William Henry Harrison. The political cam-

* See Sprague's Florida War, Giddings's Exiles of Florida, Mayne Reid's Osceola, and J. R. Donalson's Sergeant Atkins; A. B. Street's Osceola, poem, and the poem entitled The Seminole's Defiance.

What were the peculiar features of the Seminole war? How long did it continue? Give some account of Osceola.

202. Who was President after Jackson? What positions had he held? What calamity came upon the country during his term?

paign was remarkable for its immense mass meetings, processions, and novel modes of exciting the people. Harrison, the hero of Tippecanoe and the Thames, a man of thought and unusual benevolence, was greatly beloved by his fellow-citizens. He died at Washington, April 4, 1841, just one month after he had been inaugurated President.*

The Vice President, John Tyler, of Virginia, now became chief executive. To the chagrin of the Whig party, one of Tyler's first official acts was to veto a National Bank Bill, which Congress had passed. A second bank bill, based entirely on his own suggestions, he vetoed also, and thus provoked the resignation of all his cabinet members, except Webster. Tyler was denounced by the Whigs as betraying their confidence.

Daniel Webster.

In 1844, the republic of Texas,† which had thrown off its allegiance to Mexico nine years before, petitioned to be annexed to the United States. Texas was settled at San Antonio, by the Spaniards, as early as 1692. But it was not until long after this that any considerable population found residence in that state.

* See N. P. Willis's Death of Harrison, a poem.

† See Mrs. Houston's Texas and the Gulf of Mexico, Wm. Kennedy's and Doran Maillard's History of Texas.

Which party gained the election of 1840? Who was chosen President? What principles did he represent? When did Harrison die? Who then became President? In what act did he dissappoint the expectation of the Whigs? What is the meaning of *veto?*

In 1821, Stephen F. Austin established a colony between the rivers Brazos and Colorado. From this date American migration went on so rapidly, that within a single decade nearly ten thousand citizens of the United States had found homes in Texas. The boundary between Texas and Mexico had not been settled; therefore, annexation was likely to involve the United States in war with the latter. The South was almost unanimous for annexation at all hazards, since Texas would inevitably come into the Union as a slave state. The Texan question was the main issue of the political campaign of 1844, the Democrats being for, and the Whigs against, annexation. James K. Polk,* of Tennessee, the Democratic candidate, was chosen President. Before he took his seat, Texas was received into the Union. The Mexican minister at Washington declared the act of annexation the most unjust recorded in history.

203. Texas claimed the Rio Grande as her western boundary. Mexico refused to yield any territory west of the Nueces. One of the conditions of the treaty of annexation was that the United States should settle all questions of boundary—that is, should assume the quarrels of the newly adopted state, the Lone Star. War had existed between Texas and Mexico for a long time. It was now the political duty of the United States to protect her own. General Zachary Taylor,† who had gained a fine military reputation in the wars with Black Hawk and the Seminoles, was sent in the summer of 1845 to Corpus Christi, with an army to occupy the disputed territory. Receiving orders from President Polk, in April, 1846, to march to the Rio Grande, he took post opposite Matamoras, where he built Fort Brown.

* See L. Chase's History of the Administration of Polk.

† See C. F. Powell's Life of Taylor.

When did Texas apply for admission into the Union? What is the early history of Texas? What objection was made to the annexation of Texas? Why did the South favor annexation? What party gained the election of 1844? On what issue? Who was chosen President?

203. What dispute existed between Texas and Mexico?

On the 26th of April, a party of Mexicans, having crossed the Rio Grande, surprised a small body of United States dragoons, and killed or captured nearly all of them, thus inaugurating actual war. The Mexicans, with a strong force, threatened to cut off Taylor's communication with Point Isabel, where his supplies were deposited. Leaving an inconsiderable force to garrison the new fort, Taylor conducted his main army to that town, where he was re-enforced.

At the head of his army, now twenty-three hundred strong and amply provisioned, he set out on his return march. On the 8th of May, he encountered the Mexican general, Mariano Arista (å-rēs'tå), with an army numbering six thousand, on the plain of Palo Alto. Five hours' hard fighting, mostly with light artillery, gave the victory to Taylor. The Mexicans retreated, having suffered a loss of 600. The loss on the other side was 53.

On the next day, a second battle was fought by the same armies, at a ravine called Resaca de la Palma (rå-så'kå då lå pål'må). The Mexicans were routed with great loss in both killed and prisoners. The battle was short, but furious. The decisive event of the day was the brilliant and overwhelming charge of Captain May and eighty fearless dragoons upon the main battery of the enemy. "Men, we must take that battery!" exclaimed May. The assault was made with incredible fury; the gunners were cut down, the artillery was silenced, the field was won. Meanwhile, the fort opposite Matamoras had been besieged by the Mexicans. Taylor came to the relief of the well-nigh exhausted garrison. The enemy retired from the fort, and soon afterwards withdrew from Matamoras, which Taylor occupied on the 18th of May.

Other towns on the lower Rio Grande were presently taken. Volunteers flocked to the American army from all parts of the United States. To the young, the daring, the

---

What decisive action did Polk take? What was the first act of open hostility? When, where, and between what forces was the first battle of the Mexican war fought? With what results? Describe the battle of Resaca de la Palma.

adventurous, this war offered many romantic attractions. The field of operations was strange, picturesque, and renowned in Spanish history. The mountains, the cities, the peculiar products, the novel customs of Mexico, all had their share in drawing recruits. The traditional splendor of the ancient halls of the Montezumas filled the imagination, and inspired the soldiers with something of the chivalrous spirit that characterized the days of old.

General Zachary Taylor.

204. The next great event of the war was the capture of Monterey (mon-tā-rā′), a famous city not far from the Sierra Madre Mountains, very strongly fortified, and defended by a force of nine thousand men. Monterey was attacked by Taylor's army, now six thousand strong, on the 22d of September. The assault was maintained for several days. The fighting raged in the streets, and was of the fiercest character. On the 24th, the Mexican commanding general, Pedro de Ampudia (åm-poo′de-å), surrendered the city.

205. General Stephen Kearny (kar′ne), distinguished for the part he took in the battle of Queenstown, had been appointed to the command of the Army of the West. In June, he set out from Leavenworth with a force of twenty-seven hundred, mostly mounted Missouri volunteers, and on the 18th of August reached Santa Fé, after a toilsome

---

Was the Mexican war popular?

204. Tell what you can of the battle of Monterey.

march over wild prairies and desert tracts. The distance was nearly one thousand miles. Kearny, without opposition, entered the old town of Santa Fé, a place of fifteen hundred inhabitants, and proceeded to establish a provisional government for New Mexico, which, from this time forward, acknowledged allegiance to the United States.

It was part of Kearny's design to conquer California; but that state, he soon learned, had already yielded to the energetic young American explorer, John Charles Fremont,* the Pathfinder of the Rocky Mountains. Fremont was in the Sierra Nevada region with a party of sixty men, conducting a series of scientific investigations, when the war began. Before war had been declared, however, this daring man, being threatened with expulsion from California, by the Mexican military commandant at Los Angelos, conceived the idea of conquering the state on his own responsibility. He stimulated the American settlers to revolt, and in July, 1846, California was declared independent of Mexico. About the same time, Commodore Sloat bombarded and captured the town of Monterey, on the Pa-

John Charles Fremont.

* See Tuthill's History of California; also John Bigelow's Life of John C. Fremont: C. W. Upham's Life and Explorations of John C. Fremont; and Fremont's Explorations.

---

205. Recount the particulars of Kearny's campaign. Of Fremont's operations.

cific, and other less important coast towns. A little later, Commodore Stockton, joined by Fremont and his men, proceeded to Los Angelos and organized a government. A few vigorous skirmishes at different points, all disastrous to the Mexicans, established the military and civil supremacy of the United States in California. Thus easily were New Mexico and California wrested from Mexican domination.

206. Kearny arrived at Los Angelos in February, 1847, and assumed the governorship of California. His army, now in command of Colonel Doniphan, quitting Santa Fé, pursued its march southward over desolate plains, and in December reached Bracito, on the Rio del Norte. At this point an army of Mexicans had assembled. The commander, Ponce de Leon, sent Doniphan a black flag, and demanded an immediate surrender. Doniphan returned a spirited message, declaring himself ready for battle. Accordingly, on the 22d a furious encounter took place. Doniphan was victorious. The gallant little army moved onward to the pass of Sacramento, where it encountered and overcame a force of four thousand Mexicans. The battle being won, Doniphan pushed southward to the populous city of Chihuahua (che-wä'wä), capital of the province of that name, and took military possession.

207. General John E. Wool had been appointed to the duty of recruiting the service, and of organizing an Army of the Center to operate in the interior of the enemy's country. Having sent forward a force of nine thousand volunteers to join Taylor, Wool, at the head of three thousand troops whom he had thoroughly drilled, set out from San Antonio, and, after a march of nine hundred miles, reached Agua Nueva, where he encamped in December. A divi-

---

Who co-operated with Fremont? How did Fremont happen to be in the far West? When was California declared independent of Mexico? Where did Stockton establish a provisional government?

206. Describe Colonel Doniphan's campaign.

207. Relate the services of General Wool. What long march did he accomplish?

sion of Taylor's army, under General Worth, had taken Saltillo (sȧl-teel'yo) in November. The coast city of Tampico had also surrendered to an American squadron.

In the autumn of 1846, General Scott was appointed to the chief command of the army, with instructions to carry the war directly to the city of Mexico. The plan of the campaign contemplated first the capture of Vera Cruz. In order to accomplish his object, Scott drew from Taylor and Wool a large proportion of their forces, and several of their finest officers. The depleted armies were consolidated at Agua Nueva, and mustered in all less than five thousand men. This army was menaced by Antonio Lopez de Santa Anna, President of Mexico, with a force four times as great. Taylor withdrew his troops from Agua Nueva, and took a strong position at a mountain pass called Buena Vista (bwā'nah vees-tah).

Here, on the 22d of February, 1847, almost surrounded by the swarming host of the enemy, Taylor was summoned to surrender. But *Rough and Ready*, as his soldiers styled him, replied to the summons that he meant to fight and not to yield. Some preliminary skirmishing occurred the same day. The Americans slept on their arms, and on the next morning the unequal armies joined battle in terrible earnest. The sanguinary contest continued with unabated fury until dark. Nearly 800 Americans were killed and wounded. The Mexican loss was 2,000. Santa Anna was defeated. In the night he drew his forces off, and retired to San Luis Potosi. Not long after this brilliant victory, Taylor returned to the States, and his command devolved upon Wool. The army, was joined by Doniphan's illustrious Missourians, and went into garrison at Saltillo and Monterey.

208. We have now to recount the decisive events of the final campaign of the war. Scott selected the island of Lobos as a place of rendezvous, and there brought together troops to the number of twelve thousand men, the

---

What general captured Saltillo? When? What was the plan of Scott's campaign? Describe the battle of Buena Vista.

flower of the American army. These, embarking on vessels provided for them, sailed to Vera Cruz, and landed near the city on the 9th of March, 1847. The chief defense of Vera Cruz was the castle of San Juan de Ulloa (ool-yo'ä), a fortress that was deemed impregnable.

Antonio Lopez de Santa Anna.

Having erected his batteries and made all preparations for an assault, Scott demanded the surrender of the city. This being refused, the bombardment was begun, both by land and water, Commodore Conner's powerful fleet assisting. On the 27th, the besieged city and castle capitulated, yielding up 5,000 prisoners, 600 cannon, and 10,000 stand of arms.

209. Early in April the invading army took up the line of march for the capital. The road, which led through a rugged country, was guarded at the height of Cerro Gordo by twelve thousand soldiers under the command of Santa Anna. The unfortunate Mexican president and general was destined to suffer a second signal defeat. On the 18th of April, Scott made an unexpected attack, drove the enemy from their strong works, took three thousand prisoners, and utterly routed the rest of the army, killing and wounding many. His own loss was but 63 killed. Santa Anna fled

---

208. Whence did Scott embark for Vera Cruz? With what force? Give a full account of the bombardment of Vera Cruz and San Juan de Ulloa.

209. Give the particulars concerning the battle of Cerro Gordo.

on the back of a mule. From Cerro Gordo the Americans pushed on to Jalapa (hå-lå'på), and presently occupied the abandoned castle of Perote (på-ro'tå), a stronghold almost as much renowned as that of San Juan de Ulloa. By the middle of May, Scott reached the splendid city of Puebla (pwĕb'lå), next to Mexico in size, and containing a population of eighty thousand. Taking peaceable possession, the army here rested for several months.

General Winfield Scott.

210. At Puebla, Scott received re-enforcements. Early in August, he resumed his march toward the capital. His progress was through a delightful country, and the soldiers scarcely felt their fatigues, so interesting was the scenery they beheld, and so sanguine their expectation of victories that would put an end to the war. At length the army, having ascended by rough but romantic roads to the vast plateau which occupies so large a part of Central Mexico, came in view of the magnificent object of conquest—the ancient and renowned city of the Aztec kings. The approaches to the capital were guarded by strong works, defended by an aggregate force of over thirty thousand Mexicans.

About eight miles south of the capital was a hill called Contreras (kon-trå'rås). Here, entrenched behind powerful

---

From Cerro Gordo whither did the army go?

210. Describe the march from Puebla to the vicinity of Mexico. What force defended Mexico?

batteries, a force of eight thousand, awaited the coming of the Americans. On the 20th of August, at dawn of day, a detachment of Scott's men surprized the Mexicans, and within a quarter of an hour was in possession of Contreras and its artillery. The Mexican loss was 700 killed and 800 captured; that of the Americans, not above 60 in killed and wounded! From Contreras, Scott directed his course to Churubusco (choo-roo-boos′-ko), where, under cover of strong defenses, twenty-seven thousand Mexicans were stationed, with the desperate resolution of brave men at bay. Santa Anna was once more at the head of his army. A bloody battle of three hours' duration gave a second triumph to the Americans, but at the sacrifice of many lives. Thus on one day were two battles fought, and two formidable defenses captured.

An armistice was now proposed by Scott, and accepted by Santa Anna; but the latter violated its terms by taking occasion to strengthen his fortifications. When this became known to Scott, he at once resumed hostilities. On the 8th of September, the field-works surrounding Molino del Rey (mo-lee′no dĕl rà) were attacked, and the enemy driven therefrom with fearful slaughter. One strong position yet remained unconquered—the castle of Chapultepec (chă-pool′-tà-pĕk′). On the 13th, this was stormed, and at night Santa Anna and his troops fled toward Puebla. On the 14th, the American army marched to the grand plaza, or public square, in front of the cathedral and royal palace of the city of Mexico. The American banner was unfurled above the domes of the conquered capital. The Mexican war was at an end.

On the 2d of February, 1848, a formal treaty of peace was concluded, in which the Mexicans agreed to consider the Rio Grande as the western boundary of the disputed territory, and to cede to the United States the provinces of New Mexico and California for the sum of fifteen million

---

Describe the battle of Contreras. The battle of Churubusco. Of Molino del Rey. Of Chapultepec. What occurred on the 14th of September, 1847? When was peace negotiated?

dollars. The treaty having been duly ratified, peace was proclaimed on the Fourth of July, **1848.***

211. Within the thirty-three years covered by the events recorded in this chapter, six new states were admitted to the union — Arkansas in 1836, Michigan in 1837, Texas and Florida in 1845, Iowa in 1846, and Wisconsin in 1848. The increase of population was so great that in 1850 the census gave over twenty-three million as the total number of inhabitants in the United States. Internal improvement had gone on rapidly; many labor-saving machines were invented; all branches of industry thrived. Mining became an object of importance. The first railroad constructed in the United States was the Baltimore and Ohio, begun in 1828. On this the first locomotive used in America ran in 1831. In 1848, there were 6,000 miles of railroad in the United States; in 1860, more than five times as much. In 1844, Professor S. F. B. Morse† erected, between Washington and Baltimore, the first magnetic telegraph

Professor S. F. B Morse.

* See Mayer's and Mansfield's History of the Mexican War.
† See Dunlap's History of Arts and Designs in the United States.

On what terms? When was it proclaimed?

211. What states were admitted into the Union within the period embraced in this chapter? Which of these were slave states? What was the population of the states in 1850? What branch of industry was developed? Give the history of railroads.

in the world. There are now, in the United States, fifty thousand miles of railroad, enough to extend twice round the globe. There are double as many miles of telegraph.

The New England system of common school education was generally adopted in the Western states. Private institutions of learning were fostered also, and the arts and sciences received encouragement and patronage from Congress. Newspapers and school-books exercised a molding influence on the mind and character of the people. "The greatest scholars of the country," says Tuckerman, "have not deemed the production of the latter an unworthy labor; nor have the most active, enterprising, and ambitious failed to exercise their best powers in the former sphere." A galaxy of literary stars rose in this period.

Washington Irving.

Among these are, Bryant, Longfellow, Bancroft, Cooper, Irving, Sparks, Everett, Halleck, Prescott, Ticknor, and Hildreth. The great artists, Cole, Chapman, Weir, Greenough, Inman, Crawford, Hart, Powers, Page, Huntington, Leutze, and Church, were all born between the years 1800 and 1820. Audubon, the American naturalist, began his valuable scientific labors in this period.

The peculiar religious order called Mormons was started

Of telegraphy. How had education progressed? What is said of newspapers and school-books? Of literary men? Of artists?

about the year 1830.* Joseph Smith, the founder of Mormonism, a Vermonter by birth, having made several converts, went with them first to Kirtland, Ohio, then to Independence, Missouri. In 1838, the Mormons, to the number of five thousand, being expelled from Missouri for breaking the laws, bought a tract of land in Illinois, and built a town called Nauvoo, in which they erected a grand temple. Smith, defying the state laws, was guilty of outrages for which he was thrown into jail. In June, 1844, a mob broke into the jail and shot him. He was succeeded by Brigham Young, the present high-priest and prophet of the Mormons. Young conducted his adherents to Utah, where, in 1847, he founded Salt Lake City, now a place of about twenty thousand inhabitants.

Brigham Young.

In 1848, gold was first discovered in California, and soon rich deposits of this precious metal were brought to light. The news spread with amazing swiftness to all parts of the

* See Gunnison's History of Mormonism; Hyde's Mormonism: its Leaders and Designs; also Autobiography of Joseph Smith; Turner's Life of Joseph Smith; and Dixon's New America.

Give the history of Joseph Smith and Mormonism. Who is Brigham Young? When was gold discovered in California? What was the effect of this?

world. So great was the rush of population to this Eldorado, that when five years had elapsed the population of California had grown to one hundred thousand, and two years later it was more than double that number. The city of San Francisco sprang into existence as at the touch of the magician's wand.

GENERAL QUESTIONS AND DIRECTIONS.

Prepare a chronological table of the dated events mentioned in this chapter. Give a list of the states admitted to the Union, from the adoption of the Constitution to the close of 1848. Tell in what year each was admitted. Give a list of the names of the presidents from Washington to Polk. Give the date at which each began his administration. Prepare a list of the battles of the Mexican war, and the names of commanding generals. How can you account for the fact that the American armies, though small, were so uniformly victorious?

BIOGRAPHICAL REVIEW.

What is the difference between biography and history? Write a list of the names of the most celebrated American military commanders who figured before the year 1850. A list of naval commanders. Of statesmen and orators. Of literary characters. Of artists. Of divines. Of discoverers. Of inventors. Compile a sketch of the life of Monroe. Of J. Q. Adams. Jackson. Calhoun. Clay. Webster. Black Hawk. Osceola. Van Buren. Harrison. Tyler. Polk. Taylor. Scott. Santa Anna. Fremont. Morse. Cooper. Irving. Cole. Hart. Powers. Young.

Map Questions and Geographical Review.

How were the limits of the United States extended in 1819? How in 1845? When did Texas become independent of Mexico? Where was Texas first settled? By whom? When, and where was it colonized by emigrants from the United States? By what Indian family was Mexico originally occupied? By what European nation was it conquered and colonized? To what river did Texas claim that her western boundary extended? What portions of the United States were obtained by the Mexican War? What, by the Gadsden Purchase? What are the present boundaries of the United States? How much territory has been added to the country since 1802? What was the extent of Louisiana at the close of the Revolutionary War?

Locate the city of Mexico. Vera Cruz. Tampico. Matamoras. Puebla. The two Montereys. Chihuahua. Acapulco. Saltillo. San Luis. At which of these places were battles fought? Locate San Antonio. What reference is made to this place in the text? Where is Santa Fé? For what is it noted? Where is Los Angelos? What events are associated with this town?

When, and by whom was the Missouri River explored? The Colorado? The Gila? When was the Red River first visited by white men? Describe the Columbia River. The Yellow Stone. The Platte. The Brazos.

When, and by whom was the Pacific coast first explored? Who named California? New Mexico? Why is Montana so named? Arizona? Indian Territory? Dakota?

What states lie west of the Mississippi? What territories? What circumstance led to the rapid settlement of California? When was the first settlement made west of the Mississippi? By whom was Utah settled? Locate San Francisco. Salem. Denver. St. Paul. Omaha. Galveston. Astoria. Who founded Astoria?

How does the region west of the Mississippi compare in size with the region east? What mountain ranges near the Pacific?

CHAPTER FOURTEENTH.

FROM THE CLOSE OF THE MEXICAN WAR TO THE OPENING OF THE GREAT CIVIL WAR.

1848—1861.

POLK was succeeded in office by Zachary Taylor, the hero of Buena Vista. In the campaign of 1848, three distinct parties — the Whigs, the Democrats, and the Free-soilers — brought out candidates. Taylor was nominated by the Whigs; General Lewis Cass of Michigan, by the Democrats; and Martin Van Buren, by the Free-soilers. The last-named party, weak as to numbers, held that Congress should prohibit the introduction of slavery into the territories. Taylor was elected, and he took his seat March 5, 1849. When sixteen months had elapsed, his administration was abruptly closed by his death, which occurred, after a brief illness, on the 9th of July, 1850. His last words were: "I have endeavored to do my duty. I am not afraid to die." The Vice President, Millard Fillmore of New York, now became chief magistrate.

QUESTIONS.—**212.** Who were candidates for the presidency in the election of 1848? Who was elected? When did Taylor die? Who then became President?

No sooner had the Mexican war closed, than difficulties began to arise respecting the newly-acquired territory. One question in dispute was regarding the boundary between Texas and New Mexico. The most exciting topic of congressional debate, however, was slavery. California, as we have seen, had suddenly acquired a population sufficient to entitle her to the privileges of a state. At the suggestion of Taylor, the Californians held a convention in September, 1849, and adopted a state constitution, which was ratified by the people with great unanimity. It was presumable, from the geographical position of California, that she would be a slave state; but it happened that the majority of her mixed population were in favor of free labor, and the newly-adopted constitution, therefore, excluded slavery. The bill to admit California without slavery met with violent opposition at Washington. Indeed, so bitter was the feeling against it, that great fears were entertained of disunion in case of its passage.

The discussion on the admission of California, and on other subjects directly or indirectly related to slavery, continued to agitate both Congress and the people at large for many months. At length, in January, 1850, Henry Clay, the great compromiser, introduced, in the Senate, a set of resolutions soon collectively named, by the newspapers, the Omnibus bill. The measures Clay proposed were, after long delays, substantially adopted, and were the means of postponing for ten years the final conflict between the North and the South.

By this compromise California was admitted to the Union as a free state; the boundary line between Texas and New Mexico was fixed four degrees east of Santa Fé; Utah and New Mexico were erected into territorial governments, free to introduce slavery or prohibit it as the people should decide; the slave trade was abolished in the District of Col-

---

What subjects engrossed the attention of the government after the close of the Mexican war? When did California adopt a state constitution? What provision was made in it? How did Congress receive the application of California for admission into the Union? What was the Omnibus bill? When introduced? By whom?

umbia; and the fugitive slave law was passed, providing for the capture and delivery to their masters of runaway negroes who had escaped from the South to the North. The Abolitionists severely blamed Fillmore for signing the fugitive slave bill.

213. In the fall of 1852, the Democrats nominated, for President, Franklin Pierce, of New Hampshire; the Whigs nominated Winfield Scott. Both candidates were pledged to the support of the Omnibus bill. The Free-soilers, now a formidable party, nominated John P. Hale, of New Hampshire, famous for his early antagonism to slavery. Pierce was elected. He was a lawyer, had been in Congress both as representative and as senator, and had served in the Mexican war as a brigadier-general. Not long after his election, the United States bought of Mexico, for twenty million dollars, about twenty-seven thousand square miles of territory south of the Gila River. This transaction is known as the Gadsden purchase.

Stephen A. Douglas.

The great legislative event of Pierce's administration was the passage of the celebrated Kansas-Nebraska bill, brought before the Senate in 1853 by Stephen A. Douglas of Illinois, a man destined to play an important part on the

---

State the different things included in the compromise measures as adopted.

213. What political parties nominated candidates for the presidency in 1852? To what principles were the parties severally committed? Who was elected? When and by whom was the Kansas-Nebraska bill brought before Congress?

political stage. Douglas was a powerful champion of the doctrine of state sovereignty. The bill which he proposed organized Kansas and Nebraska into territorial governments, with the provision that slavery might be introduced if the majority of the settlers so willed it. In May, 1854, the bill passed. Of course, this violated the Missouri Compromise, which declared that *north of* 36° 30′ slavery should be forever prohibited. It was argued that the spirit and intent of that Compromise had already been violated by the admission as a free state of California, a large part of which lies south of 36° 30′.

Both sections now looked upon Kansas with absorbing interest. Thither from the North there was a rush of migration to swell the anti-slavery population. From the South, more especially from Missouri, multitudes poured into the contested territory, to outnumber and outvote the northern settlers. Civil war was inevitable, and it came in some of its worst aspects. Many lives were lost, and many families were left homeless. "Bleeding Kansas" was a theme of universal talk.

The excitement was at its height when the presidential canvass of 1856 claimed the public mind. Again there were three candidates, and again the Democrats triumphed, electing to the chief magistracy James Buchanan, of Pennsylvania. The Whig party was broken up. Many of its old adherents had combined with the Free-soilers, and, calling themselves Republicans, had nominated Fremont at the head of their ticket. Millard Fillmore had run as the candidate of the Know Nothings, a new party holding as a leading principle the proposition that "Americans ought to rule America." Buchanan came into power at a very critical period. The Kansas struggle continued throughout his whole administration. It did not cease until 1861, when the contested state was admitted without slavery.

What was this bill? When did it pass? How did it conflict with the Missouri Compromise? What induced rapid migration to Kansas? What followed? What was the state of parties in 1856? Who was elected President? When was Kansas admitted? Minnesota? Oregon?

Minnesota became a state in 1858, and Oregon,* in 1859. Thus three new anti-slavery states were added to the Union, while the number of pro-slavery states had not been increased.

214. In 1859, events transpired of a nature to inflame the southern mind to a degree before unknown. John Brown,† of Ossawatomie, having planned an invasion of Virginia to free the slaves, collected a supply of guns and pikes, and, with a party of twenty, on the night of October 16th, attacked the arsenal and armory at Harper's Ferry, and took twenty prisoners. The next day Brown was captured by the Virginia militia. He was tried, convicted, and hung.

215. The antagonism between the extremists of the two great sections seemed well-nigh implacable. The cotton states were strongly disposed to sever their connection with the Union. All parties looked anxiously forward to the coming political campaign. On the 23d of April, 1860, a Democratic national convention met at Charleston, South Carolina, for the purpose of adopting a political platform and nominating a presidential candidate. Nearly six hundred delegates were in attendance. The committee on resolutions reported, among other things, that neither Congress nor territorial legislatures have the power to abolish slavery in the territories, nor to prohibit the introduction of slaves therein, nor to destroy the right of property in slaves by any legislation whatever. This, being contrary to the popular democratic principle of state sovereignty, was rejected. The minority report, in which the state sovereignty doctrine was expressed, was adopted by a vote of 165 to

* See Oliphant's Minnesota and the Far West; Bond's Minnesota and her Resources; and Neill's History of Minnesota; also Dunn's Oregon Territory, and Bulfinch's Oregon and Eldorado.

† See Redpath's and Webb's Life of John Brown.

---

214. Give the particulars of John Brown's raid, and what followed.

215. Relate in full the history of the Charleston convention of 1860. On what issue did the convention divide? What was the action of the southern members?

138. Most of the southern delegates now withdrew from the convention. Thus the great Democratic party, which had been so long victorious, was split asunder; and slavery was the wedge.

The Charleston convention adjourned to meet again in June, at Baltimore, where Stephen A. Douglas was nominated for President. The seceding delegates met also in June, at Richmond, Virginia, and nominated John C. Breckenridge, of Kentucky. Another organization, called the Constitutional Union party, met at Baltimore and nominated John Bell, of Tennessee. On May 16, 1860, the Republican convention met at Chicago, and there, after adopting resolutions which declare that the normal condition of the territories is freedom; that neither Congress nor the territorial legislatures have authority to give existence to slavery in the territories; and that the traffic in slaves should be suppressed—nominated, for President, Abraham Lincoln,* of Illinois.

Every issue now hinged upon the slavery question. Lincoln denied the right of slavery to obtrude itself upon the territories, and declared Congress, by duty, bound to prevent it from intruding. Douglas affirmed that the people of a territory had the right to adopt or to reject slavery. Breckenridge represented the opinion that the slaveholder had a right to carry his slaves into a territory, and that Congress should protect him even if territorial legislation should have prohibited slavery. Bell simply declared that the United States Constitution was a sufficient guide. The Republicans under Lincoln were one mass, and, though the party was unmistakably antislavery, its doctrines contained no threat against slavery as it then existed. The Democrats under Douglas and Breckinridge were divided. The Bell party was insignificant in numbers. The elec-

* See Raymond's and Holland's Life of Abraham Lincoln; Mrs. Stowe's Men of Our Time; and Bancroft's Memorial Address on Lincoln.

Of the northern convention at Baltimore? Of the Constitutional Union party? Whom did the Republicans nominate for President? State the *platform* of each nominee. Which party gained the election?

tion in November passed off quietly, and Lincoln was chosen President.

216. Abraham Lincoln was born in Hardin County, Kentucky, February 12, 1809. His ancestors, who were Quakers, came from Pennsylvania to Virginia, and thence to Kentucky. His father was a poor man, and the youth's life was one of hard labor and great privation. At the age of seventeen, Lincoln removed to Illinois. He studied law, and in time became state representative, and then congressman. His predominant qualities were patience, firmness, honesty, and magnanimity. He had great capacity for learning from passing events. He said the war educated him.

Abraham Lincoln.

217. When the result of the election was known, the cotton states at once prepared to carry into effect the threat which had frequently been made during the campaign—that if Lincoln were elected, they would secede from the Union. A disunion convention met at Columbia, South Carolina, on the 17th of December, at which it was unanimously resolved, "that it is the opinion of the convention that the state of South Carolina should forthwith secede from the Federal Union known as the United States of America." On the 20th, the ordinance of secession passed both houses

---

216. Sketch the life of Abraham Lincoln.

217. How was the news of Lincoln's election received in the South? What was the action of the Columbia convention?

of the legislature. The example of South Carolina was soon followed by Mississippi, Florida, Alabama, Georgia, Louisiana, and Texas. On the 4th of February, 1861, delegates from the seceded states met at Montgomery, Alabama, and organized a Southern Confederacy. Jefferson Davis,* of Mississippi, was chosen President of the new government; and Alexander H. Stephens, of Georgia, Vice President. Committees were appointed on foreign relations, finance, commerce, military and naval affairs, judiciary, and other important subjects. A Confederate flag was adopted also.

Jefferson Davis was born in Kentucky, in 1808, but had removed to Mississippi in his boyhood. He received a military education at West Point. He served in the Mexican war, and was afterwards United States senator. During the administration of President Pierce, he was Secretary of War.

218. Lincoln's inauguration took place without any disturbance, as General Scott had taken the fullest military precautions to insure quiet. The President's inaugural address was calm and dispassionate in tone. It concluded with an earnest appeal to the Secessionists not to precipitate civil war. On March 5, commissioners from the Confederate Congress arrived at Washington to open negotiations, and adjust questions growing out of the separation. William H. Seward,† Secretary of State, recognized the commissioners only as citizens of the United States, and assured them that there could be no separation or secession of any state, except through the agency of a national convention, in which all the states were represented. This was the view taken by the Federal Government throughout the strife — it never recognized the right of secession,

* See Pollard's and Alfriend's Life of Jefferson Davis.

† See Bartlett's Modern Agitators; and Baker's Works of Seward.

What states followed the example of South Carolina? What organization did the seceded states form? Whom did they choose for President?

218. How did Seward answer the commissioners from the Confederate States?

and always considered that the states in rebellion were part of the Union even when unrepresented in Congress, and in arms against her powers.

219. We are now about to enter upon the history of the War of Secession. The causes of this war will be apparent to the student who carefully considers the events unfolded in preceding chapters of this book. The election of Lincoln was the occasion, not the cause, of the rupture between the North and the South. Many things contributed to array the two sections in rivalry against each other, and to develop in each interests, opinions, politics, customs, and institutions antagonistic to those of the other. Climate fostered this diversity. The laws of migration favored it. Long ago the manufacturing interests of New England came in conflict with the agricultural interests of the South; hence the bitter opposition of the South to the tariff.

William H. Seward.

Slavery, as we have seen, existed for a time in all the colonies. In the North, it was gradually given up, partly because slave labor could not be profitably employed, partly because of conscientious scruples. Many of the people in the South thought slavery to be the proper condition of the black man. The culture of the great southern staples — tobacco, rice, sugar-cane, and especially cotton — made the employment of slave labor exceeding-

219. State the causes of the civil war.

ly profitable. It was, indeed, the chief means of wealth. The Calhoun doctrine of state rights grew with the growth of the Southerners, and was bone of their bone. They honestly believed that they owed allegiance first to their own state, then to the United States. The principle of absolute state rights applied to the maintenance of slavery led to disunion.

From the time of the adoption of the Federal Constitution forward the subject of slavery was agitated. After the War of 1812, it became a subject of very frequent discussion, especially by the political press. The Missouri Compromise was thought to have averted disunion. The annexation of Texas and the Mexican war were events mainly growing out of slavery. The debate on the admission of California to the Union without slavery almost led to war; that on the admission of Kansas *did* bring local war. In the presidential campaign of 1856, the two great political parties were definitely opposed to each other on the slavery question. The tide of emigration from Europe to the North gave that section the ascendency; and the South could not compete with her in settling new territories. The slave states saw the growing preponderance of the free states, and knew that if they did not stop or equal such rapid growth, their power at Washington, and the institution of slavery at home would be in danger of extinction.

The Kansas war, the John Brown raid, the split of the Democratic party, the triumph of the Republicans, only served to fan into full blaze a fire that had been smoldering for years. The South, anticipating war, had prepared for it. During Buchanan's administration, the southern leaders had seized nearly all the custom-houses, forts, arsenals, ships, and army stores within their borders. They had also organized and trained their militia for action. A large quantity of arms and munitions had been quietly collected for the probable emergency of war.

The Secessionists saw the vast importance of securing

What preparation had the South made for probable war?

Virginia, and the other slave states which had not yet thrown off allegiance to the Union, as members of the Southern Confederacy. Something had to be done to precipitate hostilities. "I will tell you," said Roger A. Pryor, of Virginia, in a speech at Charleston, "what will put Virginia in the Southern Confederacy in less than an hour—*strike a blow!* The very moment that blood is shed, Virginia will make common cause with her sisters of the South. It is impossible that she should do otherwise." South Carolina had initiated disunion, and therefore it was fit that she should strike the first blow of the war. On April 10th, 1861, P. G. T. Beauregard (bō′re-gard′), general commanding at Charleston, received orders from the Confederate Secretary of War to demand the surrender of Fort Sumter, and, in case of refusal, to reduce it.

Jefferson Davis.

Sumter was one of the few southern posts which had not yet been seized by the Confederates. It was under command of Major Robert Anderson. The surrender of the fort was demanded on the 11th, and declined. Again, on the same day, Beauregard made another demand, to which Major Anderson replied, that, if unmolested, he

---

What state struck the first blow in the war? What occurred at Charleston, April 10, 1861? Who was Beauregard? Where is Fort Sumter? Who was in command of it at this time? What did Beauregard do on the 11th? How did Anderson reply? What message did Anderson receive on the 12th?

would evacuate the fort at noon on the 15th, should he not receive, prior to that time, controlling instructions from his government or additional supplies. A peaceful departure was not what was thought politic. The Confederates wished to commit themselves, and at twenty minutes past three o'clock on the morning of April 12, 1861, Major Anderson was notified that fire would be opened on the fort in an hour.

GENERAL QUESTIONS AND DIRECTIONS.

Prepare a chronological table of the dated events given in this chapter. Compile a sketch of the life of Fillmore. Of Pierce. Of J. P. Hale. Of Douglas. Of Buchanan. Of John Brown. Of Lincoln. Of Davis. Of Seward. Of A. H. Stephens. Give the history of the Federalist party. Of the Whig party. Of the Democratic party to the time of the Charleston convention. Of the Free-soil party. Give the history of slavery in the United States.

CHAPTER FIFTEENTH.

FROM THE BEGINNING OF THE WAR OF SECESSION TO THE PRESENT TIME.

1861—1872.

AT twenty minutes past four o'clock on the morning of April 12, **1861**, the first shot of the Civil War in America crashed against the solid granite wall of Fort Sumter. It was fired by Edmund Ruffin, of Virginia, a white-haired old man who had been a personal and political friend of Calhoun. The bombardment was continued, without intermission, for twelve hours, the garrison steadily returning the fire. At dark the firing from the fort almost ceased, but it was renewed early the next morning. Beauregard's batteries kept playing all night. The buildings in the fort were ignited by red-hot balls showered upon them, and the ammunition was in so much danger that all the powder but four barrels was thrown into the sea. Deprived of the means of defense, and unable to quench the spreading flames, Major Anderson at length displayed a signal of distress, and soon afterwards surrendered. No lives were lost on either side.

QUESTIONS.—**220.** Describe the bombardment of Fort Sumter. When did it occur?

The garrison, which numbered only about eighty men, marched out of Fort Sumter on Sunday morning, April 14, with drums beating and colors flying.

221. The Confederates had calculated that striking the first blow would precipitate affairs, and they were not mistaken. Virginia passed the ordinance of secession, April 17, three days after the evacuation of Sumter; Arkansas followed, May 6; North Carolina, May 20; and Tennessee, June 8; making, in all, eleven states in the Confederacy. Strong and well-nigh successful efforts were made to force Missouri out of the Federal Union. The legislature of Kentucky passed a resolution against both secession and abolition. Neither Delaware nor Maryland seceded, although they were slave-holding states.

The immediate effect of the news of Sumter's fall was to produce wild excitement. The Secessionists were jubilant. The Confederate banner of stars and bars was conspicuously displayed every-where in the South. Crowds collected in the towns and villages to hear enthusiastic speeches and to organize military companies. Bands of music paraded the streets of cities playing patriotic airs.

In the North, the excitement was even more intense. The people were aroused as if by an electric shock. The flag of the Union was unfurled from almost every building, public and private, in the free states. Throngs of men assembled about the newspaper offices by day and night, eager to hear every syllable of the telegraphic news. Immense meetings were held at which leading public men spoke eloquently of the momentous issue of the hour. The rostrum, the bar, the pulpit, the press, the merchants' exchange, the work-shop, and the farm had but one voice, and that was for instant redress by arms. Democrats and Republicans were fused into one glowing mass by the fire of the popular will.

222. On the 15th of April, President Lincoln issued a

---

221. Which of the slave states joined the Confederacy after the fall of Sumter? Give the date of the secession of each. What effect had the fall of Sumter in the North?

call for seventy-five thousand volunteers, and the levies were promptly filled. The northern states each freely furnished their quota of men and their proportion of money. No difficulty was experienced in collecting or supporting troops at the beginning of the war. The uprising of the people seemed spontaneous.

The Confederate Congress, soon after its organization, had passed an act calling for an army of one hundred thousand men. The southern people responded to the call with alacrity and ardor. They were willing to fight for the secession cause.

223. The limits of a school history will not permit even the mention of hundreds of the minor battles and skirmishes that took place during the great Civil War. Only the most important events are here recorded. Only vast military plans, decisive battles, and significant political acts receive particular attention. The principal outlines of the picture are traced; the student must fill in the details from more extended histories of the war.

The first blood of the war was shed on the 19th of April, **1861**, in the streets of Baltimore. The Sixth Massachusetts regiment, one of the first organized, was ordered to march directly to the national capital. Baltimore lay in the line of march, and as the soldiers filed through the streets of that city they were assailed by a mob full ten thousand strong, with sticks, stones, and pistols. At length the troops, in self-defense, fired at random into the crowd. The scene now became truly appalling. The fury of the mob increased, and the soldiers had to fight their way through the town. Three of them were killed outright. Nine of the citizens of Baltimore were killed, and many more were wounded.

224. The war now began in deadly earnest. The opening scenes of the terrible drama were enacted in Virginia. The militia of that state made haste to seize Harper's Ferry,

---

222. What is said of the great uprising of the northern people? How did the southern people respond to the call for troops?

223. Describe the conflict in the streets of Baltimore.

where there was a United States arsenal; but the officer in charge, anticipating an attack, had set fire to the buildings and destroyed most of the material. The Federal authorities at Norfolk, fearing a surprise, ordered the destruction of the vast property of the navy yard near that place. Many buildings were burned, and all the ships but one were fired and scuttled. Nevertheless, an immense quantity of shot, shell, and ordnance fell into the hands of the Confederates, who, as expected, made a rapid descent upon Norfolk. The loss of the government by the destruction of the navy yard and stores was estimated at ten million dollars. The possession of these two points was of great advantage to the Confederates.

These successes of the Virginia militia were considered preliminary to the capture of Washington City. The capital of a country represents the security, power, and dignity of the government; therefore, Washington was the great prize which the Secessionists hoped to seize, and which the Union army felt bound to protect and defend.

225. The levies from the free states began to pour into Washington by thousands. The veteran Winfield Scott had the direction of military affairs, under the President, who is commander-in-chief by virtue of his office. The Confederates put their army under the control of General Beauregard. Both sections labored under the delusion that the war would soon end, and without much bloodshed. It was believed in the North that the fear of a general slave insurrection would prevent the planters from leaving their homes.

Many southern men doubted whether the Yankees, as they commonly called their antagonists, could or would fight under any circumstances. Jefferson Davis thought that there would be no conflict of any moment. William H. Seward's frequent declaration that the war would certainly end in ninety days, went far to impair his reputation

---

224. What was done at Harper's Ferry? What at Norfolk? Why did the Confederates desire to seize Washington?

225. What commanders were put at the head of the respective armies? What opinions were held respecting the duration of the war?

as a wise and sagacious statesman. Colonel William T. Sherman* was laughed at and called crazy for his openly avowed opinion that there would be a long and sanguinary struggle, and that the number of Union forces ought to be greatly increased.

The rapid and determined aggressive movements of the Confederates had no appearance of paltering. The fact that Washington was threatened—nay, was in imminent peril—could not be ignored. Defenses were constructed on all sides of the city. Active preparations for war were every-where apparent from the long lines of bristling bayonets, the prevailing garb of army blue, and the inspiriting sound of martial music. A great majority of the troops of both armies were near the capital.

226. When Virginia went out of the Union, a convention was held at Wheeling, which proposed that the part of the state lying west of the Alleghanies should secede from the Confederacy and form a new commonwealth. This region was inhabited by hardy mountaineers, who had never owned many slaves, and whose sympathies were more with the North than with the South. Confederate troops poured in to prevent, and Union troops to secure, the desired separation. The curious spectacle was presented of a seceded state fighting against secession, and a nation at war on account of secession fighting to uphold it. The Union party was finally successful.

The contested region was eventually erected into a separate state, called West Virginia, which was formally admitted into the Union on the last day of December, 1862. During the summer of 1861, several battles were fought in Western Virginia, in which the Unionists were successful. An engagement of considerable importance at Big Bethel, in south-eastern Virginia, resulted in favor of the Confederates.

* See Bowman and Irwin's Sherman and his Campaigns.

What precautions were taken to secure the safety of the capital?

226. Relate the military and political events that transpired in West Virginia.

227. The first really great battle of the war was fought at Manassas Junction, a point on the railroad between Richmond and Washington, about thirty miles from the latter city. A branch road from the Shenandoah Valley joins the main trunk at Manassas. Here a large number of Confederate troops from all parts of the South were collected for the double purpose of shielding their own capital (which had been removed from Montgomery to Richmond) and of menacing Washington. Beauregard was in command. His entire force consisted of about twenty thousand men. The Confederate general, Joseph E. Johnston, lay at Winchester, about fifty miles distant, with an army of eight thousand.

---

227. Where is Manassas Junction? Locate Winchester on the map.

General Irwin McDowell commanded the Union forces in and about Washington. These consisted of about forty thousand men, most of them three months' volunteers, imperfectly drilled, and without experience in war. The military authorities decided that the army should advance and give battle to the enemy at Manassas. McDowell led his forces to the attack on Sunday morning, July 21, 1861. The roads from Washington to the scene of action were crowded with carriages full of people anxious to witness the coming fight, or at least to rejoice in the victory which they felt confident would crown the Union arms. The Confederate lines were eight miles long, west of the creek of Bull Run.

At nine o'clock the battle began. The fighting was fierce and terrible. After a time the Confederate line gave way, and was driven back a mile and a half to a high plateau. On this vantage ground the retreating troops turned at bay. There they were supported by a brave man whom the war made famous. This was General Thomas J. Jackson.* He had been stationed on the plateau with five regiments as a reserve. In rallying the retreating troops, General Bee shouted: "See, there's Jackson standing like a stone wall!" The name Stonewall ever after clung to Jackson, who was regarded

Stonewall Jackson.

* See Dabney's Life of Stonewall Jackson.

When was the battle of Bull Run fought? What forces were engaged?

by friends and enemies as not only a brave and able general, but also as a noble and pure-minded man. His resolute stand checked the advance of the Union soldiers. Again the struggle became furious. The ground was wet with carnage. At three o'clock in the afternoon, the fortunes of the Confederates were at the worst; but the Union troops were becoming exhausted. The day was one of the hottest in the year. Victory seemed within McDowell's grasp, when suddenly eight thousand fresh Confederate troops arrived upon the field. These were Johnston's men from Winchester. They were led by General Kirby Smith. They struck the Union line with such force that it recoiled, broke, and scattered in confusion. The battle was ended; and a long line of fugitive foot soldiers, artillery, carriages of spectators, cavalry, and camp followers fled in panic toward Washington. McDowell, seeing that all was lost, placed a rear guard of United States regulars to check the enemy, and the dismayed rout of soldiers and citizens swept on to the capital unharmed.

The results which flowed from the battle of Bull Run were more important than the battle itself. The number slain was not so great as in many subsequent actions. The Confederate loss was 378 killed, 1,489 wounded, and 80 missing. The total Union loss was about 3,000 men, 28 guns, and 6,000 muskets.

Both sections learned that the war would not terminate in sixty or ninety days, but would probably be long and bloody. The South, while victory gave her confidence, no longer doubted that the Yankees would fight. The North was taught, by humiliating experience, that an effective army was something different from an assemblage of brave men with blue coats and muskets. It was obvious that trained soldiers were wanted, and to prepare these time and systematic drilling were requisite. The Army of the Potomac was placed under the command of General George

---

Describe the engagement. What generals were in command? How did the battle end? What were the losses on each side? How did this fight affect the South? How did it affect the North?

B. McClellan, a most excellent organizer; and, until April, 1862, nothing of importance was done except to drill and practice the various military evolutions that the exigencies of actual service require. By the end of the year the forces were vastly increased. They numbered one hundred and fifty thousand men.

228. The war in 1861 was not confined to Virginia. The state of Missouri was prevented from seceding only by the most determined and persistent fighting. The governor of Missouri called out the state militia to resist the Union soldiers. Confederate troops came up from Arkansas and Texas to aid their friends. The exertions of General Nathaniel Lyon and Colonel Franz Sigel effected much for the Union cause; and, before the end of the year, the Confederate army was ejected from Missouri.

229. At the beginning of the war, President Lincoln issued a proclamation declaring the ports south of Maryland to be in a state of blockade. Stout frigates, swift steamers, and light gun-boats kept watch about the designated ports, increasing in number and vigilance, until the South was nearly deprived of intercourse with the rest of the world. The navy of the United States had a gigantic task to perform, but accomplished it most effectually. All the ports of a shore line longer than the entire distance round the globe, were almost hermetically closed. The rapid development of the naval resources of the Union was one of the astonishing phenomena of the war. In March, 1861, the number of vessels in the navy was but 42; in December, 1864, it was 671. There was not a single armed vessel in the Union service, on our great rivers, at the opening of the contest; at its close there were more than one hundred.

In 1861, two expeditions were fitted out, one of which took the forts at Hatteras Inlet; the other, after a three

---

Who took command of the Union army? What was done by it?

228. What military operations occurred in Missouri in 1861?

229. What is said of naval operations? What of the growth of the navy?

hours' fight, captured forts Walker and Beauregard, at the entrance of Port Royal Harbor. These expeditions inspired a terror of gun-boats in the South, and considerably encouraged the North. The Confederates organized no regular navy; but they fitted out a number of privateers, some of which rendered them essential aid.

In November, Captain Charles Wilkes took from the English steam-packet, Trent, J. M. Mason and J. Slidell, who had been dispatched as Confederate commissioners to the British and French governments. This was resented by the British authorities, who threatened to declare war against the United States. Captain Wilkes's action was disavowed by government, and the commissioners were allowed to proceed on their journey. The South confidently expected recognition and aid from England and France; but those powers never openly acknowledged the Confederacy as an independent nation.

230. At the close of 1861, matters with the Union stood altogether on a firmer base than in the beginning of the year. The people had begun to recover from the state of depression into which they were thrown by the reverse at Bull Run. Trade and manufactures had revived. Washington was strongly fortified; Congress had voted five hundred million dollars for war purposes; and the army, mustering in all about 661,000 men, was in a condition to do effective service.

EVENTS OF 1862.

231. In the beginning of 1862, a Union army was gathering at Cairo, Illinois. The people of the north-west had determined that the Mississippi should be free to their

---

What forts were captured in 1861? How did the United States become involved in troubles with England? What did the Confederacy expect of France and England?

230. What was the state of feeling in the North at the close of 1861? What was the financial and military prospect?

231. Describe the situation of affairs in the West at the beginning of 1862.

boats from its source to the sea. The Confederates had but one direct line of railroad from the Mississippi eastward. This ran from Memphis to Chattanooga, where it forked, one branch running thence to Richmond, the other to Charleston. It was of vital importance to the Confederates, that the line from Memphis to Chattanooga should be kept in their hands, for on it they depended for nearly all their supplies and men from beyond the Mississippi and above Vicksburg; and if they lost it, they lost Kentucky and a great part of Tennessee. Hence, they made desperate efforts to retain it. To this end they constructed a chain of forts from Columbus, on the Mississippi, to Bowling Green, Kentucky, and about one hundred and fifty miles north of the railroad. These forts and the intervening lines were defended by sixty thousand men, under the command of General Albert S. Johnston. The most important points of defense were Fort Henry, on the Tennessee, and Fort Donelson, on the Cumberland.

232. General Halleck was in command of the Department of Missouri, which included western Kentucky, and to him belongs the praise of planning the advance on forts Henry and Donelson. Draper, in his History of the Civil War, relates that, "One evening Halleck, Sherman, and Cullum were conversing at the Planter's Hotel, in St. Louis, on the proper line of invasion. They saw clearly that the Confederates meant to stand on the defensive, and Halleck asked, 'Where is their line?' Sherman replied, 'Why, from Bowling Green to Columbus.' 'Well, then, where is the true point of attack?' 'Naturally, the center.' 'Then let us see what is the direction in which it should be made.' A map lay on the table, and, with a blue pencil, Halleck drew a line from Bowling Green to Columbus, past forts Donelson and Henry, and another per-

---

What was the great object of western military operations? Why was the railroad that ran from Memphis eastward important to the South? How was it defended?

232. Who was General Halleck? Relate the conversation of Halleck and Sherman as quoted from Draper.

pendicular to its center, which happened to coincide nearly with the Tennessee River. 'There,' said he, 'that is the true line of attack.'" On that line the attack was successfully made.

Halleck ordered General Ulysses S. Grant,* who commanded the forces at Cairo, to move on the enemy in co-operation with a fleet of seven gun-boats under Commodore A. A. Foote. Grant left Cairo, January 30, 1862, with an army of seventeen thousand men. The gunboats reduced Fort Henry in about an hour, February 6; but the greater part of the garrison escaped and fled to Fort Donelson. Grant's advance was greatly hindered by miry roads and bridgeless streams; but on the 12th of February he invested Fort Donelson with fifteen thousand troops. Foote's gunboats arrived on the 14th, made an attack, and were repulsed. At five o'clock on the morning of the 15th, a column of ten thousand sallied out of the fort and attempted to force their way through Grant's lines, with the design of escaping to Nashville. After a hard fight, they were driven back. Grant had been re-enforced until his numbers were swelled to twenty-seven thousand men under arms.

Ulysses S. Grant.

* See Badeau's Military History of General Grant; also works relating to Grant by Phelps, Headley, Richardson, Coppee, and Howland.

Who commanded the forces at Cairo? Where were forts Henry and Donelson? Describe their capture.

On the morning of the 16th, he was ready to renew the attack, when General Simon B. Buckner, commander at Donelson, hung out the white flag, and surrendered the fort with fifteen thousand men. The capture of Donelson, cost the Union 2,041 men, 425 of whom were killed. It was very important in its results, for the whole line of Confederate defenses was given up. Nashville was abandoned; Columbus was presently occupied by the Union troops; and the Mississippi was free as far as Island No. 10, which was also taken soon after.

233. After the fall of Fort Donelson, Halleck assigned Grant to the command of the new district of West Tennessee, and ordered him to strike Corinth, at the intersection of the Charleston & Memphis and the Mobile & Ohio Railroads. This was a point of great importance, as it controlled the great railway communications between the Mississippi and the East, and the border slave states and the Gulf of Mexico.

On the 14th of March, Grant arrived at Pittsburg Landing, on the west bank of the Tennessee, with a force thirty-five thousand strong. Disembarking, they went into camp at Shiloh meeting-house, two miles back from the river. At early dawn on Sunday, April 6, forty thousand Confederates, under General Albert S. Johnston and General Beauregard, dashed down upon Grant's encampment, taking it completely by surprise. The battle that ensued was a confused one on the part of the Union forces. Grant was eight miles away, and did not reach the field for several hours. The Confederates steadily drove the Union soldiers down the river. At five o'clock in the afternoon, affairs were at their worst—the army was much disorganized and fast becoming a wreck; but the staunchness of Grant and the energy of Sherman saved the day.

Night came on, and Beauregard, commander in the place

How many men were lost on each side? What did the Union gain by the capture of Fort Donelson?

233. Where is Corinth? Why was Grant sent against that place? Describe the battle of Pittsburg Landing.

of Johnston, who was mortally wounded, drew back his troops and resolved to finish the destruction of the Union army in the morning. But when the morning came he found himself confronted by a vastly increased force. General Buell, who had been making forced marches from Nashville, came up in the night, and the combined Union armies, fifty thousand in number, were advancing against an opposing army of but thirty thousand. Before sunrise, an attack was made by a part of the Union troops, and soon the engagement became general. The battle raged till four o'clock in the afternoon, when the Confederates, fairly beaten, gave way at all points, but in good order, and the field was won for the Union.

This battle was the bloodiest that had yet been fought on the continent. The Confederates lost nearly 11,000, and the Federals, 15,000. It lost to the South the Mississippi down as far as Vicksburg. Island No. 10, with a large force and many guns, was taken. Corinth was evacuated after a siege of several weeks. Fort Pillow yielded, and Memphis fell, after a short and brilliant attack upon the Confederate fleet which guarded that city. The Memphis Railroad was, of course, now held by the Union army; western Tennessee was reclaimed; and northern Mississippi and Alabama were brought under Federal supremacy.

234. So many men and gun-boats had been drawn toward Corinth, that New Orleans was drained; and when Commodore David G. Farragut,* on April 24, forced his way through rafts and chains, and blazing fire-ships, past forts, up to the city, he found no such determined opposition as he would have encountered had those who were with Beauregard been present. New Orleans surrendered. "It was," says Pollard, "a terrible disaster to the Confederacy. The fall of Donelson broke our center in the West. The fall of

* See J. T. Headley's Farragut and Our Naval Commanders.

How did it end? What noted officers were engaged in it? Were the losses severe? What advantages resulted to the Union from this battle?

234. When, by whom, and in what manner was New Orleans taken?

New Orleans yet more sorely punished the vanity of the Confederates; annihilated their power in Louisiana; broke up their routes to Texas and the gulf; closed their access to the richest grain and cattle country in the South; gave to the enemy a new base of operations; and, more than any thing else, staggered the confidence of Europe in the fortunes of the Confederacy."

235. After these successful operations, Buell, commanding the Army of the Cumberland, threatened Chattanooga; then marched rapidly to the defense of Louisville; and, on the 8th of October, fought the battle of Perrysville against General Braxton Bragg, of Mexican fame. In this action the Confederates were worsted, and Bragg retreated to Chattanooga. He afterwards took a strong position at Murfreesborough.

Buell was relieved of the command of the Union army by General Rosecrans, who advanced first to Nashville, and then to Murfreesborough, where, on the last day of 1862 and the first and second of 1863, he repulsed Bragg after one of the most destructive battles of the war. The Union army numbered forty-seven thousand; the Confederate thirty-five thousand; but the latter had by far the best cavalry. Rosecrans planned, as did Bragg, to attack with the left wing. Bragg was first on the field, and struck so fierce a blow that the right wing of Rosecrans nearly crumbled to pieces. One man with his division stayed the Confederate advance, and saved the Federal army. This man was General Philip H. Sheridan. Colonel W. B. Hazen also rendered the most effective service in this battle. But much as Sheridan and Hazen did, the success of the battle greatly depended upon Rosecrans, who never gave up, even when the army seemed going to wreck, but reformed and fought his soldiers in a new position. The Confeder-

---

Give the quotation from Pollard.

235. When, and by what forces was the battle of Perrysville fought? Whither did Bragg retreat? Who superseded Buell? When was the battle of Stone River fought? How many men were engaged? Describe the engagement. What noted officers took part? What were the losses?

ates contested the field with the most heroic valor. Their loss in the battle of Murfreesborough, or Stone River, as it is also called, was ten thousand. The Federal loss was about one half as much again.

The other army of the West (that commanded by Grant), after Corinth had been secured, undertook the great task of conquering Vicksburg, in order to further the prime object of western military ambition—the opening of the Mississippi. In fact, nearly all the Union troops west of the Alleghanies were for a time either directly or indirectly working to accomplish the object mentioned. There remained no Confederate town or fort on the Mississippi, from Cairo to New Orleans, but Vicksburg, and its outpost, Port Hudson.

After the fall of New Orleans, Farragut's gun-boats made an ineffectual assault on Vicksburg, from the south. They retired after a great waste of ammunition. Toward the end of the year 1862, Grant marched on Vicksburg, and found the Confederate line two hundred miles north of the city, on the Tallahatchie River. Grant threatened to cut off the railroad in the rear of the enemy; and the Confederate general, John C. Pemberton, hastily retired with twenty-five thousand men to Granada, one hundred miles south of Grand Junction, the point where the railroad south from Memphis joins the Mississippi Central.

Grant pursued and made a depot for provisions and war materials at Holly Springs. His intention was to follow southward until he came to the rear of Vicksburg, but his plans were foiled by the capture of this grand depot at Holly Springs, by General Van Dorn, and the destruction of the supplies there. The value of the lost stores was estimated at more than four million dollars. This was a heavy blow to Grant, and compelled him to leave all the advantages he had gained and to fall back to Holly Springs.

What was done by Grant's army after the fall of Corinth? Where is Vicksburg? What general commanded at Vicksburg? What disaster did Grant suffer at Holly Springs?

Sherman, with forty thousand men, had gone down the Mississippi, and disembarked thirteen miles above Vicksburg to take the fortifications on the Yazoo. An attack was made on Haines's Bluff; but the repulse was so bloody, that, after a loss of nineteen hundred and twenty-nine men in a very short time, Sherman became convinced that the works could not be captured by direct assault; and so the whole scheme for taking Vicksburg failed on the part of both Grant and Sherman. The army, during January, 1863, was transferred to Milliken's Bend, twelve miles above Vicksburg, on the west side of the river.

236. While these events transpired in the West, the Army of the Potomac was not idle. Late in January, the President ordered a general advance of the Union armies to be made on or before February 22, 1862. In compliance with this order, McClellan moved forward on the 14th of March. He led the army to the Confederate camp at Manassas, and found no enemy there. The Confederates, now under the command of General J. E. Johnston, had retired toward Richmond. McClellan's army went back to Alexandria, and there em-

General J. E. Johnston.

What attempts did Sherman make to approach Vicksburg? What did Grant and Sherman do after this? Why was it desirable to possess Vicksburg?

236. What was the first movement of the Army of the Potomac in 1862?

barked for Fortress Monroe, on the peninsula formed by the James River and the York.

Early in March, 1862, a very remarkable naval battle was fought in Hampton Roads, the results of which were most important. The old United States frigate Merrimac, sunk at Norfolk navy yard at the beginning of the war, had been raised by the Confederates, her sides cut down to the water's edge, and a novel structure heavily cased with railroad iron built upon the hull. Her armament consisted of ten large rifled cannon. A little before noon, March 8, this strange craft, "looking like the roof of an immense building sunk to the eaves," and accompanied by several armed boats, was seen by the Union frigate Congress and the sloop of war Cumberland. The frigates Minnesota, Roanoke, and St. Lawrence, six miles away, at Fortress Monroe, were signaled, and attempted to join the Congress and Cumberland.

As the Merrimac came on she received the fire of the Congress, but held her way uninjured and unchecked. She struck the Cumberland with her iron beak, making a great hole, into which the water rushed, sinking the vessel. All on board the Cumberland remained at their posts to the last, and, firing a broadside, she went down with her flag still waving. The Congress ran ashore to avoid being sunk by the Merrimac, which raked her with heavy shells, and at length set her on fire, so that she was compelled to haul down her flag. Then the iron monster turned her attention to the other vessels, but could not strike them on account of the shallowness of the water. At seven o'clock in the evening, she steamed back to Norfolk, designing to return the next day and finish the ruin she had begun.

Strange and destructive as was this monster craft, a little vessel arrived at Fortress Monroe on the evening after the fight, still stranger in appearance. This was the Monitor. She came from New York, after two days' sail. At Fortress Monroe all shook their heads and wondered that such

---

Where is Fortress Monroe? What is the peninsula? Describe the Merrimac.

an insignificant looking thing should dare to meet the Merrimac. When the Confederates first saw the Monitor, they called her a "Yankee cheese-box on a plank." But this "cheese-box," revolving by means of machinery shielded by thick plates of iron, and worked by steam-power below the water-line, contained within its iron circle two guns of great weight, throwing eleven-inch balls.

Early Sabbath morning, March 9, the look-out on the grounded Minnesota saw the Merrimac looming up through the mist as she drew near. The Monitor was signaled. She hove anchor, and prepared for fight. As the Merrimac came sternly on to destroy the Minnesota, the Monitor steamed out and lay athwart her path. The Merrimac veered round and let fly a broadside against her audacious opposer. The heavy shot glanced harmlessly off the rounded turret. From eight o'clock till twelve, the vessels fought. Finally, one of the Monitor's shot, hitting a weak spot, caused the Merrimac to leak. The Merrimac now avoided her antagonist, and set the Minnesota on fire by a shell, but again the Monitor interposed. The huge ironclad, as if enraged, now dashed straight at the Monitor to sink her; but, though the shock was great, it did no harm. A few more shots against the Merrimac's sides determined her to withdraw from the combat. She hauled off and returned to Norfolk for repairs.

She was called the Virginia by the Confederates, and was blown up by them on the 11th of May, at which time Norfolk was surrendered to the Union soldiers. The victory of the Monitor changed the dismal forebodings of the North to exultation. Almost before the echoes of the cannon had died away, contracts were made for the construction of a squadron of monitors, which, when done, speedily patrolled the Atlantic coast, and were able to destroy any fleet of wooden vessels in the world. The invention of the Monitor, which has revolutionized naval warfare, is due to the genius of John Ericsson, a Swede.

Describe the Monitor. The combat of these vessels. What effect had this upon the minds of the people? Who invented the Monitor?

237. On April 1, 1862, General McClellan, with over one hundred and twenty-one thousand men, superbly appointed, began to move toward Richmond from Fortress Monroe. He spent about a month preparing to reduce Yorktown, which place was evacuated without a fight, on the 3d of May. There were in Virginia three other Union armies, under the respective commands of Fremont, Banks, and McDowell. General J. E. Johnston, the Confederate commander-in-chief, knew that it was the purpose of the Federals to combine McDowell's forces, some forty thousand strong, with those of McClellan, in order to swell the numbers of the already vast army that threatened Richmond. To prevent this combination, Johnston ordered Stonewall Jackson to attack the forces in the Shenandoah Valley. Jackson made a rapid march, drove a portion of Fremont's army back into West Virginia, and, defeating Banks at Winchester, forced him to retreat to the Potomac.

Alarmed at Jackson's approach, the authorities at Washington countermanded the order for McDowell to join McClellan, and instructed him to re-enforce Banks. Jackson, having neutralized sixty thousand men, hastened back to the upper part of the Shenandoah Valley, hotly pursued by the forces of Fremont, Banks, and McDowell. He escaped after sharp contests at Cross Keys and Port Republic, June 8th and 9th, and presently joined the army before Richmond.

McClellan pushed on from Yorktown toward Richmond. On the 5th of May, he encountered and repulsed a portion of the Confederate forces at Williamsburg. By the 20th of May, the Union forces had taken position about nine miles from Richmond, on the Chickahominy, a miry and sluggish stream. Three corps were placed on the south, or Richmond side of the river. These latter came into collision with the Confederates at Fair Oaks, or Seven Pines, on

---

237. What was the size of McClellan's army? How was the army employed during April, 1862? What armies were in Virginia besides McClellan's? Describe Jackson's expedition to the Shenandoah Valley. What was effected by it? What battle occurred on the 5th of May? Describe the Chickahominy.

the 31st of May. Both armies fought with the most determined courage. The battle was renewed on the 1st of June. It was not decisive, and both sides claimed the victory.

General Robert E. Lee.

The aggregate loss was about seven thousand on each side. General Johnston was seriously wounded, and the command of the Confederate army passed into the hands of General Robert E. Lee, who retained it until the close of the war. Lee was a son of the gallant Light-horse Harry Lee, of Revolutionary fame. He was regarded as one of the best, if not the best, of the southern generals. During the month of June, while preparations were made to assault Richmond, the Confederates busied themselves constructing strong fortifications, so that a small part of the army could defend the city while the rest might operate against the enemy in open field.

238. When Jackson returned from his raid, he hastened to join the Confederate forces on the north side of the Chickahominy. Without waiting for his aid, Lee gave battle to McClellan's right wing on the 26th day of June, at Mechanicsville. The Confederates were beaten back

---

When, where, by what forces, and with what result was the battle of Fair Oaks fought? What change of command was made in the Confederate army? Why? How were the Confederates employed after the battle?

238. When, and with what results was the battle of Mechanicsville fought?

with fearful carnage. Nevertheless, a general attack was renewed the next day, when the battle of Gaines's Farm took place. McClellan's forces were pushed to the Chickahominy river; and they presently crossed to the south side.

Lee got possession of McClellan's communications with White House, near West Point, the supply station of the Federals, and McClellan was obliged to change his base. Holding the enemy in check with a strong rear guard, he moved southward toward James River. The retreat was pronounced well conducted, but its progress was marked by a series of terrible battles. The first of these was the battle of Savage's Station, fought June 29; the second, the fierce battle of Glendale, or Frazier's Farm, fought June 30; the third, the battle of Malvern Hill, fought on July 1. In this last fight, which was furious and destructive in the extreme, the Union army gained a decisive victory. The Confederates gave over the pursuit. McClellan posted his army at Harrison's Landing, opposite City Point, and remained inactive. The aggregate loss of the Federals, in the seven days fight before Richmond, was fifteen thousand. The Confederates lost perhaps twenty thousand; but they saved their capital.

239. On the 11th of July, 1862, General Halleck was appointed commander-in-chief of the United States armies. The forces scattered over northern Virginia were gathered into one body under command of General John Pope. Lee, from his position between McClellan and Pope, saw the advantage of being able to strike at either. The indomitable Jackson was sent against Pope to hold him in check. When this became known to the Federal authorities, McClellan was ordered to embark his army forthwith at Harrison's Landing, and hasten to Washington. No sooner had McClellan commenced removing his troops

---

The battle of Gaines's Farm? What series of battles followed this? Where was the last one fought? Why did McClellan retreat? Give the aggregate losses of the two armies.

239. State the position of the armies after the peninsula campaign. What object had Lee in sending Jackson against Pope? What effect had Jackson's movement on McClellan's army?

than Lee learned it, and resolved to advance with all his force against Pope.

On the 9th of August, the Confederates encountered that portion of Pope's army which was under the command of Banks, at Cedar Mountain. In the battle that ensued, the Federals were defeated and driven back. Jackson now hurried onward to cut the railroad between Pope's army and Washington. He reached Manassas and captured a vast depot of stores of all descriptions without even a skirmish. Lee's whole army came up, and, on August 29 and 30, engaged Pope's forces in the bloody Second Battle of Bull Run. The Federals were swept in disastrous rout off the field. Lee pursued for two days.

Another fight took place on September 2, known as the battle of Chantilly, in which the Confederates were checked. Night closed the battle; and on the next day the broken and demoralized army of the Federals was drawn within the fortifications of Washington. Pope's loss during the campaign was not less than thirty thousand men, many of whom were stragglers and deserters. He was relieved of the command at his own request, and McClellan was placed at the head of the troops at the capital.

On the night of the battle of Chantilly, Lee formed the daring resolution of invading Maryland, and on the 4th day of September he crossed the Potomac with three army corps, commanded by generals Jackson, Longstreet, and Hill. On the 6th, the ubiquitous "Stonewall" was riding at the head of his dusty columns through the streets of Frederick. Here he was instructed by Lee to march directly to Harper's Ferry; and, in the meanwhile, Longstreet and Hill were to hold McClellan's advance in check. Lee's plan of march fell into McClellan's hands at Frederick, thus enabling him to direct his movements with promptness. Being too closely pressed, the Confederates

---

What did Lee now do? Give an account of Jackson's operations. When did the Second Battle of Bull Run occur? How did it end? What took place afterwards? What was Pope's entire loss in the campaign? When and with what forces did Lee invade Maryland? What enterprise was intrusted to Stonewall Jackson? How was it accomplished?

made a stand, on the 14th, at Boonesborough Gap, or South Mountain. They were defeated; and next day Lee retreated across the mountain. But time had been saved for Jackson to capture Harper's Ferry, which place surrendered on the same day that the battle of South Mountain was fought. Twelve thousand prisoners, as many stand of arms, seventy-three pieces of artillery, and over two hundred wagons fell into Jackson's hands.

On the 15th, Lee again turned at bay in the beautiful valley of Antietam, and there resolved to endeavor to beat back his pursuers while he concentrated his army. He had at the time but forty thousand soldiers, while McClellan was pressing on with an army not far from ninety thousand strong. Jackson, however, by forced marches from Harper's Ferry, re-joined Lee on the 16th, with his gallant corps of about five thousand men; and other re-enforcements coming up next day, the Confederate army numbered in all, perhaps, sixty thousand men. The terrific battle of Sharpsburg, or Antietam, commenced at dawn on the morning of the 17th, and continued for fourteen dreadful hours. Five hundred pieces of artillery were engaged. McClellan's loss was over twelve thousand; that of Lee much greater. The result was indecisive.

On the night of the next day, the Confederates quietly re-crossed the Potomac into Virginia. The moral effect of this great battle was favorable to the North, and injurious to the reputation of Lee. The Confederates were taught that they could gain nothing by invasion. Their total loss from the time they crossed into Maryland until the end of the battle of Antietam is estimated at thirty thousand men.

240. There was an event at this juncture greater and of more lasting importance than many battles. Repeated disasters had prepared the people of the North for the radical policy of striking the Confederates a paralyzing blow by destroying slavery. "I made a solemn vow be-

---

When was the battle of South Mountain fought? With what result? Describe the battle of Antietam. How did it end, and what were its moral effects?

fore God," said the President, "that if General Lee was driven back from Maryland, I would crown the result by the declaration of freedom to the slaves." On September 22, 1862, Lincoln issued his celebrated Emancipation Proclamation, in which it was declared that on the first day of January, 1863, "all persons held as slaves within any state or designated part of a state, the people whereof shall be in rebellion against the United States, shall be then, thenceforward, and forever free."

241. After the battle of Antietam, General McClellan stood still, receiving re-enforcements until he had one hundred and fifty thousand men. General Halleck repeatedly sent him orders to advance; but these orders were disregarded. At length, after six long weeks of delay, McClellan moved down to Manassas, where, on November 7, he was relieved and ordered to turn his command over to General Ambrose Burnside. Burnside, believing that the direct line from Washington was the one on which to attack Richmond, changed the base of the army to the north bank of the Rappahannock, opposite to Fredericksburg.

"On to Richmond" was now the popular cry throughout the North. The Federals threw pontoon bridges across the Rappahannock, and, on the 12th of December, crossed over to Fredericksburg. They were a hundred thousand strong. Lee's army, numbering about eighty thousand, was strongly intrenched on the bluffs and hills back of the city. On the morning of the 13th, Burnside ordered his men to attack. They did so, but only to be repulsed with horrible slaughter. The Union loss in the battle of Fredericksburg was over thirteen thousand, being nearly three times as great as the loss of the Confederates. The Army of the Potomac presently returned to the north side of the Rappahannock.

---

240. What is said of Lincoln's Emancipation Proclamation?

241. What was done by the Union army this fall before Burnside took command? What was Burnside's plan of taking Richmond? Describe the battle of Fredericksburg.

EVENTS OF 1863.

242. Burnside resigned, January 26, 1863, and General Hooker was put in command. The troops were in a very disorganized condition, and about three months were consumed in preparing them to renew hostilities. Many disapproved of the Emancipation Proclamation. At one time, as shown by the Congressional Inquiry into the state of the war, two hundred men were deserting each day. Nearly three thousand commissioned officers and eighty-two thousand privates were reported absent.

By the middle of April, Hooker was ready for an advance. His army was then one hundred and twenty thousand strong. Lee's forces were not half so numerous. Hooker crossed the Rappahannock, and succeeded in reaching the rear of Lee's army with about seventy thousand men, having detached a part of his troops to make a feint on Lee's right. He halted at Chancellorsville, some ten miles from Fredericksburg. Here he was met by Lee and thoroughly beaten in a great battle, fought on the 2d and 3d of May, 1863. The Union loss was seventeen thousand men. Lee lost about thirteen thousand men; but he compelled his antagonist to recross the Rappahannock. In this battle, Stonewall Jackson was accidentally shot by his own men. The loss of this brave and efficient officer was deeply felt throughout the Confederacy.

243. The Union cause in the East seemed to have fallen on evil days. Almost every important movement had failed. The Army of the Potomac, after two such defeats as at Fredericksburg and Chancellorsville, was fast becoming demoralized. On the other hand, the Confederate cause seemed prosperous. Lee, with a victorious and self-confident army lately much re-enforced, boldly crossed the Po-

---

242. Who succeeded Burnside in the command of the eastern army? What was the condition of the troops? When did Hooker move? Where did he encounter the enemy? What was the result of the battle? What noted man was killed?

243. When did Lee make his second invasion?

tomac into Maryland, on the 26th of June, and marched through that state into Pennsylvania.

The wildest excitement seized upon the northern people. Hooker was ordered to repel the invaders at any cost. He demanded the soldiers that Halleck had placed at Harper's Ferry. Halleck refused to comply with the demand. Hooker resigned, and on the same day, June 28, General G. G. Meade was appointed in his stead. The Union army, equal in numbers to the opposing one, but not so in experience or in prestige, marched northward to intercept the enemy. The armies met at Gettysburg, Pennsylvania. Here, on the 1st, 2d, and 3d of July, 1863, the greatest and most important battle of the whole war was fought. The fury of the third day's engagement is indescribable. Whole brigades were almost utterly destroyed. The slope of Cemetery Hill, upon which the hardest struggle occurred, was literally heaped with the slain. The loss of the Unionists was twenty-three thousand; that of the Confederates, thirty thousand. Both sides fought with desperate determination, but the Confederates were finally overcome.

The possibility that the Secession cause could triumph was entirely destroyed by the Union victory on the field of Gettysburg. Lee retreated, and, on the 13th, once more crossed the Potomac into Virginia, having lost sixty thousand men in seventeen days.

244. We now resume the narration of events in the West. After the battle of Murfreesborough, the army under Rosecrans did not move until June 25, 1863. It did not then rest until it had gained, by some brilliant movements, the entire state of Tennessee, with the mountain fastness of Chattanooga. This point, very important on account of its railroad connections and nearness

---

What effect did his appearance in Pennsylvania produce? When and why did Hooker resign? Who succeeded him? Give an account of the great battle of Gettysburg.

244. When did the army of Rosecrans move from Murfreesborough? What did it accomplish?

to the passes through the mountains, was ever afterward firmly held for the Union. The Confederates, under General Bragg, had retreated to the heights south of Chattanooga. Here they received re-enforcements, and turned at bay in the valley of the Chickamauga. A battle ensued on the 19th and 20th of September, in which Rosecrans was defeated, and the town and the army were saved only by the masterly soldiership of General George H. Thomas. After the battle, Rosecrans took refuge in Chattanooga, where he was besieged for two months by General Bragg. His supplies were cut off, and his soldiers were threatened with starvation.

General George H. Thomas.

245. It has already been related that the other army of the West was transferred to Milliken's Bend, in January, in furtherance of Grant's designs upon Vicksburg. Various expedients were tried in February and March to capture that city, but without success. Finally, the Union army marched down the west bank and crossed the river below Grand Gulf. It then swung loose from its base, and, after a series of rapid marches and telling victories, gained the rear of Vicksburg in eighteen days. The railroad was destroyed, and Pemberton, with nearly thirty thousand men, was driven back and securely fastened up in the town, which was then closely besieged. On the 4th of

---

When and where was it defeated? Where is Chattanooga?
245. Recount Grant's operations against Vicksburg.

July, 1863, Pemberton surrendered, and Grant received the paroles of twenty-seven thousand Confederates.

Port Hudson yielded to Banks as soon as its commander learned of the capture of Vicksburg; and thus, after two years of bloody battle and weary siege, the men of the north-west made good their vow, for the Mississippi, the great artery of the continent, was open to the sea, and the Confederacy was rent in twain. After this no battle of great importance was fought in the central valley.

Grant was promoted to the command of the Division of the Mississippi, which comprised three departments—that of the Tennessee, under Sherman; of the Cumberland, under Thomas; and of the Ohio, under Burnside. Rosecrans was relieved of his command, October 16.

246. Vicksburg having fallen, the next object of prime importance was to defeat Bragg, and relieve the Federal soldiers shut up in Chattanooga. The Union armies of the West were combined and also strengthened by the addition of Hooker's corps, twenty-three thousand strong, from the Army of the Potomac. Grant's whole force at the opening of the fall campaign was about eighty thousand. The Confederate army under Bragg numbered about sixty thousand, and held positions of great strength extending from the summit of Missionary Ridge to that of Lookout Mountain. On the night of November 23, Sherman occupied the northern end of Missionary Ridge; and Hooker, by 12 o'clock on the 24th, had stormed and carried Lookout Mountain, fighting above the clouds. Descending the eastern slope next morning at break of day, Hooker swept across the Chattanooga Valley; while Sherman advanced so vigorously that Bragg thrust forward all his available troops to check him.

When did Pemberton surrender? How did the capture of Vicksburg greatly aid the Union cause? How was the western army divided and commanded in the autumn of 1863?

246. What was Grant's entire force in October? Whence had he obtained re-enforcements? How large was the opposing army? Where was it stationed? What was accomplished on the 23d of November? By whom? On the 24th? By whom? On the 25th?

While these movements of both wings were going on, Grant stood on Orchard Knob, an isolated hill that commanded a clear view of the battle. He saw that the critical moment had come, and ordered his center, under Thomas, to move forward and take the rifle-pits at the foot of Missionary Ridge. Sheridan's and Wood's division advanced, took the rifle-pits, and then, without halting to reform, without any orders or any regular lines, they dashed up the steep hill—privates, captains, colonels, generals—all together. They gained the crest, wheeled round the cannon there, fired them on their late owners, who fled with precipitation, pursued by the flushed victors. The day was won, the Chattanooga campaign was ended, and Bragg was in rapid retreat southward. The Union losses amounted to five thousand; the Confederate, to ten thousand. Bragg was removed, and his command was given to General J. E. Johnston. After the battle of Chattanooga, Sherman was sent to the relief of Knoxville, where Burnside had been besieged by a detachment of Bragg's army under Longstreet.

EVENTS OF 1864-65.

247. From January 1, 1864, until May 5, there was no important movement in either army. On the 3d of March, Grant was appointed Lieutenant General of the Armies of the United States. This rank had been borne by only two men—George Washington and Winfield Scott. As soon as Grant received the order which placed him in command of all the armies, he summoned Sherman to meet him at Nashville for consultation. The two went to Cincinnati together, and in a few days a plan of operations was mapped out. The plan was to let go every thing unimportant, and to strike directly at the principal armies of the enemy. There were two of these—Lee's, in Virginia;

What was the result of the campaign? What were the losses?

247. To what position was Grant promoted in March, 1864? What was his first act after receiving his appointment? What plan of operations was decided upon?

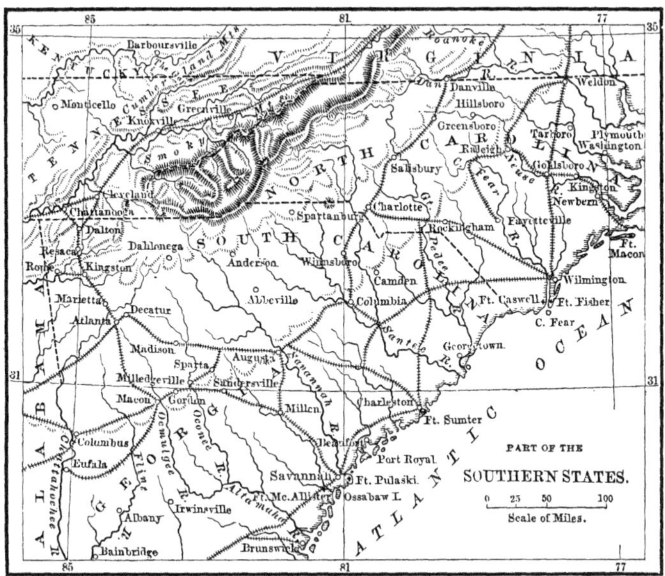

PART OF THE SOUTHERN STATES.

and Johnston's, in Georgia. Each army had a vital point to defend. Lee aimed to guard Richmond; Johnston, to protect Atlanta, the great military store-house and manufactory of the South. In a letter to Sherman, dated April 14, Grant says: "My directions would be, if the enemy in your front shows signs of joining Lee, follow him up to the extent of your ability. I will prevent the concentration of Lee upon your front, if it is in the power of this army to do it."

So from henceforward there are but two campaigns to chronicle—that of Sherman in the West, and that of Grant in the East. Both armies were to act in unison, for previously, as Grant said, "the armies in the East and West acted independently and without concert, like a balky team, no two pulling together.". The Lieutenant General joined the army of the Potomac, and, having crossed the Rapidan,

---

What two points did the Confederates aim to defend? What instructions did Sherman receive on April 14?

he telegraphed to Sherman, May 4, directing him to advance at once against Johnston, who was lying at Dalton with about 45,000 veterans.

248. Sherman's three armies—the Cumberland, led by Thomas; the Tennessee, by McPherson; and the Ohio, by Schofield—numbered altogether 98,000 men, with 254 guns. They immediately began a march memorable both for its extreme length and for the victories which marked its progress. Their desolating career could be traced along a broad belt of the fairest region of the South, by ruined towns, abandoned intrenchments, and blackened chimneys standing amid the ashes of once pleasant country homes.

Sherman's desire, when he rode out of Chattanooga, May 7, 1864, was to fall upon Johnston and crush him by superior numbers in a great battle; but Johnston, a very able soldier, was too prudent to risk such an engagement. By a series of bold and rapid flank movements on Johnston's communications, Sherman forced him to abandon, in quick succession, all the strongholds along the line of railroad from Chattanooga to Atlanta. Although compelled to fall back, Johnston was watchful and circumspect. He gathered his forces so compactly around him, that, when directly assailed in the strong positions which he had selected and fortified, he always repulsed Sherman, and then, being flanked, steadily continued his retreat to Atlanta.

From May 7 to July 17, there were the same rapid flanking movements met by as rapid and clean retreats. Sherman himself bore testimony to the masterly manner in which this retreat was conducted.

It is said that the Atlanta campaign was fought by the skirmish line and won by the spade. This is partly true. The men thrown out to the extreme front were accustomed to construct temporary works, which saved the lives of thousands, and sometimes turned the tide of battle. When the skirmish line was ordered out, many of the men

---

248. What three armies did Sherman command? What was their combined force? What was Johnston's force? Give an account of the advance from Chattanooga to Atlanta.

carried forward rails and poles, and, seizing some easily defended position, built a low fence of these materials; then, under the protection of their comrades' rifles, some would throw up the earth on the outside, while others dug a like trench on the inside. This method of intrenchment is said to have been purely the invention of the privates. The loss of the Union army in the campaign from Chattanooga to Atlanta was about thirty thousand; that of the Confederates, about forty thousand, with over forty guns.

General W. T. Sherman.

The Confederate authorities were much dissatisfied with Johnston's conduct during the retreat, and when the army reached the fortifications around Atlanta, he was removed, and Hood, who was reputed a fighting general, was appointed to the command in his stead. Hood made a bold attempt to drive Sherman back in the battles of the 20th, 22d, and 28th of July, but was repulsed with a loss of nearly twenty thousand men. Sherman broke up his siege on the 25th of August, and moved by the right around Atlanta to destroy the railroads from the west and south. His movements were so successful that the western road was entirely destroyed for several miles. Hood, deceived by Sherman's movements, sent a part of his army to defend the railroad to Macon. Sherman slipped his force between

---

What was the loss of each army? Who was appointed to supersede Johnston at Atlanta?

the two halves of the Confederate army, and prepared to defeat them in detail. Hood now saw that the campaign was lost. He destroyed such ammunition and stores as could not be removed, and abandoned Atlanta on the night of September 1. Both armies were quiet for nearly a month. Hood then started on a disastrous expedition north. He drove Schofield's corps back before him until they reached Nashville. Here Thomas, whom Sherman had sent northward, had collected together a force of nearly thirty thousand men.

On the 15th of December, Thomas sallied forth from his intrenchments and defeated the Confederates in a hard fought battle of two days. The retreating army was closely pursued, and was almost annihilated before it secured itself in central Mississippi. Hood had hoped to compel Sherman to follow him north by cutting the single line of railroad by which he had, during half a year, supplied his entire army; but Sherman had conceived other plans. Following Hood until he was fairly under way, and then leaving a portion of his army with Thomas to defend Tennessee, Sherman again turned his face southward.

On November 12, 1864, his army, numbering over sixty-five thousand men in compact fighting trim, swung itself clear from all communications and started on its famous march to the sea. Several columns moved on parallel roads from Atlanta, in the direction of Augusta, destroying the railroads in the most thorough manner. The merciless conscription had so drained the South of men, that their advance met very little opposition. The Confederates collected their forces at Augusta against the expected attack; but Sherman turned south after passing Sandersville, passed through Millen, and, before the Confederate authorities were well aware of his intention, appeared west of Savannah. Fort McAllister was gallantly stormed, and the army opened free communication with

---

When and how was General Hood defeated near Atlanta? What, after this, were the movements of Hood's army? When did Sherman set out on his celebrated march to the sea? Give the course of this march.

the fleet in Ossabaw Inlet, on the 13th of December. Savannah was evacuated a few days after, and Sherman sent the following dispatch to President Lincoln: "I beg to present you, as a Christmas gift, the city of Savannah, with 150 guns and plenty of ammunition, and also about 25,000 bales of cotton." Sherman remained nearly a month at Savannah resting and refitting his army.

249. Grant crossed the Rapidan, May 4, 1864, at the head of the Army of the Potomac, numbering one hundred and forty thousand men. He met the Confederate army, sixty thousand strong, in a tangled thicket of pines and cedars, called the Wilderness. A battle was fought on the 5th of May, and another on the 6th. The dense forest allowed no scope for maneuvering. It was a hand to hand encounter with musketry; neither artillery nor cavalry could be employed. The battle closed without decisive advantage to either side. Both North and South were confident that the Union army would now fall back and rest for a month or two, as had been its wont; but Grant brought his lines in order at once, and determined to put himself between Lee and Richmond by moving southward to Spottsylvania Court-house. Lee, guessing his intention, was there before him, with his army in position. Severe actions took place during the next four days, and the losses on both sides were very heavy.

On the 11th of May, Grant sent to Washington these resolute words: "I propose to fight it out on this line, if it takes all summer." On the 19th, he renewed his stubborn advance to the North Anna River, where Lee disputed the crossing. Flanking him by a rapid march to the south, Grant crossed the river and took position at Cool Arbor. Here again bloody engagements occurred. On the 3d of June, after losing eight thousand men in a half hour, by a

---

What was Sherman's Christmas gift to the President?

249. Where did Grant conduct the Army of the Potomac? When did he encounter Lee? What was the character of the battles in the Wilderness? How was Grant affected by defeat? What was the result of the fight at Cool Arbor?

vain assault upon the Confederate works, the Union forces, when ordered to renew the charge, silently disobeyed.

Grant now decided to cross the James River and attack Richmond from the south. Twelve days later the troops were safely passed over, and the siege of Petersburg was begun. The losses of the Union army during this most sanguinary campaign were over fifty-four thousand killed, wounded, and missing, against a Confederate loss of about thirty-two thousand. During the advance from the Rapidan to the James, supporting movements were ordered to be made by the forces in the Shenandoah Valley; by the cavalry under Sheridan; and by the army under Butler at Fortress Monroe. Very little was achieved that had any important bearing on the campaign, except the destruction of the railroad from Richmond to Gordonsville, by the dashing Sheridan.

About the middle of June, Lee sent General Early through the Shenandoah Valley, with a strong force, to invade Maryland and threaten Washington, hoping thus to draw Grant north and relieve Petersburg. Early swept rapidly down the valley, crossed the Potomac, and advanced toward the capital. He was delayed, however, long enough for re-enforcements to reach Washington, and secure it against his attack. Foiled in his design, Early, after a few days, retreated to the valley.

To prevent a recurrence of these raids, an effective force was organized under General Sheridan and sent against Early. By the middle of October, after several sharp battles, Early's army was virtually destroyed, and the beautiful valley of the Shenandoah utterly laid waste.

250. New-year's day, 1865, found the Confederate cause in a very precarious state. The Union troops were closing in around Richmond. Farragut had sailed up Mobile Bay on August 5th, 1864, and closed that valuable port to the

---

How did Grant change his plans? What city was besieged? What were Grant's losses up to this time? Relate the facts concerning Early's raid into the Shenandoah Valley.

250. When was Mobile taken?

Southerners. Every-where but about Richmond could the Union cavalry ride without much fear of opposition. The Confederates saw the condition of affairs, and in their Congress debated the question of arming their slaves. Fort Fisher, on the coast of North Carolina, was captured, January 15, 1865; and Wilmington, of necessity, in a few weeks, also fell into the possession of the Federals.

Lee's situation was now extremely critical. Should Grant sever, or get possession of, the Danville Railroad, the Confederates would be entirely cut off from their supplies. Nothing, therefore, remained for Lee but to abandon the cities of Petersburg and Richmond, and join his fifty thousand veterans to Johnston's forty thousand, who were in North Carolina, and, with the whole force, take to the fastnesses of the Alleghany Mountains. This it was determined to attempt, and this Grant resolved to prevent. Hoping to break through the Union lines, Lee struck first on the right wing at Fort Steadman, and surprised that work. But the fort was soon retaken with nineteen hundred Confederate prisoners. On the first of April, General Sheridan, having returned from the Shenandoah Valley, began a movement against Five Forks, a very important

General P. H. Sheridan.

What was the condition of affairs about Richmond at the beginning of 1865? What capture was made on January 15? What did Lee now determine to do? Where did he attempt to break the Union line? What was the result?

point. He captured Lee's works with five thousand prisoners and four guns. His own loss was trifling.

At four o'clock in the morning of April 2, Grant assaulted the enemy's lines from the Appomatox to Hatcher's Run. Lee's intrenchments were forced at almost every point; thousands of prisoners and many guns were taken. By eight o'clock in the morning, the exterior net-work of defenses around Petersburg was in the hands of Grant, and the fate of the city was decided. In Richmond, while President Davis was in church, a messenger came swiftly up the aisle and handed him a paper. It was from Lee, who informed him that Richmond must be evacuated at once. The congregation soon surmised the contents of the dispatch when they saw the spare form of Davis bent and his face ashen as he passed rapidly down the aisle and out of the church. He gave orders to remove what coin belonged to the government, to Danville, and to take away or burn all archives. Lee hastily evacuated Petersburg and Richmond, and fled westward, intending to join Johnston; but he was intercepted by the vigilant Sheridan. Changing his course, Lee moved to the Appomatox, and crossed that stream. For want of time, the bridge over which he crossed was not destroyed, and soon over the planks thundered the hoofs of the pursuing cavalry.

On the 7th of April, Grant sent a note to Lee, urging him to surrender to save the useless shedding of blood; but at night Lee marched off again, and, on the 8th, answered Grant's proposition by saying that he thought neither the time nor the emergency had come that made necessary the surrender of the Army of Northern Virginia. He then pushed on for Appomatox Station, where supply trains were awaiting him. But Sheridan was before him, having reached that station, by forced marches, at daylight on the 9th. Seeing that his condition was desperate, Lee

---

What important gain was made by Sheridan on the 1st of April? When did Grant make his grand assault on the defenses of Petersburg? What message did Lee dispatch to Davis at Richmond? With what intention did Lee evacuate Richmond? By whom was his army intercepted? What was done on the 7th of April? On the 8th? On the 9th?

sought a conference with Grant. The latter demanded an immediate surrender, and his terms were accepted.

After the Confederate soldiers were paroled, Lee addressed them in these simple words: "Men, we have fought through this war together. I have done the best I could for you." There were nearly 28,000 paroled, and all immediately started for their homes. The surrender of Lee's army was virtually the ending of the war.

Sherman, after having remained at Savannah until February 1, moved northward in pursuit of Johnston. Several hot engagements took place, from which the Confederates retreated. Eight days after Lee had surrendered, Johnston sent in offers of capitulation to Sherman, and, on the 26th of April, his troops laid down their arms on the same terms as Lee's had done. The last Confederate army—that west of the Mississippi—surrendered to General Canby, May 26, and the War of Secession was over.

251. At the November election of 1864, Abraham Lincoln had been re-chosen President, and Andrew Johnson, of Tennessee, had been elected Vice President. On the night of the 14th of April, 1865, while the President was sitting in a private box of a theater in Washington, he was killed by a pistol-shot fired at his head by John Wilkes Booth. The assassin sprang from the box to the stage of the theater, escaped by a back way, and fled. He was pursued and shot. The tragic fate of Lincoln caused the profoundest grief and mourning all over the North.

252. Jefferson Davis attempted to escape to the sea-shore, but was taken prisoner at Irwinsville, Georgia, on the 10th of May. He was imprisoned at Fortress Monroe, whence, after two years' confinement, he was released on the bail of several prominent persons, Horace Greeley, the famous

---

Repeat Lee's parting words to his soldiers. How many soldiers were paroled? What fighting occurred after Lee's surrender? When, and to whom did Johnston surrender? When, and to whom did the last Confederate army surrender?

251. How did the presidential election of 1864 result? Describe the assassination of the President.

journalist and politician being of the number. Davis was included in the amnesty proclaimed by President Johnson in December, 1868.

Horace Greeley.

253. There were raised for the defense of the Union, during the civil war, 2,688,523 men. Owing to the fact that some of these were mustered in twice, and some three times, and that many deserted, perhaps not more than 1,500,000 took part in actual service. The Confederates had about 600,000 in the field. Each side lost about 300,000 men, who fell in battle or perished from their wounds. If to this number we add 400,000 crippled and permanently disabled by sickness, we have, from North and South together, a grand total of 1,000,000 men destroyed in four years of civil war.

254. The cost of supporting this tremendous conflict is shown by the amount of the national debt. On the 30th of June, 1860, this was but $64,770,000; on the 1st of January, 1866, it was $2,750,000,000. To this last should be added the sums paid by states, counties, cities, and towns, for raising local levies. The sum of $200,000,000 was paid in bounties, and $100,000,000 were given to sol-

---

252. What was the career of Davis after the fall of Richmond?

253. How many men were raised for the defense of the Union? How many of these actually engaged in the war? How many served in the Confederate army? How many died from all causes in both armies? How many were permanently disabled?

diers' widows or other heirs, making the whole amount of money paid out for the war more than $4,000,000,000.

255. What became of the Union army when no longer needed in the field? European writers thought that riots and other evils would arise when so many soldiers, familiar with scenes of violence and blood, were freed from military restraint. But these men came from the people, not as choosing the barbarous experiences of war, but to sacrifice themselves for the sake of Union and Liberty. Their duty bravely done, they returned to the people, and gladly resumed the vocations of peace. Within eighteen months, over a million men were disbanded and transported to their homes.

256. Humanity had its beautiful victories even in the midst of the deadliest strife. More was done to alleviate pain and succor the dying than during any previous war in the world's history. Sanitary fairs were organized on a stupendous scale, by means of which $14,000,000 were raised in cash and supplies. Every body contributed to them—the rich with money, the poor with work. Women in every neighborhood, from the coast of Maine to the shores of California, put up delicate food, or made garments for the brave men fighting in the South. The Sanitary Commission had its hospital cars on railroads, its steamers on every river, its wagons and ambulances on every battle-field. It collected in depots great stores of provisions; it gave great dinners to regiments passing through cities; it took care of soldiers not yet in charge of the government; and furnished homes to soldiers' wives and children, who were, from any cause, in destitute circumstances.

The Christian Commission, in co-operation with the Sanitary, raised four million five hundred thousand dollars for benevolent work in camp, field, and hospital.

---

254. How much did the war cost?

255. How did the soldiers employ themselves when disbanded?

256. Give an account of the Sanitary Commission, and what it did. What was done by the Christian Commission?

The Southern people were not behind the Northern in their care and tenderness. They did what they could for their own soldiers, but were unable, with their inadequate means, to accomplish what was done in the rich and populous North.

257. Reviewing the grand features of the war in a military light, we are impressed by several important facts, which alike illustrate the resources of modern science and the inventive faculty of the American people. Until this war, troops were never moved with such facility in this country, or massed so suddenly in large numbers at points where they were required. Instead of marching from place to place, entire armies frequently went by railroad, thus saving both time and labor. Steamboats and sailing vessels were much employed in the transportation of troops. A striking instance of rapid military movement was afforded at the opening of Grant's final campaign against Bragg, when twenty-three thousand men were brought west from the Army of the Potomac, a distance of eleven hundred and ninety-two miles, in seven days. They traveled by railroad and steamboat, eating and sleeping on the way.

The changes wrought in the construction of war vessels have been mentioned. Great improvement was made in ordnance and projectiles, requiring corresponding alterations in the structure of defenses. The improvement in small arms was such that a regiment provided with breech-loading guns, could do more in battle than five or six regiments armed in the usual way.

EVENTS SINCE THE WAR.

258. Abraham Lincoln expired, April 15, 1865, and, on the same day, Vice President Andrew Johnson was sworn into office as chief magistrate. Two subjects of paramount importance claimed prompt attention. One of these was,

---

How did the Southern people provide for their soldiers?

257. What improvements were made during the civil war in modes of transportation, war vessels, small arms, etc.?

what disposition to make of the public debt. Congress pledged the nation's honor to the discharge of this vast sum, principal and interest, and forthwith set about raising a revenue from duties and taxes. Nothing more forcibly illustrates the recuperative energy of the republic than the manner in which her enormous liabilities have been funded and reduced. Every demand on the treasury for interest or on general account has been promptly met. Moreover, the principal of the public debt has been decreased, since March 1, 1869, at the rate of nearly one hundred million dollars per annum, or over one-fourth of a million a day.

259. The other absorbing subject for instant consideration was, how to reconstruct the shattered Union — on what terms to restore the late belligerent states to their former privileges. On this troublesome question the President was at variance with Congress. In February, 1865, the Thirteenth Amendment to the Constitution had been proposed, abolishing slavery. This was subsequently ratified by a sufficient number of states, and was declared adopted, December 18th. The President held that the seceded states should be re-admitted to the Union upon voting for this amendment, rescinding their ordinances of secession, and declaring the Confederate war debt void. Congress insisted on these and several other terms, one of which was that the states in question should pledge themselves to protect the civil rights of the Freedmen, their late slaves.

During the years 1865–66, the conflict between the President and Congress became more and more violent. Early in 1867, Congress passed, over the President's veto, a reconstruction act, defining the conditions upon which the seceded states might return to the Union, and placing them under military government until those conditions were complied with.

---

258. When did Andrew Johnson become President? What important subjects agitated Congress? How has the public debt been diminished?

259. What was the Thirteenth Amendment to the Constitution? How did the President and Congress differ on the subject of reconstruction? What act was passed over the President's veto?

A bill regulating the tenure of office was passed also, making it unlawful for the President to remove from civil office, without consent of the Senate, any person whose appointment by the President required the confirmation of the Senate. After the adjournment of Congress, Johnson suspended from office Edwin M. Stanton, Secretary of War. Congress assembled early in 1868, and re-instated Stanton. Johnson again ordered him to vacate his office. Stanton, backed by Congress, refused obedience, and kept his place. So strong now was the feeling against Johnson that he was impeached of high crimes and misdemeanors. After a tedious trial, in which he narrowly escaped conviction, the President was acquitted, May 23, 1868.

On the 24th of June, the states of Arkansas, Alabama, Georgia, Louisiana, North Carolina, and South Carolina, having complied with the requirements of Congress, were restored to the Union. Tennessee had already been readmitted. Before the close of another year the rest of the seceded states came back; and, as before the war, the motto, *E Pluribus Unum*, appropriately inscribed the American banner and shield.

260. At the November election of 1868, U. S. Grant was chosen President. He was the Republican candidate, and ran in opposition to Horatio Seymour, of New York, the nominee of the Democrats. Grant entered upon the duties of his high position under favorable auspices. Previous to his inauguration, Congress proposed to the several states the ratification of the Fourteenth and Fifteenth amendments, which, being acceded to by three-fourths of the state legislatures, became, March 30, 1870, a part of the Federal Constitution.

261. The territory of Nevada became a state in 1864; that of Nebraska, in 1867; making the entire number of states thirty-seven. By treaty with Russia, negotiated in

---

When and why was the President impeached? Which of the seceded states returned first to the Union?

260. Who was elected President in 1868? What is the Fifteenth Amendment? What two amendments were ratified in 1870?

March, 1867, and ratified in April, Alaska was purchased for the sum of seven million dollars, and thereupon became a part of the republic. The area of the whole United States is, at present, over three and a half million square miles.

262. According to the ninth census, the entire population of the United States is 38,555,983. Of these, 5,566,546 are of foreign birth; 4,880,009 are colored; about 380,000 are Indians. Since 1860, the immigration of Chinese has rapidly increased, and there are now probably 100,000 of these people in the country, most of whom are located in California and Oregon. Shortly after the close of the war, migration began from the Eastern, Middle, and Central states to the new states and unclaimed territorial lands west of the Mississippi.

About the year 1870, this migration was greatly accelerated. From Ohio and other populous states large colonies moved to Kansas, Nebraska, Colorado, and adjacent regions. Such is now the demand for transportation to the far West, that special emigrant trains are run on the railroads leading toward the frontier. Cities and towns are springing up on the chief lines of western travel; and, from present appearances, all the habitable lands in the United States will be occupied within a very few years.

263. The year 1871 is memorable for a conflagration so great and terrible that it must be regarded as a national calamity. This was the burning of Chicago, a city whose rapid growth was one of the marvels of our country. The fire broke out on the 8th of October, and continued its ravages for three days, desolating an area of twenty-four hundred acres, and consuming eighteen thousand buildings. The pecuniary losses caused by this awful visitation were estimated at two hundred million dollars.

---

261. What territory became a state in 1864? What in 1867? What is the whole number of states? The extent of the United States? What is said of Alaska?

262. What is the population of the United States? How many Chinese? What has been the recent course and extent of migration?

263. What is said of the great fire at Chicago?

264. The material prosperity of the United States, during the period measured by the events recorded in the last two chapters — 1848 to 1871 — has been extraordinary. It was American enterprise, sustained and directed by an American merchant, Cyrus W. Field, that in 1866 accomplished the difficult work of laying the Atlantic cable, by means of which telegraphic communication was established with Europe. It was American enterprise that in 1869 completed the Great Pacific Railroad across the continent. It was an American machinist — Elias Howe — who invented the sewing machine, the general introduction and use of which marks an era in our domestic history. To the genius of American inventors, the world is indebted for the type-revolving press, by which twenty-five thousand copies of a newspaper may be struck off in an hour. What need to mention the improvements that have been made in engineering, bridge-building, machinery, farm implements, furniture, and the useful arts dependent upon the applications of chemistry and other practical sciences?

William Cullen Bryant.

265. The intellectual, moral, and æsthetic progress of the republic, though not commensurate with her amazing

---

264. Give an account of American enterprise in the construction of the telegraph. Of railroads. Sewing machines. Printing-presses.

material development, has, nevertheless, been creditable. The press has continued to exercise a powerful influence, and its field of operations has been much enlarged. The energy and ability of such journalists as William Cullen Bryant, Horace Greeley, and James Gordon Bennett, have raised the American newspaper to an enviable position among the agencies that forward civilization and elevate man. The whole number of periodicals issued in the United States is nearly 6,000. There are 548 papers which print more than 5,000 copies each issue, and eleven which print more than 100,000 copies. The whole number of copies of newspapers printed annually exceeeds one billion! The number of books published in the United States averages three thousand a year.

The cause of education has gone forward of late with great rapidity. The common school system, long since adopted in the North, is gaining popularity in the South. More than 7,000,000 children already attend the American free schools, and are taught by about 200,000 teachers. Many thousands attend private schools and academies. There are in the country 369 colleges, 93 theological seminaries, 88 medical schools, 28 law schools, and 81 normal schools.

Within the last quarter of a century, many public libraries have been established in our cities and towns, while those of earlier foundation have greatly increased in size and usefulness. One American library contains over two hundred thousand volumes, and at least ten contain over fifty thousand volumes each.

266. In science and literature encouraging achievements have been made, and present indications justify the hope that these departments are rising to a higher plane of excellence. The professions of authorship, lecturing, and teaching are well sustained. In the æsthetic world, the

---

265. What can you say of the American press? Of public and private education? Of public libraries?

266. What can you say of science and literature? Of American artists?

name of Powers, and of other excellent American artists, shine with a brilliant luster.

Hiram Powers.

Since the close of the war, a tendency prevails to revolutionize and reconstruct institutions, and to make the new republic nobler, grander, and purer than the old. Evidence of this tendency is seen in the extension of the privileges and influence of woman; in the multiplication of schools, churches, and benevolent institutions; and in the popular attention given to sanitary science, domestic economy, and the right ordering of the Family, the true unit of American society. In a word, the best people in the country are acting upon the conviction that a nation is bettered only by bettering her individual citizens, and that public welfare depends upon the wise regulation of private life.

Compared in age with the nations of the old world, the United States is but an infant. The kingdom of England, for example, had been growing in civilization for about seven hundred years before Columbus discovered America. Half as many more years elapsed ere our hardy forefathers declared themselves a free and independent people, and organized a separate national government. Let the student note how short the time, historically considered, since the

---

What is the general tendency of the people of the republic at the present time? What is said of the growth of the United States?

Revolutionary War, and he will realize with what energy and rapidity the Republic has risen to her present position among the great powers of the world. When we review the history of our country, and reflect how prosperous has been her career hitherto, it is reasonable and right to entertain glowing hopes of the future, mingled with emotions of gratitude to the Divine Providence who rules the destinies of nations.

> This land is like an Eagle, whose young gaze
> Feeds on the noontide beam, whose golden plume
> Floats moveless on the storm, and in the blaze
> Of sunrise gleams when earth is wrapt in gloom;
> An epitaph of glory for the tomb
> Of murdered Europe may thy fame be made,
> Great People! As the sands shalt thou become;
> Thy growth is swift as morn, when night must fade;
> The multitudinous earth shall sleep beneath thy shade.
>
> SHELLEY.

APPENDIX.

THE DECLARATION OF INDEPENDENCE.

IN CONGRESS, JULY 4, 1776.

THE UNANIMOUS DECLARATION OF THE THIRTEEN UNITED STATES OF AMERICA.

WHEN, in the course of human events, it becomes necessary for one people to dissolve the political bands which have connected them with another, and to assume, among the powers of the earth, the separate and equal station to which the laws of nature and of nature's God entitle them, a decent respect to the opinions of mankind requires that they should declare the causes which impel them to the separation.

We hold these truths to be self-evident: that all men are created equal; that they are endowed, by their Creator, with certain inalienable rights; that among these are life, liberty, and the pursuit of happiness; that to secure these rights, governments are instituted among men, deriving their just powers from the consent of the governed; that whenever any form of government becomes destructive of these ends, it is the right of the people to alter or abolish it, and to institute a new government, laying its foundation on such principles, and organizing its powers in such form as to them shall seem most likely to effect their safety and happiness. Prudence, indeed, will dictate, that governments long established should not be changed for light and transient causes; and, accordingly, all experience hath shown, that mankind are more disposed to suffer while evils are sufferable, than to right themselves by abolishing the forms to which they are accustomed. But when a long train of abuses and usurpations, pursuing invariably the same object, evinces a design to reduce them under absolute despotism, it is their right, it is their duty to throw off such a government, and to provide new guards for their future security. Such has been the patient sufferance of these colonies; and such is now the necessity which constrains them to alter their former systems of government. The history of the present king of Great Britain is a history of repeated injuries and usurpations, all having in direct object the establishment of an absolute tyranny over these states. To prove this, let facts be submitted to a candid world.

He has refused his assent to laws the most wholesome and necessary for the public good.

He has forbidden his governors to pass laws of immediate and pressing importance, unless suspended in their operations, till his assent should be obtained; and when so suspended, he has utterly neglected to attend to them.

He has refused to pass other laws for the accommodation of large districts of people, unless those people would relinquish the right of representation in the legislature — a right inestimable to them, and formidable to tyrants only.

He has called together legislative bodies at places unusual, uncomfortable, and distant from the repository of their public records, for the sole purpose of fatiguing them into compliance with his measures.

He has dissolved representative houses repeatedly for opposing, with manly firmness, his invasions on the rights of the people.

He has refused, for a long time after such dissolutions, to cause others to be elected; whereby the legislative powers, incapable of annihilation, have returned to the people at large, for their exercise, the state remaining, in the meantime, exposed to all the dangers of invasions from without, and convulsions within.

He has endeavored to prevent the population of these states, for that purpose obstructing the laws for the naturalization of foreigners; refusing to pass others to encourage their migration hither, and raising the conditions of new appropriations of lands.

He has obstructed the administration of justice by refusing his assent to laws for establishing judiciary powers.

He has made judges dependent on his will alone for the tenure of their offices, and the amount and payment of their salaries.

He has erected a multitude of new offices, and sent hither swarms of officers, to harass our people, and eat out their substance.

He has kept among us, in times of peace, standing armies, without the consent of our legislatures.

He has affected to render the military independent of, and superior to, the civil power.

He has combined with others to subject us to a jurisdiction foreign to our constitution, and unacknowledged by our laws; giving his assent to their acts of pretended legislation:

For quartering large bodies of armed troops among us;

For protecting them, by a mock trial, from punishment for any murders which they should commit on the inhabitants of these states;

For cutting off our trade with all parts of the world;

For imposing taxes on us without our consent;

For depriving us, in many cases, of the benefits of trial by jury;

For transporting us beyond seas to be tried for pretended offenses;

For abolishing the free system of English laws in a neighboring province, establishing therein an arbitrary government, and enlarging its boundaries, so as to render it at once an example and fit instrument for introducing the same absolute rule into these colonies:

For taking away our charters, abolishing our most valuable laws, and altering, fundamentally, the forms of our governments;

For suspending our own legislatures, and declaring themselves invested with power to legislate for us in all cases whatsoever.

He has abdicated government here by declaring us out of his protection, and waging war against us.

He has plundered our seas, ravaged our coasts, burned our towns, and destroyed the lives of our people.

He is at this time transporting large armies of foreign mercenaries to complete the works of death, desolation, and tyranny, already begun with circumstances of cruelty and perfidy, scarcely paralleled in the most barbarous ages, and totally unworthy the head of a civilized nation.

He has constrained our fellow-citizens, taken captive on the high seas, to bear arms against their country, to become the executioners of their friends and brethren, or to fall themselves by their hands.

He has excited domestic insurrection among us, and has endeavored to bring on the inhabitants of our frontiers, the merciless Indian savages, whose known rule of warfare is an undistinguished destruction of all ages, sexes, and conditions.

In every stage of these oppressions we have petitioned for redress in the most humble terms. Our repeated petitions have been answered only by repeated injury. A prince, whose character is thus marked by every act which may define a tyrant, is unfit to be the ruler of a free people.

Nor have we been wanting in attentions to our British brethren. We have warned them, from time to time, of attempts by their legislature to extend an unwarrantable jurisdiction over us. We have reminded them of the circumstances of our emigration and settlement here. We have appealed to their native justice and magnanimity, and we have conjured them by the ties of our common kindred to disavow these usurpations, which would inevitably interrupt our connections and correspondence. They, too, have been deaf to the voice of justice and of consanguinity. We must, therefore, acquiesce in the necessity which denounces our separation, and hold them, as we hold the rest of mankind—enemies in war; in peace, friends.

We, therefore, the representatives of the UNITED STATES OF AMERICA, in general congress assembled, appealing to the Supreme

Judge of the world for the rectitude of our intentions, do, in the name and by the authority of the good people of these colonies, solemnly publish and declare, That these United Colonies are, and of right ought to be, *Free* and *Independent States;* that they are absolved from all allegiance to the British crown, and that all political connection between them and the state of Great Britain is, and ought to be, totally dissolved; and that, as *Free* and *Independent States*, they have full power to levy war, conclude peace, contract alliances, establish commerce, and do all other acts and things which *Independent States* may of right do. And for the support of this Declaration, with a firm reliance on the protection of DIVINE PROVIDENCE, we mutually pledge to each other our lives, our fortunes, and our sacred honor.

JOHN HANCOCK.

NEW HAMPSHIRE.—Josiah Bartlett, William Whipple, Matthew Thornton.

MASSACHUSETTS BAY.—Samuel Adams, John Adams, Robert Treat Paine, Elbridge Gerry.

RHODE ISLAND, ETC.—Stephen Hopkins, William Ellery.

CONNECTICUT.—Roger Sherman, Samuel Huntington, William Williams, Oliver Wolcott.

NEW YORK.—William Floyd, Philip Livingston, Francis Lewis, Lewis Morris.

NEW JERSEY.—Richard Stockton, John Witherspoon, Francis Hopkinson, John Hart, Abraham Clark.

PENNSYLVANIA.—Robert Morris, Benjamin Rush, Benjamin Franklin, John Morton, George Clymer, James Smith, George Taylor, James Wilson, George Ross.

DELAWARE.—Cæsar Rodney, George Read, Thomas M'Kean.

MARYLAND.—Samuel Chase, William Paca, Thomas Stone, Charles Carroll, of Carrollton.

VIRGINIA.—George Wythe, Richard Henry Lee, Thomas Jefferson, Benjamin Harrison, Thomas Nelson, Jr., Francis Lightfoot Lee, Carter Braxton.

NORTH CAROLINA.—William Hooper, Joseph Hewes, John Penn.

SOUTH CAROLINA.—Edward Rutledge, Thomas Hayward, Jr., Thomas Lynch, Jr., Arthur Middleton.

GEORGIA.—Button Gwinnett, Lyman Hall, George Walton.

CONSTITUTION OF THE UNITED STATES.

WE, the People of the United States, in order to form a more perfect union, establish justice, insure domestic tranquillity, provide for the common defense, promote the general welfare, and secure the blessings of liberty to ourselves and our posterity, do ordain and establish this Constitution for the United States of America.

ARTICLE I.

SECTION 1. All legislative powers herein granted shall be vested in a congress of the United States, which shall consist of a senate and house of representatives.

SEC. 2. The house of representatives shall be composed of members chosen every second year by the people of the several states, and the electors in each state shall have the qualifications requisite for electors of the most numerous branch of the state legislature.

No person shall be a representative who shall not have attained to the age of twenty-five years, and been seven years a citizen of the United States, and who shall not, when elected, be an inhabitant of that state in which he shall be chosen.

Representatives and direct taxes shall be apportioned among the several states which may be included within this union, according to their respective numbers, which shall be determined by adding to the whole number of free persons, including those bound to service for a term of years, and excluding Indians not taxed, three-fifths of all other persons. The actual enumeration shall be made within three years after the first meeting of the congress of the United States, and within every subsequent term of ten years, in such manner as they shall by law direct. The number of representatives shall not exceed one for every thirty thousand, but each state shall have at least one representative; and until such enumeration shall be made, the state of New Hampshire shall be entitled to choose three; Massachusetts, eight; Rhode Island and Providence Plantations, one; Connecticut, five; New York, six; New Jersey, four; Pennsylvania, eight; Delaware, one; Maryland, six; Virginia, ten; North Carolina, five; South Carolina, five; and Georgia, three.

When vacancies happen in the representation from any state, the executive authority thereof shall issue writs of election to fill such vacancies.

The house of representatives shall choose their speaker and other officers, and shall have the sole power of impeachment.

SEC. 3. The senate of the United States shall be composed of two senators from each state, chosen by the legislature thereof, for six years; and each senator shall have one vote.

Immediately after they shall be assembled in consequence of the first election, they shall be divided, as equally as may be, into three classes. The seats of the senators of the first class shall be vacated at the expiration of the second year; of the second class, at the expiration of the fourth year; and of the third class, at the expiration of the sixth year: so that one-third may be chosen every second year; and if vacancies happen, by resignation or otherwise, during the recess of the legislature of any state, the executive thereof may make temporary appointments until the next meeting of the legislature, which shall then fill such vacancies.

No person shall be a senator who shall not have attained to the age of thirty years, and been nine years a citizen of the United States, and who shall not, when elected, be an inhabitant of that state for which he shall be chosen.

The vice president of the United States shall be president of the senate, but shall have no vote unless they be equally divided.

The senate shall choose their other officers, and also a president *pro tempore*, in the absence of the vice president, or when he shall exercise the office of president of the United States.

The senate shall have the sole power to try all impeachments. When sitting for that purpose, they shall be on oath or affirmation. When the president of the United States is tried, the chief justice shall preside; and no person shall be convicted without the concurrence of two-thirds of the members present.

Judgment, in cases of impeachment, shall not extend further than to removal from office, and disqualification to hold and enjoy any office of honor, trust, or profit under the United States; but the party convicted shall nevertheless be liable and subject to indictment, trial, judgment, and punishment, according to law.

SEC. 4. The times, places, and manner of holding elections for senators and representatives, shall be prescribed in each state by the legislature thereof; but the congress may, at any time, by law, make or alter such regulations, except as to the places of choosing senators.

The congress shall assemble at least once in every year, and such meeting shall be on the first Monday in December, unless they shall by law appoint a different day.

SEC. 5. Each house shall be the judge of the elections, returns, and qualifications of its own members; and a majority of each shall constitute a quorum to do business; but a smaller number may adjourn from day to day, and may be authorized to compel the attendance of absent members, in such manner and under such penalties as each house may provide.

Each house may determine the rules of its proceedings, punish its members for disorderly behavior, and, with the concurrence of two-thirds, expel a member.

Each house shall keep a journal of its proceedings, and from time to time publish the same, excepting such parts as may in their judgment require secrecy; and the yeas and nays of the members of either house, on any question, shall, at the desire of one-fifth of those present, be entered on the journal.

Neither house, during the session of congress, shall, without the consent of the other, adjourn for more than three days, nor to any other place than that in which the two houses shall be sitting.

SEC. 6. The senators and representatives shall receive a compensation for their services, to be ascertained by law, and paid out of the treasury of the United States. They shall, in all cases, except treason, felony, and breach of the peace, be privileged from arrest during their attendance at the session of their respective houses, and in going to and returning from the same; and for any speech or debate in either house, they shall not be questioned in any other place.

No senator or representative shall, during the time for which he was elected, be appointed to any civil office under the authority of the United States which shall have been created, or the emoluments whereof shall have been increased, during such time; and no person holding any office under the United States shall be a member of either house during his continuance in office.

SEC. 7. All bills for raising revenue shall originate in the house of representatives; but the senate may propose or concur with amendments, as on other bills.

Every bill which shall have passed the house of representatives and the senate, shall, before it become a law, be presented to the president of the United States. If he approve, he shall sign it; but if not, he shall return it, with his objections, to that house in which it shall have originated, who shall enter the objections at large on their journal, and proceed to reconsider it. If, after such reconsideration, two-thirds of that house shall agree to pass the bill, it shall be sent, together with the objections, to the other house, by which it shall likewise be reconsidered, and if approved by two-thirds of that house, it shall become a law. But, in all such cases, the votes of both houses shall be determined by yeas and nays, and the names of the persons voting for and against the bill shall be entered on the journal of each house respectively. If any bill shall not be returned by the president within ten days (Sundays excepted) after it shall have been presented to him, the same shall be a law in like manner as if he had signed it, unless the congress, by their adjournment, prevent its return, in which case it shall not be a law.

Every order, resolution, or vote, to which the concurrence of the senate and house of representatives may be necessary, except on a question of adjournment, shall be presented to the president of the United States; and, before the same shall take effect, shall be approved by him, or, being disapproved by him, shall be repassed by two-thirds of the senate and house of representatives, according to the rules and limitations prescribed in the case of a bill.

SEC. 8. The congress shall have power—

To lay and collect taxes, duties, imposts, and excises; to pay the debts and provide for the common defense and general welfare of the United States; but all duties, imposts, and excises, shall be uniform throughout the United States:

To borrow money on the credit of the United States:

To regulate commerce with foreign nations, and among the several states, and with the Indian tribes:

To establish an uniform rule of naturalization, and uniform laws on the subject of bankruptcies throughout the United States:

To coin money, regulate the value thereof, and of foreign coin, and fix the standard of weights and measures:

To provide for the punishment of counterfeiting the securities and current coin of the United States:

To establish post offices and post roads:

To promote the progress of science and useful arts, by securing for limited times, to authors and inventors, the exclusive right to their respective writings and discoveries:

To constitute tribunals inferior to the supreme court:

To define and punish piracies and felonies committed on the high seas, and offenses against the law of nations:

To declare war, grant letters of marque and reprisal, and make rules concerning captures on land and water:

To raise and support armies, but no appropriation of money to that use shall be for a longer term than two years:

To provide and maintain a navy:

To make rules for the government and regulation of the land and naval forces:

To provide for calling forth the militia to execute the laws of the union, suppress insurrections, and repel invasions:

To provide for organizing, arming, and disciplining the militia, and for governing such part of them as may be employed in the service of the United States, reserving to the states, respectively, the appointment of the officers, and the authority of training the militia according to the discipline prescribed by congress:

To exercise exclusive legislation, in all cases whatsoever, over such district, not exceeding ten miles square, as may, by cession of particular states, and the acceptance of congress, become the seat of government of the United States, and to exercise like authority over all places purchased by the consent of the legislature of the state in which the same shall be, for the erection of forts, magazines, arsenals, dock-yards, and other needful buildings; and,

To make all laws which shall be necessary and proper for carrying into execution the foregoing powers, and all other powers vested by this constitution in the government of the United States, or in any department or officer thereof.

SEC. 9. The migration or importation of such persons as any of the states now existing shall think proper to admit, shall not be prohibited by the congress prior to the year one thousand eight hundred and eight, but a tax or duty may be imposed on such importation not exceeding ten dollars for each person.

The privilege of the writ of *habeas corpus* shall not be suspended, unless when, in cases of rebellion or invasion, the public safety may require it.

No bill of attainder, or *ex post facto* law, shall be passed.

No capitation or other direct tax shall be laid, unless in proportion to the census or enumeration hereinbefore directed to be taken.

No tax or duty shall be laid on articles exported from any state. No preference shall be given by any regulation of commerce or revenue to the ports of one state over those of another; nor shall vessels bound to or from one state be obliged to enter, clear, or pay duties in another.

No money shall be drawn from the treasury, but in consequence of appropriations made by law; and a regular statement and account of the receipts and expenditures of all public money shall be published from time to time.

No title of nobility shall be granted by the United States, and no person holding any office of profit or trust under them, shall, without the consent of the congress, accept of any present, emolument, office, or title of any kind whatever, from any king, prince, or foreign state.

SEC. 10. No state shall enter into any treaty, alliance, or confederation; grant letters of marque and reprisal; coin money; emit bills of credit; make any thing but gold and silver coin a tender in payment of debts; pass any bill of attainder, *ex post facto* law, or law impairing the obligation of contracts, or grant any title of nobility.

No state shall, without the consent of the congress, lay any imposts or duties on imports or exports, except what may be absolutely necessary for executing its inspection laws; and the net produce of all duties and imposts, laid by any state on imports or exports, shall be for the use of the treasury of the United States, and all such laws shall be subject to the revision and control of the congress. No state shall, without the consent of congress, lay any duty of tunnage, keep troops or ships of war in time of peace, enter into any agreement or compact with another state, or with a foreign power, or engage in war, unless actually invaded, or in such imminent danger as will not admit of delay.

ARTICLE II.

SEC. 1. The executive power shall be vested in a president of the United States of America. He shall hold his office during the term of four years, and, together with the vice president, chosen for the same term, be elected as follows:

Each state shall appoint, in such manner as the legislature thereof may direct, a number of electors, equal to the whole number of senators and representatives to which the state may be entitled in the congress; but no senator or representative, or person holding an office of trust or profit under the United States, shall be appointed an elector.

[The electors shall meet in their respective states, and vote by ballot for two persons, of whom one at least shall not be an inhabitant of the same state with themselves. And they shall make a list of all the persons voted for, and of the number of votes for each; which list they shall sign and certify, and transmit sealed to the seat of the government of the United States, directed to the president of the senate. The president of the senate shall, in the presence of the senate and house of representatives, open all the certificates, and the votes shall then be counted. The person having the greatest number of votes shall be the president, if such number be a majority of the whole number of electors appointed; and if there be more than one who have such majority, and have an equal number of votes, then the house of representatives shall immediately choose, by ballot, one of them for president; and if no person have a majority, then, from the five highest on the list, the said house shall, in like manner, choose the president. But, in choosing the president, the votes shall be taken by states, the representation from each state having one vote. A quorum for this purpose shall consist of a member or members from two-thirds of the states, and a majority of all the states shall be necessary to a choice. In every case, after the choice of the president, the person having the greatest number of votes of the electors shall be the vice president. But if there should remain two or more who have equal votes, the senate shall choose from them, by ballot, the vice president.]

The congress may determine the time of choosing the electors, and the day on which they shall give their votes, which day shall be the same throughout the United States.

No person except a natural born citizen, or a citizen of the United States at the time of the adoption of this constitution, shall be eligible to the office of president: neither shall any person be eligible to that office who shall not have attained to the age of thirty-five years, and been fourteen years a resident within the United States.

In case of the removal of the president from office, or of his death, resignation, or inability to discharge the powers and duties of the said office, the same shall devolve on the vice president, and the congress may, by law, provide for the case of removal, death, resignation, or inability, both of the president and vice president, declaring what officer shall then act as president, and such officer shall act accordingly, until the disability be removed, or a president shall be elected.

The president shall, at stated times, receive for his services a compensation, which shall neither be increased nor diminished during the period for which he shall have been elected, and he shall not receive within that period any other emolument from the United States, or any of them.

Before he enter on the execution of his office, he shall take the following oath or affirmation:

"I do solemnly swear (or affirm) that I will faithfully execute the office of president of the United States, and will, to the best of my ability, preserve, protect, and defend the constitution of the United States."

SEC. 2. The president shall be commander-in-chief of the army and navy of the United States, and of the militia of the several states when called into the actual service of the United States. He may require the opinion, in writing, of the principal officer in each of the executive departments, upon any subject relating to the duties of their respective offices; and he shall have power to grant reprieves and pardons for offenses against the United States, except in cases of impeachment.

He shall have power, by and with the advice and consent of the senate, to make treaties, provided two-thirds of the senators present concur; and he shall nominate, and, by and with the advice and consent of the senate, shall appoint embassadors, other public ministers, and consuls, judges of the supreme court, and all other officers of the United States, whose appointments are not herein otherwise provided for, and which shall be established by law. But the congress may, by law, vest the appointment of such inferior officers as they think proper, in the president alone, in the courts of law, or in the heads of departments.

The president shall have power to fill up all vacancies that may happen during the recess of the senate, by granting commissions which shall expire at the end of their next session.

SEC. 3. He shall, from time to time, give to the congress information of the state of the union, and recommend to their consideration such measures as he shall judge necessary and expedient; he may, on extraordinary occasions, convene both houses, or either of them, and, in case of disagreement between them with respect to the time of adjournment, he may adjourn them to such time as he shall think proper; he shall receive embassadors and other public ministers; he shall take care that the laws be faithfully executed; and shall commission all the officers of the United States.

SEC. 4. The president, vice president, and all civil officers of the United States, shall be removed from office on impeachment for, and conviction of, treason, bribery, or other high crimes and misdemeanors.

ARTICLE III.

SEC. 1. The judicial power of the United States shall be vested in one supreme court, and in such inferior courts as the congress may, from time to time, ordain and establish. The judges, both of the supreme and inferior courts, shall hold their offices during good behavior; and shall, at stated times, receive for their services a compensation which shall not be diminished during their continuance in office.

SEC. 2. The judicial power shall extend to all cases in law and equity, arising under this constitution, the laws of the United States, and treaties made, or which shall be made, under their authority; to all cases affecting embassadors, other public ministers and consuls; to all cases of admiralty and maritime jurisdiction; to controversies to which the United States shall be a party; to controversies between two or more states; between a state and citizens of another state; between citizens of different states; between citizens of the same state claiming lands under grants of different states; and between a state, or the citizens thereof, and foreign states, citizens, or subjects.

In all cases affecting embassadors, other public ministers and consuls, and those in which a state shall be a party, the supreme court shall have original jurisdiction. In all the other cases before mentioned, the supreme court shall have appellate jurisdiction, both as to law and fact, with such exceptions, and under such regulations, as the congress shall make.

The trial of all crimes, except in cases of impeachment, shall be by jury; and such trial shall be held in the state where the said crimes shall have been committed; but when not committed within any state, the trial shall be at such place or places as the congress may, by law, have directed.

SEC. 3. Treason against the United States shall consist only in levying war against them, or in adhering to their enemies, giving them aid and comfort. No person shall be convicted of treason unless on the testimony of two witnesses to the same overt act, or on confession in open court.

The congress shall have power to declare the punishment of treason, but no attainder of treason shall work corruption of blood or forfeiture, except during the life of the person attainted.

ARTICLE IV.

SEC. 1. Full faith and credit shall be given in each state to the public acts, records, and judicial proceedings of every other state. And the congress may, by general laws, prescribe the manner in which such acts, records, and proceedings shall be proved, and the effect thereof.

SEC. 2. The citizens of each state shall be entitled to all privileges and immunities of citizens in the several states.

A person charged in any state with treason, felony, or other crime, who shall flee from justice, and be found in another state, shall, on demand of the executive authority of the state from which he fled, be delivered up, to be removed to the state having jurisdiction of the crime.

No person held to service or labor in one state under the laws thereof, escaping into another, shall, in consequence of any law or regulation therein, be discharged from such service or labor, but shall be delivered up on claim of the party to whom such service or labor may be due.

SEC. 3. New states may be admitted by the congress into this union; but no new state shall be formed or erected within the jurisdiction of any other state; nor any state be formed by the junction of two or more states, or parts of states, without the consent of the legislature of the states concerned, as well as of the congress.

The congress shall have power to dispose of, and make all needful rules and regulations respecting, the territory or other property belonging to the United States; and nothing in this constitution shall be so construed as to prejudice any claims of the United States, or of any particular state.

SEC. 4. The United States shall guarantee to every state in this union a republican form of government, and shall protect each of them against invasion, and on application of the legislature, or of the executive (when the legislature can not be convened) against domestic violence.

ARTICLE V.

The congress, whenever two-thirds of both houses shall deem it necessary, shall propose amendments to this constitution, or, on the application of the legislatures of two-thirds of the several states, shall call a convention for proposing amendments, which, in either case, shall be valid, to all intents and purposes, as part of this constitution, when ratified by the legislatures of three-fourths of the several states, or by conventions in three-fourths thereof, as the one or the other mode of ratification may be proposed by the congress; provided, that no amendment which may be made prior to the year one thousand eight hundred and eight, shall in any manner affect the first and fourth clauses in the ninth section of the first article; and that no state, without its consent, shall be deprived of its equal suffrage in the senate.

ARTICLE VI.

All debts contracted, and engagements entered into, before the adoption of this constitution, shall be as valid against the United States under this constitution as under the Confederation.

This constitution, and the laws of the United States which shall be made in pursuance thereof, and all treaties made, or which shall be made, under the authority of the United States, shall be the supreme law of the land; and the judges in every state shall be bound thereby, any thing in the constitution or laws of any state to the contrary notwithstanding.

The senators and representatives before mentioned, and the members of the several state legislatures, and all executive and judicial officers, both of the United States and of the several states, shall be bound by oath or affirmation to support this constitution: but no religious test shall ever be required as a qualification to any office or public trust under the United States.

ARTICLE VII.

The ratification of the conventions of nine states, shall be sufficient for the establishment of this constitution between the states so ratifying the same.

Done in Convention, by the unanimous consent of the states present, the seventeenth day of September, in the year of our Lord one thousand seven hundred and eighty-seven, and of the Independence of the United States of America the twelfth. In witness whereof, we have hereunto subscribed our names.

GEORGE WASHINGTON, PRESIDENT,
and Deputy from Virginia.

NEW HAMPSHIRE.—John Langdon, Nicholas Gilman.

MASSACHUSETTS.—Nathaniel Gorham, Rufus King.

CONNECTICUT.—William Samuel Johnson, Roger Sherman.

NEW YORK.—Alexander Hamilton.

NEW JERSEY.—William Livingston, David Brearly, William Patterson, Jonathan Dayton.

PENNSYLVANIA.—Benjamin Franklin, Thomas Mifflin, Robert Morris, George Clymer, Thomas Fitzsimons, Jared Ingersoll, James Wilson, Gouverneur Morris.

DELAWARE.—George Read, Gunning Bedford, Jr., John Dickinson, Richard Bassett, Jacob Broom.

MARYLAND.—James McHenry, Daniel of St. Thomas Jenifer, Daniel Carroll.

VIRGINIA.—John Blair, James Madison, Jr.

NORTH CAROLINA.—William Blount, Richard Dobbs Spaight, Hugh Williamson.

SOUTH CAROLINA.—John Rutledge, Charles Cotesworth Pinckney, Charles Pinckney, Pierce Butler.

GEORGIA.—William Few, Abraham Baldwin.

Attest:

WILLIAM JACKSON, *Secretary.*

AMENDMENTS TO THE CONSTITUTION.

ARTICLE I.

Congress shall make no law respecting an establishment of religion, or prohibiting the free exercise thereof; or abridging the freedom of speech, or of the press; or the right of the people peaceably to assemble, and to petition the government for a redress of grievances.

ARTICLE II.

A well regulated militia being necessary to the security of a free state, the right of the people to keep and bear arms shall not be infringed.

ARTICLE III.

No soldier shall, in time of peace, be quartered in any house without the consent of the owner, nor in time of war but in a manner to be prescribed by law.

ARTICLE IV.

The right of the people to be secure in their persons, houses, papers, and effects, against unreasonable searches and seizures, shall not be violated, and no warrants shall issue but upon probable cause, supported by oath or affirmation, and particularly describing the place to be searched, and the persons or things to be seized.

ARTICLE V.

No person shall be held to answer for a capital or otherwise infamous crime, unless on a presentment or indictment of a grand jury, except in cases arising in the land or naval forces, or in the militia when in actual service, in time of war or public danger; nor shall any person be subject, for the same offense, to be twice put in jeopardy of life or limb; nor shall be compelled in any criminal case to be a witness against himself; nor be deprived of life, liberty, or property, without due process of law; nor shall private property be taken for public use without just compensation.

ARTICLE VI.

In all criminal prosecutions, the accused shall enjoy the right to a speedy and public trial, by an impartial jury of the state and district wherein the crime shall have been committed, which district shall have been previously ascertained by law, and to be informed of the nature and cause of the accusation; to be confronted with the witnesses against him; to have compulsory process for obtaining witnesses in his favor; and to have the assistance of counsel for his defense.

ARTICLE VII.

In suits at common law, where the value in controversy shall exceed twenty dollars, the right of trial by jury shall be preserved; and no fact tried by a jury shall be otherwise re-examined in any court of the United States, than according to the rules at the common law.

ARTICLE VIII.

Excessive bail shall not be required, nor excessive fines imposed, nor cruel and unusual punishments inflicted.

ARTICLE IX.

The enumeration in the constitution of certain rights, shall not be construed to deny or disparage others retained by the people.

ARTICLE X.

The powers not delegated to the United States by the constitution, nor prohibited by it to the states, are reserved to the states respectively, or to the people.

ARTICLE XI.

The judicial power of the United States shall not be construed to extend to any suit in law or equity, commenced or prosecuted against one of the United States by citizens of another state, or by citizens or subjects of any foreign state.

ARTICLE XII.

The electors shall meet in their respective states, and vote by ballot for president and vice president, one of whom, at least, shall not be an inhabitant of the same state with themselves; they shall name in their ballots the person voted for as president, and in distinct ballots the person voted for as vice president; and they shall make distinct lists of all persons voted for as president, and of all persons voted for as vice president, and of the number of votes for each, which lists they shall sign and certify, and transmit sealed to the seat of the government of the United States, directed to the president of the senate; the president of the senate shall, in the presence of the senate and house of representatives, open all the certificates, and the votes shall then be counted; the person having the greatest number of votes for president shall be the president, if such number be a majority of the whole number of electors appointed; and if no person have such majority, then from the persons having the highest numbers, not exceeding three, on the list of those voted for as president, the house of representatives shall choose immediately, by ballot, the president. But in choosing the president, the votes shall be taken by states, the representation from each state having one vote; a quorum for this purpose shall consist of a member or members from two-thirds of the states, and a majority of all the states shall be necessary to a choice. And if the house of representatives shall not choose a president, whenever the right of choice shall devolve upon them, before the fourth day of March next following, then the vice president shall act as president, as in the case of the death or other constitutional disability of the president.

The person having the greatest number of votes as vice president shall be the vice president, if such number be a majority of the whole number of electors appointed; and if no person have a majority, then from the two highest numbers on the list, the senate shall choose the vice president; a quorum for the purpose shall consist of two-thirds of the whole number of senators, and a majority of the whole number shall be necessary to a choice.

But no person constitutionally ineligible to the office of president, shall be eligible to that of vice president of the United States.

ARTICLE XIII.

SEC. 1. Neither slavery nor involuntary servitude, except as a punishment for crime, whereof the party shall have been duly convicted, shall exist within the United States, or any place subject to their jurisdiction.

SEC. 2. Congress shall have power to enforce this article by appropriate legislation.

ARTICLE XIV.

SEC. 1. All persons born or naturalized in the United States, and subject to the jurisdiction thereof, are citizens of the United States, and of the state wherein they reside. No state shall make or enforce any law which shall abridge the privileges or immunities of citizens of the United States; nor shall any state deprive any person of life, liberty, or property, without due process of law, nor deny to any person within its jurisdiction the equal protection of the laws.

SEC. 2. Representatives shall be apportioned among the several states according to their respective numbers, counting the whole number of persons in each state, excluding Indians not taxed. But when the right to vote at any election for choice of electors for president and vice president of the United States, representatives in congress, the executive and judicial officers of a state, or the members of the legislature thereof, is denied to any of the male inhabitants of such state being twenty-one years of age, and citizens of the United States, or in any way abridged, except for participation in rebellion or other crime, the basis of representation therein shall be reduced in the proportion which the number of such male citizens shall bear to the whole number of male citizens twenty-one years of age in such state.

SEC. 3. No person shall be a senator, or representative in congress, or elector of president and vice president, or hold any office, civil or military, under the United States, or under any state, who, having previously taken an oath as a member of congress, or as an officer of the United States, or as a member of any state legislature, or as an executive or judicial officer of any state, to support the Constitution ot the United States, shall have engaged in insurrection or rebellion against the same, or given aid or comfort to the enemies thereof; but congress may, by a vote of two-thirds of each house, remove such disability.

SEC. 4. The validity of the public debt of the United States authorized by law, including debts incurred for payment of pensions and bounties for services in suppressing insurrection or rebellion, shall not be questioned. But neither the United States nor any state shall assume or pay any debt or obligation incurred in aid of insurrection or rebellion against the United States, or any claim for the loss or emancipation of any slave; but all such debts, obligations, and claims, shall be held illegal and void.

SEC. 5. The congress shall have power to enforce, by appropriate legislation, the provisions of this article.

ARTICLE XV.

SEC. 1. The right of citizens of the United States to vote shall not be denied or abridged by the United States, or by any state, on account of race, color, or previous condition of servitude.

SEC. 2. The congress shall have power to enforce this article by appropriate legislation.

INDEX.

THE FIGURES REFER TO THE PAGES.

D

T

U

WILSON, HINKLE & CO'S

NEW PUBLICATIONS.

Venable's United States: A SCHOOL HISTORY OF THE UNITED STATES, BY W. H. VENABLE. 12mo., 288 pp., finely illustrated and accompanied with carefully drawn Maps and Charts.

Contains VALUABLE FOOT-NOTES, referring to literary matter relating to subjects discussed in the text; an original system of General Questions; an original system of Biographical Reviews, illustrated with authentic portraits; numerous Maps, *unequaled* for illustrative value, accuracy, and beauty; and sustains throughout a unity of design and execution, presenting a complete, though concise, artistic, and pleasing narration of the leading facts of the history of our country, in an attractive form.

Thalheimer's Ancient History: A MANUAL OF ANCIENT HISTORY, from the earliest times to the fall of the Western Empire, A. D. 476. BY M. E. THALHEIMER, formerly Teacher of History and Composition in Packer Collegiate Institute, Brooklyn, N. Y. 8vo., 360 pp., with complete Index and Pronouncing Vocabulary. Illustrated.

The present work, without attempting to furnish that voluminous information which can only be gained by many years' familiarity with historical literature, aims to place the leading characters and events of antiquity in a clear light; and to present the student with such a symmetrical and accurate outline as will best serve to systematize his more discursive reading. The author has sought to keep a just medium between the extremes of historical skepticism and a blind acceptance of tradition.

THALHEIMER'S ANCIENT HISTORY is handsomely illustrated with full-page engravings of Ancient Temples and other historical objects, charts of the principal cities, and with accurate and finely executed double-page Maps of the various countries considered in the text.

The Publishers are confident that these important features, in connection with the pleasing style of narration adopted by the author, and the strict conformity in statement to the very latest and most reliable authorities, will serve to render the work exceedingly valuable and interesting, not only to students, for whom it is specially designed, but to all classes of readers.

The Parser's Manual: BY JOHN WILLIAMS, A. M. Embracing classified examples in nearly every variety of English construction. 12mo., cloth, 265 pp.

[*From the Preface:*] . . . "The introduction into a text-book of such an amount of drill exercises as would be necessary to make learners perfectly familiar with the parsing and analysis of all kinds of sentences, would either make a volume too large to be conveniently handled, or it would crowd out every thing else that should find a place in a text-book on Grammar. It seems, therefore, indispensably necessary that we should have a book specially devoted to the subject of parsing.

"The present volume is designed to be a companion of any of the text-books used in our schools. It is not intended that the articles shall be taken up and studied consecutively in the order in which they stand in the book, but that such articles shall be taken up, or referred to from day to day, as will serve to impress more deeply on the minds of the pupils the lesson of their text-book."

Pinneo's Guide to Composition (New edition, in cloth): BY T. S. PINNEO, A. M., M. D., author of "Primary Grammar," "Analytical Grammar," etc. 12mo., 162 pp.

A series of practical lessons, designed to simplify the art of writing Composition. Contains over 250 carefully graded lessons, commencing with the simplest sentences, and instructing in all the essentials to a forcible, easy style; also, full instruction on the use of capital letters, punctuation marks, etc.

The Eclectic Series of Geographies: *Complete in Three Books*—PRIMARY, INTERMEDIATE, and SCHOOL GEOGRAPHY. By A. VON STEINWEHR and D. G. BRINTON. For the use of Schools and Colleges. Profusely illustrated with new Engravings, and distinct and accurate Maps.

Each book is divided into a *general* and a *descriptive* part: the general part containing the necessary definitions and explanations of the three branches of the science—Mathematical, Physical, and Political Geography; the descriptive part treating of the continents, their physical features, political divisions, inhabitants, etc.

The descriptive part treats of geographical topics in the following order: (1) Position, (2) Surface, (3) Rivers and Lakes, (4) Climate and Vegetation, (5) Inhabitants, (6) Political Divisions and Cities. Questions on the text are added.

Special attention is called to the MAPS, which, in correctness and artistic execution, are greatly superior to those of any other series of school geographies. Our own country is fully represented on seven SECTIONAL MAPS. The old historical division into four groups has been discarded, the addition of new States and Territories in the West having made those groups so very unequal in extent. The division adopted is *based upon the physical features of the country*, a grouping at once natural and useful for purposes of instruction.

The PRIMARY GEOGRAPHY contains the first principles of the science, stated in plain, simple language.

The INTERMEDIATE GEOGRAPHY contains sufficient materials for a complete course in a majority of schools; thus rendering more than two books unnecessary, except in the more closely graded schools of cities and villages.

The *Map Drawing Lessons* are placed after the descriptions of the continents and political divisions.

The SCHOOL GEOGRAPHY is designed to complete the course. The various topics are more fully treated in this book than in the Intermediate, and it contains a complete outline of Mathematical and Physical Geography.

Review Questions and a *Pronouncing Vocabulary* have been added to each book, and very full *Physical* and *Statistical Tables* to the Intermediate and School Geographies.

The numerous wood-cut illustrations of the Series have been designed and engraved by the best artists of the country, and no expense has been spared to render the Series beautiful, interesting, and, in a marked degree, teachable and instructive.

Specimen pages of the Eclectic Geographies mailed to any address.

The Eclectic System of Penmanship: Including COPY-BOOKS, EXERCISE-BOOK, WRITING-CARDS, and HAND-BOOK or KEY. By MESSRS. THOMPSON & BOWLERS. A practical system, designed for the use of schools and commercial colleges.

GENERAL FEATURES.—*The simplest, most legible,* and *business-like* style of capitals and small letters is adopted, in the conviction that this standard will be the most acceptable to teachers, and valuable to students. Each letter is given separately at first, and then in combination. The *spacing* is open, making the writing legible, and easily written. *The analysis is simple*, and indicated in every letter when first presented. Explanations are clear, concise, and complete, and are given on the cover of each book.

SPECIAL FEATURES.—The Copy-Books include a *Primary Book*, designed for use during the second year of school life. Contains all the small letters, figures, and capitals, each given separately and of large size, the object being to teach the form of the letter.

The higher numbers of the Copy-Books are duplicated for *Girls*, the copies being the same as in the *Boys'* books, but in smaller handwriting.

The *Exercise-Book* is intended to accompany each Copy-Book, and is made larger, with heavy paper cover, so that the latter may be placed within it.

The *Writing-Cards*, 36 in number, present but one letter or principle on each card. The letters are white, on a black ground, and sufficiently large to be easily read across the school-room.

White's Graded School Arithmetics: UNITING MENTAL AND WRITTEN EXERCISES IN A NATURAL SYSTEM OF INSTRUCTION. By E. E. WHITE, M. A., former State School Commissioner of Ohio. Complete in Three Books: "Primary," "Intermediate," and "Complete Arithmetic."

The GREAT WANT in Arithmetic is a practical combination of the analytic and inductive methods of teaching—a complete and philosophic union of Mental and Written Arithmetic. The preparation of the GRADED SCHOOL SERIES OF ARITHMETICS was undertaken to meet this urgent need, and is submitted to American teachers in the hope that it may be found a practical solution of one serious difficulty which has so long prevented the adoption of more rational courses of study in graded schools. Attention is invited to the following important features:

1. The Series combines Mental and Written Arithmetic in a practical and philosophical manner.
2. The inductive method of teaching is faithfully followed.
3. The successive books are adapted, both in matter and method, to the grades of pupils for which they are respectively designed.
4. The problems are sufficiently numerous, varied, and progressive, to afford the requisite drill and practice.
5. The Series is adapted to the present condition of education, science, and business.
6. The omission of useless and obsolete subjects affords room for a full presentation of all important topics.

Schuyler's Complete Algebra, for Schools and Colleges. By A. SCHUYLER, M. A., Professor of Mathematics and Logic, in Baldwin University. 12mo., sheep, 368 pp.

Though this work is sufficiently elementary for beginners, it is not a mere Elementary Algebra under the name of "Complete:" neither has the attempt been made to give every thing which might be brought under the head of Algebra. The author believes it better to teach thoroughly the essentials of the science, than to attempt, in a limited time, to exhaust the subject.

Schuyler's Logic: The Principles of Logic, for High Schools and Colleges. By A. SCHUYLER, M. A. 12mo., cloth, 168 pp.

The valuable results of the labors of former investigators in this department of science have been carefully sought for and retained, including the recent developments of Hamilton, with criticisms by Thompson and De Morgan, and Hamilton's replies. Original improvements, either in matter or in method, have been made in the following subjects: Fundamental Laws of Thought, Opposition, Conversion, Principles warranting the Conclusions, (A), (E), (I), (O), Determination of the Valid Moods, Discussion of the Figures, and Induction.

Norton's Philosophy: The Elements of Natural Philosophy, embracing latest discoveries to date of publication. By SIDNEY A. NORTON, A. M. Illustrated with 360 engravings. 12mo., cloth, 368 pp.

While fully impressed that "there is no royal road to science," the author has yet endeavored to make the labor of the student as attractive and invigorating as possible. To this end the subject has been treated, not merely as a science to be learned, but also as a means of educational discipline: the topics are considered in their logical order, methodically developed, thoroughly illustrated and enforced.

Such *illustrative experiments* are suggested as can be performed by the pupil with materials which are always obtainable.

A *copious index* at the end of the book renders the volume valuable for reference in pursuing other branches of the natural sciences.

Cole's Institute Reader AND NORMAL CLASS-BOOK. For the use of Teachers' Institutes and Normal Schools, and for self-training in the art of Reading. By WM. H. COLE. 12mo., cloth, 360 pp.

The INSTITUTE READER is based on an entirely new plan, and designed to occupy a new field among educational text-books. No work hitherto published at all resembles it, either in design or execution. It presents a variety of drill exercises and practical instruction in reading, covering all grades of progress.

Part I. contains practical directions to primary teachers, followed by exercises from the Primer and First and Second Readers.

Part II. continues the directions, and contains a Manual of Articulation for drill purposes, and a series of reading lessons from the Third, Fourth, and Fifth Readers.

Part III. is intended to be a complete Reader for advanced classes, and to furnish those who desire to pursue the study of Elocution without a master, with the necessary instructions and exercises.

Part IV. is added to enable those who have little or no experience in such organizations, to form and conduct a successful Institute.

Kidd's Rhetorical Reader: For Class Drill and Private Instruction in Elocution. By ROBERT KIDD, author of KIDD'S ELOCUTION. 12mo., cloth, 384 pp.

A book of reading exercises, with plain directions to the student what to do, and how to proceed so as to obtain, with the least difficulty and in the shortest time, a pure, full, rich, flexible voice, and a practical knowledge of all the principles involved in the art of correct reading.

The elementary principles are presented in a simple, clear, and attractive manner. The majority of the selections which constitute the reading lessons, in the body of the book, have never before appeared in any text-book on the subject.

The compiler has ignored nearly all the rules relating to inflection, emphasis, modulation, and gesture, believing that these rules are indefinite, unreliable, and impracticable, and that their observance will inevitably result in a lack of that directness and naturalness of expression, which is the crowning excellence of every department of reading and speaking.

Ray's Elements of Astronomy: Written for the Mathematical course of JOSEPH RAY, M. D., by S. H. PEABODY, A. M., Prof. of Physics and Civil Engineering, Amherst College, Mass. Illustrated. 8vo., sheep, 336 pp.

In this work the higher analysis, intricate geometrical demonstrations, and tedious arithmetical computations have been omitted, and the author has restricted himself to plain statements of facts, principles, and processes, presuming only that his readers are familiar with elementary algebra and geometry, and the simplest principles of mechanics and physics.

Great pains have been taken to bring the statements of the text in accordance with the latest authenticated discoveries.

Many important experiments are described for the first time in a work of this grade. Among them are Foucault's experiment for showing the rotation of the earth, Fizeau's for determining the velocity of light, and Plateau's for showing the rotation of fluids when relieved from the influence of terrestrial gravitation. The methods of measuring and weighing the earth, with the apparatus of Bach, Cavendish, etc., are described.

The illustrations are unusually full and excellent, and all have been drawn specially for this work.

Ray's Analytic Geometry: A Treatise on Analytic Geometry, especially as applied to the Properties of Conics: including the Modern Methods of Abridged Notation. Written for the Mathematical course of JOSEPH RAY, M. D., by GEO. H. HOWISON, M. A., Prof. in Mass. Institute of Technology. 8vo., sheep, 574 pp.

With a view to the wants of special students, more than usual FULLNESS OF DETAIL has been admitted, particularly in the treatment of the Conics. But, while this has been done, such properties as are of less immediate importance to the general reader, have been presented in FINER TYPE than is used in the remainder of the work.

With a reference to special students also, the MODERN GEOMETRY has been introduced, being now, *for the first time*, presented to the American reader. Every well-read mathematician will admit that the discoveries of STEINER and PONCELET, together with the corresponding adaptations of analysis, invented by MOBIUS and PLUCKER, fill so remarkable a place in the history of mathematics, that they can not be omitted by students who wish to obtain complete views of the subject. A pretty full account, both of TRILINEAR and of TANGENTIAL CO-ORDINATES, has accordingly been given. But this is presented in SEPARATE CHAPTERS, so as not to interrupt the progress of general readers whose time is limited.

A large collection of EXAMPLES, selected with great care from the best sources, has been interspersed with the corresponding topics. The lack of such a body of illustrative problems, has been a serious defect in previous treatises, almost without exception.

Teachers and friends of education generally, are invited to send for our *Illustrated Catalogue*, 128 pp., containing full descriptions of all the text-books of the *Eclectic Educational Series*, with opinions of well-known educators concerning them, and information as to their extensive use, etc.

Liberal terms on supplies for first introduction, or sample copies for examination, of any of the Eclectic Series.

WILSON, HINKLE & CO.,
CINCINNATI and NEW YORK.

TO EDUCATORS.

Probably in no respect has the agitation generally pervading educational matters during the last few years been more noticeable than in that of school text-books. The adoption of more advanced ideas as to the scope and methods of instruction proper in many branches of study has necessitated a corresponding change in the scope and methods of the text-books treating of them, and, as a result, the issue of new works, embracing almost every subject of the common-school course and the university curriculum, has been with a rapidity and to an extent before unknown. In the struggle for preferment of the new competing books, which has ensued, not only have their claims been individually and relatively examined, but also the intrinsic worth and adaptation of those previously before the public have been carefully scrutinized.

It is therefore with no little gratification that we call the attention of our friends and patrons, and educational men generally, to the continued retention, during this period of activity, of McGuffey's Readers in the large territory occupied by them, and where schools and school systems are in their most advanced and flourishing state; to the almost universally favorable testimony of those who have used and are now using them; and to the numerous introductions they have received over all competition, into districts where they have been before unused.

The resolution passed by the School Board of St. Louis upon the late adoption of McGuffey's Readers for the Public Schools of that city; the recent official adoptions by the State Boards of California, Nevada, Arkansas, and Virginia, and recommendations by the State Boards of Kentucky, Maryland, and Wyoming; the *re-adoptions* by the School Boards of New York City, Brooklyn, Harrisburg, and other cities, for terms of years; and the action of more than 5,000 schools in *resuming* the use of McGuffey's Readers after having laid them aside for a trial of some of the latest works in this branch of study, are undeniable testimony that they continue to hold, as they unquestionably have held for years, the foremost place as reading books among those who give their time, energies, and abilities to the best interests of education.

www.ingramcontent.com/pod-product-compliance
Lightning Source LLC
LaVergne TN
LVHW010218110826
845151LV00004B/1125

* 9 7 8 1 4 2 5 5 2 6 1 0 8 *